Polish Romantic Drama

Polish Theatre Archive

A series of books edited by Daniel Gerould, Graduate School,
City University of New York, USA

Volume 1
To Steal a March on God
Hanna Krall
translated and with an introduction by Jadwiga Kosicka

Volume 2
Alternative Theatre in Poland
1954–1989
Kathleen Cioffi

Volume 3
Country House
Stanisław Ignacy Witkiewicz
translated and with an introduction by Daniel Gerould

Volume 4
The Trap
Tadeusz Różewicz
translated by Adam Czerniawski

Volume 5
Polish Romantic Drama
Three plays in English translation
selected, edited and with an introduction by Harold B. Segel

Additional volumes in preparation

The Mannequins' Ball
Bruno Jasieński
translated and with an introduction by Daniel Gerould

Encounters with Tadeusz Kantor
Krzysztof Miklaszewski

This book is part of a series. The publisher will accept continuation orders which
may be cancelled at any time and which provide for automatic billing and
shipping of each title in the series upon publication. Please write for details.

Polish Romantic Drama

Three plays in English translation

Selected, edited
and with an introduction by
Harold B. Segel

harwood academic publishers
Australia • Canada • China • France • Germany • India
Japan • Luxembourg • Malaysia • The Netherlands • Russia
Singapore • Switzerland • Thailand • United Kingdom

Applications for licenses to perform *Forefathers' Eve*, Part III,
The Un-Divine Comedy and *Fantazy* should be addressed to
Harold B. Segel, c/o Harwood Academic Publishers.

Amsteldijk 166
1st Floor
1079 LH Amsterdam
The Netherlands

British Library Cataloguing in Publication Data
Polish romantic drama: three plays in English translation.
  – (Polish theatre archive; v. 5)
  1. Polish drama – 19th century – Translations into English
  I. Segel, Harold B. II. Mickiewicz, Adam, 1798–1855. Forefathers'
  eve III. Krasiński, Zygmunt. Un-Divine comedy IV. Słowacki, Juliusz.
  Fantazy
891. 8′5′2′6′08

ISBN 90-5702-088-2

Cover: The Improvisation, in Adam Mickiewicz's *Forefathers' Eve*,
scene ii. Photo: Wojciech Plewinski

CONTENTS

Introduction to the Series   vii

List of Plates   ix

Preface   xi

Introduction   1

Forefathers' Eve, Part III
Adam Mickiewicz   45

The Un-Divine Comedy
Zygmunt Krasiński   151

Fantazy
Juliusz Słowacki   215

Selected Bibliography   281

INTRODUCTION TO THE SERIES

The *Polish Theatre Archive* makes available in English translation major works of Poland's dramatic literature as well as monographs and critical studies on Polish playwrights, theatre artists and stage history. Although emphasis is placed on the contemporary period, the *Polish Theatre Archive* also encompasses the nineteenth-century roots of modern theatre practice in Romanticism and Symbolism. The individual plays will contain authoritative introductions that place the works in their historical and theatrical contexts.

DANIEL GEROULD

LIST OF PLATES

1. The stage director Konrad Swinarski   41
2. The Improvisation, in Adam Mickiewicz's *Forefathers' Eve*, scene ii   82
3. The ball, in *Forefathers' Eve*, scene viii   129
4. The blind mother's plea, in *Forefathers' Eve*, scene viii   136
5. The final scene from *Forefathers' Eve*, scene ix   144
6. The finale of *Forefathers' Eve*, at the Teatr Polski, Warsaw, 1934   146
7. Preparation for battle, in Zygmunt Krasiński's *The Un-Divine Comedy*, Part III   177
8. The dance of the free people, in *The Un-Divine Comedy*, Part III   181
9. Among the revolutionaries, in *The Un-Divine Comedy*, Part III   184
10. The gallows scene from *The Un-Divine Comedy*, Part III   186
11. The confrontation scene from *The Un-Divine Comedy*, Part III   194
12. The final scene from *The Un-Divine Comedy*, Part IV   213
13. A chance meeting, in Juliusz Słowacki's *Fantazy*, Act II, scene iii   238
14. The graveyard scene from *Fantazy*, Act V, scene i   269
15. The "suicide" scene from *Fantazy*, Act V, scene i   272

PREFACE

When we speak of European Romantic drama, the names of Byron, Shelley, Kleist, and Hugo come to mind. Further reflection, and those of Musset, Grillparzer, Büchner, and Pushkin follow. We think also of a lofty tradition of verse drama, often poetically brilliant but somehow unsuited for theatrical production, a drama to be read in the solitude of a study rather than watched on stage. We recall the Romantics' interest in ancient Greek and medieval drama, in Shakespeare, and in Calderón, and their attempts to fuse elements of these traditions with the new Romantic ethos. Although they regarded drama as an extension of poetry, which to them was the supreme verbal art, the Romantics yearned nonetheless to create new dramatic forms, above all a new tragedy after the long hegemony of the lifeless pseudotragedies of eighteenth-century classicism. Yet, despite their well-intentioned efforts, when we try to recollect when we last saw or heard a production of Romantic drama, we realize that were it not for Antonin Artaud's famous version of Shelley's *The Cenci* (his production, after all, dates from 1935) and the still more famous operas based on Pushkin's *Boris Godunov*, Hugo's *Hernani*, and Büchner's *Woyzeck*, Romantic drama would be the exclusive concern of the library or the classroom.

Perhaps the greatest paradox in the history of Romantic drama is that while the major poets consciously strove to originate a new dramatic tradition which would come to life in the theatre – and failed – other dramatists wrote independently of the contemporary stage and produced plays which not only have proven eminently adaptable to the stage but have had a decisive impact on twentieth-century dramaturgy, particularly that of the avant-garde.

Best representative in the West of this latter current, which we can regard as a de facto as opposed to a programmatic avant-garde within the Romantic drama, were Alfred de Musset (1810–1857) in France and Georg Büchner (1813–1837) in Germany. After the public failure of *La Nuit vénitienne* ("The Venetian Night", 1830), Musset simply stopped writing for the theatre. His fondness for dialogue remained strong, however, and found an outlet in plays devised principally for his own amusement. Liberated from the restraints of the contemporary stage or, better said, of contemporary theatrical traditions and techniques, Musset could now permit his imagination freer rein. The happy result was plays such as *Les Caprices de Marianne* (usually known in English as *Marianne*, published 1833), *Fantasio* (published 1834), and *On ne badine pas avec l'amour* ("There's No Trifling with Love" – sometimes known in English as *Camille and Perdican* – published 1834), which live to this day in the French theatre.

The case of Büchner, a rebel and iconoclast by nature, is more striking still. Büchner's most imaginative plays, *Dantons Tod* (*Danton's Death*, published 1835) and *Woyzeck* (published posthumously in 1850), were considered so outrageous both formally and ideologically that they were staged for the first time only in the early twentieth century. *Danton's Death* was first produced in Berlin in 1902, and *Woyzeck* in Munich in 1913. Their premieres were electrifying. Because of the representation of history and the human condition, the psychological depth, and the very loose, "open", episodic structure, which invests them with an almost kaleidoscopic movement, the plays at once were hailed for their modernity and contemporary relevance. Their most obvious appeal was to the avant-garde; the dramatist Bertolt Brecht admired their social content as well as their form, and a whole string of theatrical innovators, including Brecht himself, Erwin Piscator, and Max Reinhardt, recognized the formidable challenge to their creative skills posed by the stage production of such plays. Büchner may not have been well known in his lifetime, but his plays have since become important sources of twentieth-century German-language drama ranging from the early avant-garde expressionism and "epic theatre" to the plays of such contemporaries as Peter Weiss and Peter Handke.

The unusual factors in the career of Büchner were surpassed in the evolution of Polish Romantic drama. Both Musset and Büchner, like other Western Romantics, had theatres available for which they could have written had they been less independent. The Poles did not. Polish Romantic drama, which includes the plays primarily of Adam Mickiewicz (1798–1855), Juliusz Słowacki (1809–1849), and Zygmunt Krasiński (1812–1859), reached its apogee not in Poland but in the West after the defeat of the Polish Insurrection of November 1830. The suppression of the revolt, which erupted in the part of Poland then dominated by Russia, resulted in the mass exodus of thousands of Poles. They sought refuge in Western Europe; most settled in France. From late 1831 to January 1863, when the Poles again tried unsuccessfully to liberate their country by force of arms, a lively, important, and highly interesting Polish culture developed among the émigrés.

The most resonant expression of the émigré community was the drama of the great Romantic poets. Although, in exile, they had no stage to write for, the Polish Romantics were no less dedicated to the renovation of the art of drama than their Western counterparts. Their plays were in many ways even more daring and unusual than those of Musset and Büchner, and when they were eventually mounted, like Büchner's, in the twentieth century, they became the foundation on which arose the splendid Polish theatre of the present age – including the experiments of such internationally renowned directors as Jerzy Grotowski and Tadeusz Kantor.

The importance of the Romantic drama for later Polish drama as well as theatre far exceeds that of Büchner in the German-speaking countries. Apart from the impact of their formal innovations, which actually anticipated those of Büchner, the Polish Romantic plays gave rise to an entire tradition of modern Polish dramatic writing, extending from the works of Stanisław Wyspiański in the early years of the twentieth century to such contemporary dramas as Ernest Bryll's, in which the ideological and philosophical issues raised in the Romantic plays have been newly evaluated, and then reaffirmed or rejected. The Romantic drama became the spirit of the emigration and, ultimately, of Poland itself; in the name of the Polish nation and even more universally in the name of all enslaved people, it cried out for liberty, for justice, for fundamental human rights. Angry at a world in which a great nation, as Poland had once been, could be dismembered and effaced from the map of Europe, it did not shrink from indicting a God who could permit such evil to exist. Since poets constituted the highest spiritual authority among the émigrés, the Romantic concepts of the poet, poetry, society, and history became subject to startling redefinition and to a realization unparalleled elsewhere in Europe at the time. Indeed, romanticism itself and its meaning for the real world of oppression and exile in which they lived became a focus of inquiry for the creators of Polish Romantic drama.

This first collection of Polish Romantic drama in English has several objectives. Because much modern Polish drama and theatre are rooted in the Romantic tradition, and especially because Polish drama and theatre are being ever more widely disseminated abroad (Fredro, Wyspiański, Witkiewicz, Gombrowicz, Mrożek, Różewicz, Grotowski, Kantor), it seemed desirable to make available a few of the most representative and outstanding Romantic plays as an indispensable frame of reference for fuller understanding of later developments.

But the importance of Polish Romantic drama is not limited to its contributions to the twentieth century. It stands, along with lyric poetry, as the greatest achievement of Polish romanticism itself and is well worth studying both for its own merits and for what it enables us to learn about the Romantic movement in Europe as a whole. Moreover, the tradition of Romantic drama is very much alive in the contemporary Polish theatre: Polish Romantic dramas, which were not written for the stage and were never, to be sure, staged in the lifetime of their authors, are now not only performed regularly on Polish stages but constitute a self-renewing tradition. Directors are finding new ways of staging them in conformance with new visions and interpretations; and audiences are discovering new meanings and relevance in them. The following excerpt from an account of a new version of one of Słowacki's best plays, *Balladyna* (1839), illustrates my point:

> The second Hanuszkiewicz production was Słowacki's *Balladyna*, a bold and controversial but very spirited and original presentation. This drama of the struggle for power, tinged with irony, is usually played in a bland and maudlin manner. Hanuszkiewicz did not hesitate to give a radically new reading of the story inspired by Shakespeare. The modern costumes worn by the characters of the play, the skin-tight black leather pants and jackets in which the young men and women from prehistoric Poland moved with such agility, delineated the external framework of the play. ... Hanuszkiewicz went a step further and set his *Balladyna* in the 20th century. Authorities in Polish literature were horrified when the Slavic goddess Goplana and her retinue roared onto the stage on Japanese-made Honda motorcycles and then circled the auditorium over a specially built track that reached up to the first balcony. Although this fact did not deeply influence the interpretation, it did create the kind of publicity that even the most sensational analysis of the text could not have done. Young people stormed the Teatr Narodowy to see Goplana ride a motorcycle.[1]

The last objective of this book is more personal in nature. The Romantic period brought the first notable achievements in Polish drama before the ebullient and variegated growth of Polish theatre arts in the twentieth century. In partitioned Poland, Count Alexander Fredro (1793–1876) emerged as the finest comic dramatist in the Polish language. While Fredro, a former Napoleonic officer, was writing his best comedies in Poland proper in the 1830s, the leading poets of the post-1831 emigration in France were creating the tradition of Polish Romantic drama which has since come to be known in Polish literary and theatrical historiography as "monumental". In 1969, my study of Fredro together with translations of five of his major comedies was published; with the present volume, my work on the drama of the Polish Romantic period is completed.

---

[1] Roman Szydłowski, "The Thirtieth Anniversary Season", *Le Théâtre en Pologne/ The Theatre in Poland*, 1, No. 197 (1975), 11.

PREFACE

A word about my choice of plays for inclusion in this collection of English translations. With one exception, my selection offers no surprises. The foremost dramatic works of Mickiewicz and Krasiński are, respectively, *Dziady, Część III* (*Forefathers' Eve*, Part III), and *Nie-Boska komedia* (*The Un-Divine Comedy*). Both are included. To anyone familiar with Polish drama, the obvious Słowacki choice would be *Kordian*. But despite a strong third act and the play's overall ideological importance in the development of Polish émigré romanticism, it remains an overpoeticized, unripe Romantic play dealing with many of the same issues as the Mickiewicz and Krasiński works. To show a different aspect of Polish Romantic drama, I chose Słowacki's later comedy (or tragicomedy) *Fantazy*. Today regarded as one of his best plays and often performed in Poland, it is particularly interesting for its Romantic irony and its treatment of the theme of spiritual triumph through self-sacrifice within the context of a social satire.

In preparing this volume, I was greatly aided by various sources, which I am happy to acknowledge here. Rather than attempt a new verse translation of Mickiewicz's *Forefathers' Eve*, Part III, or a straight prose translation which would at this time seem a step backward, I decided to use the reliable and readable verse translation edited by George Rapall Noyes and published by the Polish Institute of Arts and Sciences in America in the volume *Poems of Adam Mickiewicz* (New York, 1944). I have, however, made a number of changes in the translation in the hope of improving its fidelity to the original and its readability in English. I was also helped in my work on Mickiewicz by the able, if more idiosyncratic, translation into English verse of the whole of *Forefathers' Eve* by Count Potocki of Montalk, published by the Polish Cultural Foundation of London in 1967. Count Potocki kindly provided me with a new, slightly revised version of his translation and in this and other ways showed his interest in my project and his willingness to be of assistance. My new translation of Krasiński's *The Un-Divine Comedy* was made easier by the earlier translation, long out of print, by Harriette E. Kennedy and Zofia Umińska, which was published (apparently in 1924; the publication itself is undated) by George G. Harrap & Co. Ltd. of London and the Książnica Polska of Warsaw. Thanks are also due to Daniel Gerould of the City University of New York for his reading of the entire manuscript and his valuable suggestions, to the late Wiktor Weintraub of Harvard University for his wise counsel, and to the American Council of Learned Societies for its support of research for the project.

H. B. S.

INTRODUCTION

In writing about a lesser-known literary culture, one is usually obliged, at the outset, to appeal to the sympathetic interest of the reader. The literature in question may not be familiar – so the plea goes – but its merits justify greater dissemination. The reader is asked to accept the argument on faith until proof is provided. For the most part, this proof takes the form of translations. If the translation is good, many of the qualities of the original penetrate the language barrier. If, on the other hand, the translation is weak, the reader is alienated. Even when the foreign literary work is available in good translation, the struggle for recognition is still not over. Differences in culture also erect barriers. If the foreign culture is appreciably different from that of the reader, the hurdles are sometimes impossible to clear. Where the work of art exhibits a strong parochial character – that is, it deals with events, personalities, and issues of primarily local significance – the cultural gap is bridged only in rare instances. Here the motivation of the reader or unusual aesthetic qualities become decisive factors. Sometimes, however, the work of art of distinct national character succeeds in transcending parochial limitations and in achieving a sufficient degree of universality to attract the interest of, and even become meaningful to, the foreign public.

I should like now to suggest that Polish Romantic drama falls into the latter category. The plays presented in this volume in English translation are among the most important in the history of the Polish theatre. Their importance, however, is determined not only by aesthetic criteria – within the context of Polish literary and theatrical tradition – but also by external cultural and political circumstances. These circumstances prevailed in the period when the plays were written and clearly leave their traces in the works themselves. To different degrees they impart to the plays an undeniable national character. Yet, at the same time, a remarkable concatenation of nation, spirit, and art spares these works an inhibiting parochialism and achieves the transcendence to which I previously referred. To appreciate this, some understanding of the elements out of which Polish Romantic drama was shaped is necessary.

By the conventional concept of "great powers", Poland was, historically, a great power. In political, economic, and military terms it was at its zenith in the sixteenth and seventeenth centuries. Although geographically a part of eastern Europe, its culture belongs to the West. This was virtually assured by its Roman Catholicism and its participation in European Latin civilization. Not surprisingly then, humanism, the Renaissance and Reformation, and the Enlightenment were well represented in Polish history. To regard this as merely the result of a vigorous policy of assimilation like that pursued, let us say, by Russia in the eighteenth century would be erroneous. Humanism, the Renaissance, and later stages in the development of Western civilization as we know it were not graftings in the case of Poland but organic phases of Polish cultural evolution.

Foreign wars, unwise policies, and domestic upheaval eroded Polish strength throughout the later seventeenth and eighteenth centuries. As the power of Poland steadily declined, that of its neighbors grew. By the later eighteenth century – despite vigorous efforts to reverse the downward spiral in the reign of the last sovereign, Stanislas August Poniatowski (1732–1798; reigned 1764–1795) – Prussia, Austria, and Russia were powerful enough to intervene in Polish affairs. Emboldened by the sight of Polish political instability and uneasy over the democratic reform movement in the country which culminated in the Constitution of May 3, 1791, Poland's neighbors undertook its systematic dismemberment. The first partition came in 1772; the second in 1792; and the third in 1795. Once a great multinational and multiethnic commonwealth, Poland in 1795 no longer existed on the map of Europe. Independence was to come again only after World War I and the dissolution of the Austro-Hungarian, German, and Russian empires.

Throughout the long period of bondage, various attempts were made to restore Polish statehood. A few years after the third partition the Poles avidly supported Napoleon. By contributing soldiers to his campaigns they believed that they were working toward the ultimate goal of national independence. Napoleon lamented the plight of Poland and made promises in return for men. When the emperor's politics moved eastward, he seemed to be making good his promises and Polish support increased. Preparatory to his great campaign against Russia, Napoleon in 1807 created the miniature state of the Duchy of Warsaw out of captured territories. This action was not much more than a gesture, but it reaffirmed Polish faith in the French. In gratitude the Poles raised an army of nearly eighty thousand men to fight under Napoleon's banners in the invasion of Russia. They fought hard and well and even after the debacle many remained so loyal that they followed the emperor back to France and participated in all his later campaigns. The fall of Napoleon in 1815 brought an end to the Duchy of Warsaw and the Poles were back where they started. In one sense, their plight was worse. After Napoleon, there were no other "deliverers" in whom the Poles could invest their hopes for liberation. They had to fall back, therefore, on their own resources. On the threshold of the Romantic age this meant rebellion.

The Poles made two major attempts to regain independence by means of arms in the nineteenth century: in November 1830 (the so-called November Insurrection, Powstanie Listopadowe), and in January 1863 (the January Insurrection, Powstanie Styczniowe). Both insurrections erupted in the Russian-occupied part of the country; both failed.

For the study of Polish Romantic literature, and Polish Romantic drama in particular, the November Insurrection is the central historical event.[1] Literary romanticism came to Poland in the early 1820's, that is, a few years after the dissolution of the Duchy of Warsaw. Inspired by Byron and German idealistic philosophy, the new Romantic literature marked a radical departure from the senescent classicism of the French-oriented Duchy. The traditional date for the appearance of romanticism in Polish literature is 1822, the year of publication of the first book of poetry by Poland's greatest poet, Adam Mickiewicz (1793–1855).[2]

Between 1822 and the outbreak of the November Insurrection Polish literature showed every indication of conforming to dominant European trends. This is not to deny, of course, certain specific Polish features. The political reality gave a special relevance to the Romantic appeals for individuality and liberty. The Romantic interest in the folk brought to prominence two border areas from which Polish Romantic regionalism derived most of its material – Lithuania and the Ukraine, historically parts of the old Polish Commonwealth. Drawing on the history of the dynastic union of the Kingdom of Poland and the Grand Duchy of Lithuania, the early Polish Romantics often used ancient Lithuanian settings for the plays and verse narratives they wrote in response to the Romantic medievalism of the West. The centuries-long domination of the Ukraine by Poland offered license to mine the rich folkloric treasures of the area in the elaboration of a Polish Romantic primitivism. In consonance with Western practice, the genres of the ballad and romance were enthusiastically cultivated. Mickiewicz's first volume of poetry in 1822 was, in fact, called *Ballady i romanse* ("Ballads and Romances"). His second volume, published in 1823, includes a two-part verse play entitled *Dziady* (*Forefathers' Eve*), in which

---

[1] For a general history of Polish literature in English, see Czesław Miłosz, *The History of Polish Literature* (London and New York, 1969; 2nd ed., 1983).

[2] The best account of Mickiewicz's poetry in English is Wiktor Weintraub, *The Poetry of Adam Mickiewicz* (The Hague, 1954).

Mickiewciz appears to be endeavoring to create a new type of drama out of folk motifs. Neither of the two parts of *Forefathers' Eve* is independently suitable for theatrical production. Their importance lies instead in their reflection in this first stage of his career of Mickiewicz's closeness to early European romanticism and his desire to bring together common Romantic themes and techniques and Polish regional folklore – here the pagan ancestor celebration of the peasants of his own native Lithuania.

The November Insurrection and its aftermath transformed the nature of this early evolving Polish romanticism. Because of their participation in the revolt or their sympathy for it, thousands of Poles became exiles. Many of the luminaries of Polish political, intellectual, and cultural life joined their ranks. Refuge was sought primarily in the West, where the November Insurrection was followed closely and where public opinion strongly supported the Polish cause. Although there were important centers of Polish émigré life in London, Geneva, and Rome, the focus of the emigration was Paris. French enthusiasm for the Insurrection (never, to be sure, translated into concrete assistance) and Polish enthusiasm for the traditions of the Revolution of 1789 and for Napoleon made the French capital the obvious place of resettlement for the majority of the émigrés.

The Great Emigration, as it is known in Polish history, had a profound effect on literature. With few exceptions, all the prominent writers were part of the emigration. This meant that after 1831, when the Insurrection had been crushed and thousands of Poles had fled to the West, Polish literature – like Polish politics – would be dominated by the émigré community. In effect, a new Poland, that of the emigration, with its capital in Paris, was created by the failure of the Insurrection. The uncrowned head of state was Prince Adam Jerzy Czartoryski (1770–1861), former minister of foreign affairs under Tsar Alexander I and the most respected Polish political figure of the time.[3] It was from Prince Czartoryski's head-quarters at the Hotel Lambert in Paris that contacts were maintained with the émigré communities elsewhere in Europe and the Near East (Constantinople, for example), that missions were sent into occupied Poland, and that plans were formulated for the political cooperation of the great states of the West, England and France, in the liberation of Poland.

Paris now became the center of Polish cultural life.[4] Polish schools were established, newspapers and journals launched, a library opened (it is

---

[3] On Czartoryski and his policies, see Marian Kukiel, *Czartoryski and European Unity, 1770–1861* (Princeton, N.J., 1955).

[4] The most comprehensive study of Polish émigré literary life in this period is Maria Straszewska's *Życie literackie Wielkiej Emigracji we Francji, 1831–1840* (Warsaw, 1970)

still in existence), and serious publishing begun. With the leading writers in the emigration, it was understandable that their works would henceforth be printed in Paris and that Paris would be the hub of the post-Insurrection Polish literary world. This was also the perspective of Poles in the occupied country. Although literary activity – and cultural life in general – continued in Poland after the partitions, freedom of expression obviously was curtailed. The situation became bleaker after the November Insurrection, especially in the Russian area where the revolt had occurred. Anxious to avoid further outbreaks, the partitioning powers maintained a close watch over publications in Polish for the slightest sign of any encouragement of revolutionary sentiment. Writers were forced, therefore, to be circumspect; that they and the reading public in the occupied lands came to view Paris and the émigré literary community located there as a haven of the free Polish word was entirely natural. Helpless themselves to change their situation, people in partitioned Poland looked to the West, and to the emigration, for guidance, for political as well as spiritual leadership. The great figures of the emigration sought to provide that leadership.

This émigré period in Polish history had definite chronological boundaries. In the first decade of the emigration belief in the imminent rebirth of Polish independence was widespread. To hasten the day, a formidable variety of political enterprises – ranging from cooperative ventures with England, France, and the Ottoman Empire, to subversion and overt conflict – were undertaken. There was no single, unified émigré approach to politics. Rival factions sprang up, some supporting the diplomatic initiatives of the conservative Czartoryski, others contemptuous of diplomacy and eager for armed intervention of one sort or another. The failure of the revolutions of 1848, in which the Poles placed great hope, took much of the steam out of émigré politics. It was becoming all too clear that Polish independence could not be achieved quickly, that a long, hard road lay ahead. The inconclusive resolution of the Crimean War – the fact that the Russian Empire (or its grip on Poland) was not toppled – increased frustration among the émigrés. In many cases, frustration gave way to despair. What finally ended the hegemony of the Great Emigration in nineteenth-century Polish political and cultural life was the disastrous January Insurrection of 1863. Encouraged both by émigré ideology and the failure of the emigration to regain national independence, Poles in Poland proper took matters into their own hands and tried for a second time in the nineteenth-century to liberate their country by insurrection. Again the revolt broke out in the Russian partition. With suppression of the revolt came a sterner administration of the region, a more aggressive policy of Russification, tighter censorship, and a greater curtailment of Polish culture.

The Great Emigration as a prime source of political initiative, spiritual leadership, and literary direction also died in the fires of the January Insurrection. By 1863 many of the leading actors in the émigré drama had either left the stage of history or were too old too remain active on it. Its great writers were no more. The greatest of them, Mickiewicz, had died of cholera in Constantinople in 1855. It was also evident, in Poland and beyond, that the day of the emigration had passed, that henceforth it would be just another emigration, no longer Great. The political programs, enterprises, and undertakings of the émigrés had come to naught; thirty-three years after the November Insurrection a second uprising was launched and failed, and Poland was still partitioned. Among the émigrés, it was time to recognize that the foreign lands in which they had sought temporary refuge would have to be their permanent homes. In Poland, it was time to understand that nothing more was to be expected from the emigration, that insurrection would bear only more bitter fruit, and that some *modus vivendi* with the reality of indefinite partition had to be found. Further alienating the population in Poland from the émigrés was the common belief that much of the inspiration for the ill-fated January Insurrection came from the Romantic ideology of the emigration. Thus the emigration, which in one way or another had fostered the insurrection, had to bear the responsibility for its failure and for the subsequent repression visited on the occupied country.

With the passing of the dominant personalities of the emigration it became easy to dismiss any further initiatives by the émigrés as futile from the outset and to seek solutions henceforth within Poland proper and within the context of partition. A reaction against the Great Emigration and the Romantic politics and poets of the emigration welled up in Poland, stimulated greatly by the social and philosophical positivism that became predominant in Polish thought in the country itself after 1863.

Reference was made earlier to the view held widely in Poland after 1831 that because the masses of émigrés who sought shelter in the West were unaffected by the restraints operative in partitioned Poland, they enjoyed unlimited freedom of expression. But in fact restraints did exist within the émigré literary community. In Poland a rigorous censorship was imposed from above by the partitioning authorities. In the Great Emigration, the restraints originated in the very fact of the emigration. In other words, the emigration qua emigration imposed a burden on its writers because the community as a whole tended to look to them for spiritual guidance as a component of its solidarity.

For at least the first decade of the emigration most of the émigrés believed that their exile would be shortlived and that they soon would be able to return to a reborn Poland. In the light of such an attitude, which was the rule rather than the exception, the cohesion of the émigré community became an absolute necessity. The emigration saw itself as the instrument through which the rebirth of an independent Poland would be achieved. To function effectively in this capacity, therefore, unity in the ranks had to be maintained. Literature could play an enormously influential role in achieving this goal by combating divisiveness and keeping the grand purpose of the Great Emigration ever in view. There resulted a literary climate wherein the Polish cause and the emigration, regarded as its moving spirit, became the central preoccupations of writers. Aesthetic criteria did not diminish in importance because of this, but the popular success or failure of a literary work often rested on the degree of manifest commitment to the national struggle.

The special relationship of the literary community to the Polish émigré milieu as a whole becomes clearer if the prevailing romanticism is taken into account. The November Insurrection, like its immediate Decembrist predecessor in Russia in 1825, was a romantic act on the part of young revolutionary idealists. The Great Emigration which followed reached the West at a time when the Romantic movement was still vital. The writers who joined the emigration or later in one way or another became identified with it were the principal architects of Polish romanticism. The confluence of these various currents, this interaction of Romantic ethos and emigration, had so great an impact on the creative writing of the Polish exiles at the peak of the emigration between 1831 and 1848 that any serious study of the émigré literature and Polish Romantic drama has to reckon with it.

By the time of the November Insurrection the Polish writers who were to dominate the literary landscape of the emigration were already strongly oriented in the direction of European romanticism. If a Polish Romantic literature was initiated with the publication of Mickiewicz's first book of poetry in 1822, then, in the eight years from this major literary event to the major political event of the Insurrection of 1830, there was ample time for the dominant Anglo-German impulses to be absorbed and the clear outlines of a well-developed Polish romanticism adumbrated. Judging from the actual literature written between 1822 and 1830 we can say that this fledgling Polish Romantic movement gave every indication of adhering to the main patterns of Western romanticism. The literature was Polish yet very European at the same time.

With the outbreak of the November Insurrection, its suppression, and the subsequent Great Emigration, this early Polish romanticism was forced to alter course dramatically. Paradoxically, when the base of this literature was dislocated and resettled in the West, the literature itself lost much of its supranational and European character and became more parochial. The emigration, after all, was a Polish phenomenon; a literature born of it and reflecting its anxieties and aspirations could not avoid parochialism. Yet, despite this, something quite striking and unexpected began to occur. The more the émigré literature made itself the spirit of the emigration, the more it assumed the heavy burden of the national struggle, the more intense became its romanticism. Realizing tendencies latent or undeveloped elsewhere in European romanticism, the Polish émigré literature of the period 1831 to 1848 evolved into the foremost manifestation of the Romantic ethos itself. It is in this way, above all, that Polish romanticism transcends parochialism and achieves universal significance.

The European Romantic saw himself as a rebel, dissatisfied with existing social and political systems. His belief in the power of the human will to effect change was profound. The sense of alienation often accompanied or inspired an urge to revolt. Generally, however, domestic political conditions made the realization of this urge impossible. The result was usually idealistic abstraction or sublimation. In some cases an outlet was found in the assumption of an alien cause. When European romanticism was crystallizing in the second decade of the nineteenth century, the Greek liberation struggle became the quintessential Romantic political revolt. Byron's identification with it was a characteristic response of the Romantic artist as activist. For the Poles, however, no alien outlets were necessary. The November Insurrection offered ample opportunity for engagement either through actual combat or through relocation in the emigration that it spawned. The emigration itself, at its peak, can also be considered a concretization of the will to rebel and resistance to status quo.

Romantic primitivism, the sense of spiritual affinity with peoples invested with a romantic aura the greater their distance from European civilization, assumed more than mere literary significance among the writers of the Polish emigration. Because of their own dispersion, the Poles were able to relate directly to the themes of exile and wandering in pre-Mohammedan Bedouin poetry, for example; in the Polish instance, Romantic literary orientalism already took on another dimension.[5]

Much the same can be said for the "Hebraicism" of European romanticism inspired by the Old Testament and Prophets. In searching for historical parallels to their own plight, the Polish émigrés quickly discovered how closely their own situation resembled the Diaspora of the Jews. In view of this "discovery", the appearance of Hebraic–Judaic motifs in Polish postinsurrectionary romanticism, which goes far beyond

---

[5] See Harold B. Segel, "Mickiewicz and the Arabic Qasidah in Poland", in *American Contributions to the Fifth International Congress of Slavists* (The Hague, 1963), pp. 279–300.

the conventional "Hebrew Melodies" poetry of the Western Romantics, should come as no great surprise. Again, literary mode fuses with existential experience.

The metaphysical propensities of romanticism offer a still more productive area of inquiry. Romantic cosmology and epistemology placed great emphasis on the supernatural and nonrational. Mystic vision, as in the case of Blake, was highly valued. If it came naturally, all the better. If not, there was the possibility of narcotic assistance, as with Coleridge and DeQuincey.

The actual literary reworking of mystic exploration was rare in European romanticism. But it was conspicuous among the Poles and again was something that came about, in the outstanding instances, through direct experience. A few of the leading Polish Romantics, above all Mickiewicz and Juliusz Słowacki, studied at the University of Wilno in Lithuania. For a long part of its history Wilno was a prominent center of Polish culture. It was also the greatest center of Orthodox Jewish culture in Europe during the nineteenth century and the home especially of Jewish mysticism when Mickiewicz, Słowacki, and other future Polish Romantic writers were students at the university there. Attracted to Romantic literature and Romantic supernaturalism – Rosicrucianism and Franz Mesmer's ideas on animal magnetism were much in vogue at the time[6] – the Poles eventually came across Jewish mystic lore (the Cabala, above all) in Wilno. This was not, to be sure, their sole exposure to mysticism, but it had a twofold appeal. First, because it was Jewish and hence non-Christian it was exotic; and second, because to a great extent it was an "underground" activity frowned on by the ecclesiastical hierarchy of the Jewish community, it enjoyed the aura of the forbidden.

Another opportunity for direct contact with mystic activity was afforded by Russia and the capital city of St. Petersburg in particular toward the end of the reign of Tsar Alexander I. The emperor's personal inclinations in his late years encouraged a great deal of occultism both in the court and outside. Masonic lodges and Rosicrucian societies served as the principal outlets for such interests. But there were other generally smaller groups of more informal character devoted, in the main, to communal mystic experience. Poles exiled to Russia in the first half of the nineteenth century occasionally found their way into such circles. The most striking case in the history of Polish romanticism involved a painter named Oleszkiewicz and Mickiewicz. Deported from November 1824 to

---

[6] See, for example, Harold B. Segel, "Animal Magnetism in Polish Romantic Literature", *Polish Review*, VII (Summer 1962), 16–39.

May 1829 for alleged anti-Russian political activism during his student days in Wilno, Mickiewicz at some point encountered Oleszkiewicz, a former acquaintance and fellow exile, and was presumably introduced into mystic circles in Russia through him. The friendship with Oleszkiewicz, who played a considerable role in helping Mickiewicz shape a mystic vision of his own future, served to reinforce the young poet's earlier contacts with mysticism, both Christian and Jewish.[7] Thus, when we find the poetic transmutation of the mystical in Mickiewicz's major dramatic work *Forefathers' Eve*, Part III, we must realize that we are dealing with more than literary pose or fashion.

Mysticism also reappeared as an important current in Polish émigré society and literature in Paris in the early 1840s. As the bleak reality of their status gradually but inexorably took hold of their consciousness, the émigrés turned from ever less fruitful stratagems for the reacquisition of Poland's independence by political or military means to sources of spiritual relief. For a frustrated people facing despair, the development was psychologically as well as emotionally understandable. Only by strengthening the spirit could the disasters of the recent past be understood and reconciled and the uncertain future that lay ahead be faced resolutely.

The role of the literary community in this turning inward to the spirit was central and decisive. As early as 1832, in his *Księgi narodu i pielgrzymstwa polskiego* (*The Books of the Polish Nation and Pilgrimage*), Mickiewicz had presented his fellow émigrés with a spiritual guidebook on how they were to interpret the Polish past and at the same time to conduct themselves in the period of their emigration.[8] In short, the émigrés were called upon to regard the emigration as a pilgrimage, for they were indeed on a spiritual mission. What was their goal? Nothing less than the re-Christianization of a Christian Europe that had become so derelict in its faith that it could permit and even participate in the dismemberment of a sister Christian nation such as Poland. This restoration of Christianity in a lapsed Europe could be effected by the émigrés

---

[7] The interest in and literary use of Christian and Jewish mysticism by Mickiewicz in particular have been the subject of several studies. Of special relevance for Mickiewicz's major drama, *Forefathers' Eve*, Part III, is Abraham G. Duker's "Some Cabbalist and Frankist Elements in Adam Mickiewicz's *Dziady*", in *Studies in Polish Civilization*, ed. Damian Wandycz (New York, 1966), pp. 213–235.

[8] The most thorough study of *The Books* is Zofia Stefanowska's *Historia i profecja: Studium o Księgach narodu i pielgrzymstwa* (Warsaw, 1962). A translation of *The Books* appears in *Poems by Adam Mickiewicz*, translated by various hands and edited by George Rapall Noyes (New York, 1944).

as the collective representation of the entire Polish nation which had been sacrificed, martyred as Christ had been in order to fulfill a higher, divine purpose. The partitions of Poland were viewed then as a political crucifixion which ultimately would bring about the redemption of Europe just as, in Christian thought, Christ's martyrdom was necessary for the redemption of man. Since the emigration was conceived of as the vanguard of the Polish nation, it was the émigrés' presence in the West that bore the burden of Poland's messianic destiny. In Mickiewicz's conception, the emigration represented both the spirit of Poland and the conscience of Europe. To be worthy of their truly noble role, the émigrés-pilgrims had to attain spiritual perfection. Once this was achieved, they would bring about a general revolution of the spirit that would return Europe to Christianity. The nations responsible for the perpetration of Poland's dismemberment would then perceive the sin into which they had fallen and would seek atonement in Poland's political resurrection.

Mickiewicz's Romantic messianism had a certain basis in history. In the seventeenth-century wars against the Ottoman Turks the Poles saw themselves as an instrument of divine will by serving as a bulwark against the infidel engulfment of European Christendom. Their sizable contribution to the lifting of the siege of Vienna in 1683, which ended for all time the Turkish threat to Central and Western Europe, easily lent itself to interpretation in messianic terms. That Poland was chosen (by God, of course) for this exalted role was attributed to the Poles' unswerving fidelity to the faith. Polish messianism thus may have lain dormant for nearly a century and a half after Vienna, but the partitions, the November Insurrection, and the Great Emigration were sufficiently powerful stimuli to reactivate it in the 1830s.

The messianic conception of Poland was amply elaborated by the Romantics. Mickiewicz may have been among the first to renew the tradition, but he was hardly the only one to do so. Much of Zygmunt Krasiński's poetry and philosophical writing developed along similar lines. But the most intriguing exponent of this ideology in the emigration was an enigmatic figure named Andrzej Towiański (1799–1878). Controversial to this day, Towiański (like Mickiewicz) was of Polish Lithuanian origin and appeared in 1840 to become a powerful voice among the émigrés. Some still insist that he was a tsarist agent assigned to Paris to sow discord among the Polish émigrés in order to render them ineffectual in influencing Western policy on Russia. Agent or mystic, Towiański was a magnetic speaker who quickly won the commitment of several leading figures of the emigration, above all, its poets. Preaching a messianic vision of Poland's destiny as a nation, Towiański appealed for a spiritual regeneration of the émigrés as a precondition to their assumption of the great mission ordained for them. The timing could not have been better. Towiański seemed like another Moses come to lead the chosen people out of the wilderness of their exile. Until he became an embarrassment to the French government and was duly banned from France in July 1842, he was the center of a Polish émigré cultism that counted such outstanding personalities as Mickiewicz and Słowacki among the faithful. To attain the inner perfection which Towiański called for, a Circle (Koło) of initiates was formed in June 1842 for the practice of spiritual exercises of marked mystic character. Although some members of the group (Słowacki, for example) defected after a year or so, the appeal of Towiański's thought was so powerful that his "work" continued even after his expulsion from France. As the most steadfast of the apostles, Mickiewicz was the logical choice to assume the direction of the Circle in the absence of the "Master".

The emigration not only activated the latent proclivity of the Romantic writer toward the mystic, it also created an appropriate climate for the full realization of the poet as seer. To the Romantics, poetry was both the highest form of art and the privileged endowment of the very few, the select. By virtue of his gift the poet was, therefore, an extraordinary individual. Possessed of powers denied ordinary mortals, the poet could penetrate the mysteries of the universe. Through his art he could share with others glimpses of the higher realm, the greater reality. He could present fresh perspectives on the past and insights into the future. By uplifting his readers, by raising their spirits far above the mundane to higher levels of being and knowing, he could through the magic of poetic creation ultimately achieve a transformation of both man and society.

This exalted conception of the poet and poetry was universal among the Romantics throughout Europe. Few, however, were afforded an environment in which it could evolve into more than an abstract ideal. The Polish Romantics were among those few. Because of the nature of the emigration, leadership became an issue of vital concern. The longer the émigrés remained in the West, the more fragmented and disunited they became as a community. In the beginning, Prince Czartoryski was the acknowledged political leader. But as time went on and the various schemes and strategies for Polish independence proved fruitless, political dissension spread among the émigrés. Czartoryski's conservatism, which counseled against outright military action, was opposed by a revolutionary faction that saw military action as the only way to break the bonds of partition. When dissension and frustration gave rise to despair, others saw only religious devotion and spiritual self-perfection as the guarantors of Poland's resurrection. As political authority dissolved into strident factionalism, a crisis of leadership developed. The situation was now ripe for the poet.

In the absence of effective political guidance the poet would step in to fill the vacuum. Through his art he would supplant the crumbling political leadership with a spiritual one. And by means of this spiritual leadership factionalism and fragmentation would finally be overcome and a new sense of unity forged among the émigrés. Without this unity, it was rightly perceived that the emigration would indeed be rendered mute and ineffectual. Mickiewicz's major dramatic work, *Forefathers' Eve*, Part III (1832), must be interpreted, on one level, as a declaration by the foremost Polish Romantic poet of his intention to assume precisely that kind of spiritual leadership.

At the outset of his literary career in the early 1820s, Mickiewicz wrote two dramatic works in verse of unequal importance as Romantic poems and of slight value as drama. Both were based on the folklore of the poet's native region – the rural area around the town of Nowogródek in Polish Lithuania which contained a large number of Belorussian peasants of the Orthodox faith. Mickiewicz linked the two short plays together by calling them parts of a larger unfinished drama named simply *Dziady* (*Forefathers' Eve*). The Polish title refers to the pre-Christian Belorussian rite of ancestor worship. Twice a year peasants would come together in cemeteries or chapels, summon the spirits of the dead, and regale them with food and drink to ease their life in the next world. Since it was pagan in origin, the ceremony was officially frowned on by the Church but was not totally suppressed because of the ease with which it could be related to the Christian celebration of the deceased on All Souls' Day. In its fusion of folklore, folk ritual, and a Wertherian tale of unrequited love culminating in madness and suicide *Forefathers' Eve* reads like a paradigm of romanticism.

The two short plays comprising *Forefathers' Eve* were published in Wilno in 1823 in Mickiewicz's second volume of poetry and were numbered Parts II and IV, respectively; a fragmentary first part, apparently written in the same period, was discovered and published only posthumously.[9] Nine years later, Mickiewicz wrote another play which he designated *Forefathers' Eve*, Part III (*Dziady*, Część III). Why he numbered the early parts of the play II and IV, instead of I and II, and the very different *Forefathers' Eve* of 1832 Part III remains a mystery. Also a mystery is the fact that Part III – complete in itself – states at the end that it

---

[9] For translations of the early parts of *Forefathers' Eve*, see Adam Mickiewicz, *Forefathers*, trans. Count Potocki of Montalk (London, 1968).

is the "first act" of something longer. Although Mickiewicz thought of further work on the drama, to which he felt a deep personal attachment, no continuation was ever written nor have any important fragments of a sequel been discovered. The most plausible explanation for the eccentric numbering of *Forefathers' Eve* seems to be that the poet wanted to suggest a fragmentary structure for the drama as a whole in a literary mystification that was by no means untypical of the Pre-Romantics and Romantics – Sterne, Goethe, Coleridge, and Keats had already provided models of such mystification. Doubtless following Mickiewicz's example, Słowacki similarly subtitled his play *Kordian* (1834) the first part of a trilogy which never came into being.

Much had happened to Mickiewicz between the first two parts of *Forefathers' Eve* and the third. He had been arrested, jailed, then exiled to Russia for four and a half years on unsubstantiated charges of membership in a Polish prorevolutionary society while a student at the University of Wilno. His fame as a poet, however, had preceded him to Russia where he was accepted and lionized in the most fashionable literary and polite society; exile, in other words, was anything but hardship. After Russia, Mickiewicz traveled through Western Europe, finally settling in Rome, where he again moved freely in the best circles. It was in Rome that word reached him of the outbreak of the November Insurrection. Although he was expected, as the leading Polish writer of the day and one, moreover, who had been imprisoned and exiled for his Polish nationalism, to make his way posthaste to the battlefield, if only to serve as a symbol, he did not do so. He lingered awhile in Rome and then went to Paris, presumably to learn more about the uprising. Months later, when he had at last resolved to head for embattled Poland, he got as far as Poznań on the Prussian-Polish border only to discover that Warsaw was under siege and that no passage across the Russian frontier was possible.

Mickiewicz remained in the Poznań area until March 1832, thereafter proceeding to Dresden. He stayed here until June and in August was back in Paris. The long residence in Prussia and Saxony was spent mostly in socializing and hunting. This carefree life ended, however, when Mickiewicz began meeting remnants of the Polish army that had crossed into Prussia to lay down their arms and other exiles streaming after them on their way to safety in the West. Confronted thus with the reality of the Insurrection and his own ambivalence toward it, the poet fell into a state of agonizing self-scrutiny. It was at this time and in these circumstances that the new *Forefathers' Eve* was conceived.

While in Russia as an exile Mickiewicz had entry into Russian or Russo-Polish mystic circles, as we have already seen. His earlier interest in mysticism going back to his student days in Wilno had prepared him

for such contacts. One result of these new experiences was the conviction
that his place in Polish literature was destined to be that of a *wieszcz* (from
the Latin *vates*), that is, a poet who is at the same time a seer. The
opportunity to fulfill his destiny, as it were, was provided by the defeat
of the November Insurrection. As Mickiewicz encountered the Poles
fleeing westward after the suppression, he gradually saw himself serving
them in the emigration as a spiritual leader. Without such direction,
which he doubtless felt himself best able to offer, Mickiewicz feared that
the emigration would soon sink into despair and be unable to assist the
Polish cause in any meaningful way. If such thinking should seem to us
an act of profound conceit, we have to remember that Mickiewicz was a
Romantic imbued with the high sense of the poet's mission in the age of
romanticism. But because of the Polish circumstances at the time, he
could move from the realm of abstract ideals to deed.

Before becoming fully active as poet-seer, however, a major problem (at
least in his own mind) had to be resolved and that was his absence from
the field of battle during the Insurrection. How could his fellow émigrés,
after all, look to him for leadership of any kind if he bore a stigma of
indifference or cowardice for his failure to throw himself headlong into
the struggle of 1830? To clear this hurdle, Mickiewicz, once decided on
his future course of action, composed the third part of *Forefathers' Eve*
while in Dresden in a surge of creative energy. He took the completed
work with him to Paris, where he established permanent residence
among the Polish émigrés and where the drama was printed in December
1832 as the fourth volume of the Paris edition of his collected poems.

Apart from its many remarkable qualities as an innovative Romantic
drama combining contemporary history and traditions of the medieval
mystery play, *Forefathers' Eve*, Part III, also has to be read as a personal
apologia. Mickiewicz had prepared such an apologia as early as 1828 in
the most curious and ideologically revealing work he wrote during his
Russian exile, the historical narrative poem *Konrad Wallenrod*.[10] Clearly
the most outstanding figure in the poem is the Lithuanian *wajdelota* or
poet-seer Halban who refuses to join the "hero" (Konrad Wallenrod) in a
suicide pact. A Lithuanian patriot, Wallenrod has finally succeeded in
defeating the German Order of the Teutonic Knights – who have conquered and ravaged his native Lithuania – from within, after having
become by subterfuge the Order's grand master. When Wallenrod's game
is up at the end of the poem, he chooses suicide over certain execution
and urges Halban, his lifelong companion and mentor, to join him.

---

[10] A translation of it appears in *Poems by Adam Mickiewicz*.

15

Halban refuses on the grounds that as a poet-seer he must live in order to immortalize Wallenrod. Through his art, in other words, Halban will pass on to future generations the courage and heroism of Wallenrod. He will transform his deeds into myth and as myth Wallenrod will live again to inspire Lithuanians from one generation to the next.

Despite the risk of reading too much into the text, it seems fair to assume that the figure of Halban in *Konrad Wallenrod* reflects a projection of Mickiewicz's own feelings at the time about the relationship of the poet, poetry, and history. His subsequent posture during the November Insurrection would appear to confirm this view. The link between *Konrad Wallenrod* and the third part of *Forefathers' Eve* offers additional evidence. In the Prologue to the play, the central character undergoes a transformation in his prison cell; under the impress of the dreadful events he experiences, Gustav becomes Konrad. The names are important here. From the earlier *Forefathers' Eve* we know that Gustav connotes the Romantic poet as ill-starred lover, Goethe's Werther. Konrad, of course, immediately evokes an association with Konrad Wallenrod, the avenger. In transforming his protagonist from Gustav to Konrad, Mickiewicz is showing, in effect, the spiritual metamorphosis of his hero from poet, Romantic lover, solitary singer, to *wieszcz*, or *vates*, the poet-seer who transcends personal feelings, identifies himself with his nation, makes its cause his own, and becomes its prophet.

In approaching *Forefathers' Eve*, Part III, as apologia the transformation of Gustav into Konrad can be applied directly to Mickiewicz himself. The play obviously traces Mickiewicz's own career from autumn 1823 to autumn 1824. Mickiewicz and several of his university friends were arrested and charged with belonging to an anti-Russian student political organization. They were detained for some six months in a monastery of the Basilian Fathers in Wilno that had been temporarily converted into a jail. In November 1824, Mickiewicz arrived in St. Petersburg to begin the Russian exile that was to last until spring 1829. What the later *Forefathers' Eve* depicts is the partial metamorphosis of Mickiewicz himself – in reaction to the events of 1823 and 1824 – from the young Romantic poet of the first published poetry of 1822 and 1823 into the émigré poet ready to make his debut as *wieszcz* in 1832. I say "partial metamorphosis" because the process is incomplete in *Forefathers' Eve*, Part III; the play ends with the hero en route across the snows of Lithuania from Wilno to St. Petersburg. What lies ahead we already know: the lionization of Mickiewicz by the Russians as the greatest Polish poet of his age, his contacts with Pushkin and poets soon to take part in the Decembrist Revolt, his entry into Russian occultist circles, the mystic interpretation of his own destiny as an artist, and the projection of that destiny in *Konrad Wallenrod*, the major literary work of his Russian period (which, in fact, was published in St. Petersburg in 1828). But before Mickiewicz can become worthy of mystic revelation, of attaining the full prophetic power of the true *vates*, he must first be made to expiate the sin of pride through suffering. It is this process of spiritual maturation that the poet traces in the third part of *Forefathers' Eve*. The psychic predisposition to mystic experience of Gustav-become-Konrad or Mickiewicz become-seer is definitely established in the drama in the hero's preference for nocturnal solitude, the "strangeness" of the songs he sings, and, above all, the so-called "little" and "great" improvisations in the play. The latter is especially noteworthy as a fine example of mystic ecstasy reconstituted as poetry.

The more transparent elements of apologia in *Forefathers' Eve*, Part III, appear in Mickiewicz's treatment of history. The play's subject is the jailing of the poet and his friends in Wilno in 1823 and 1824 and their subsequent exile to Russia. Since Mickiewicz must show that he had already become identified with the national cause and indeed had been made to suffer for it – despite his later behavior during the November Insurrection – it behooves him to portray his Wilno experiences as a national calamity. Yet the fact remains that however exaggerated the case against Mickiewicz and his friends and however brutal their arrest, imprisonment, and later dispersion throughout Russia might have been, the episode itself was of predominantly local significance. Broader humanitarian and political issues were involved, to be sure, but the Wilno events themselves simply did not represent a Polish national calamity, disaster, or anything of the sort. To place them on the same footing as the November Insurrection, which I believe Mickiewicz does by implication, may be poetic license but there is no mistaking the poet's intention. This is manifest, for example, in the play's geographic settings. The scene shifts from Wilno, in Lithuania, to Warsaw, in central Poland, and to Lwów, in the Ukraine. This simultaneity of events in disparate locations and the episodic structure of *Forefathers' Eve* situate the drama artistically in the forefront of avant-garde Romantic drama alongside the works of Christian Dietrich Grabbe and especially Büchner in Germany. But if Mickiewicz, in fact, surpasses a dramatist such as Büchner in the depth and range of his architechtonic conception, his motivation can be attributed to ideological as well as aesthetic considerations. By moving the action from Wilno, to Warsaw, and to Lwów, the poet suggests the national dimensions of the Wilno affair.

The treatment of Russian politics in the drama reflects the same ideological spirit. Mickiewicz and his friends were little more than pawns in a power struggle involving the Russian Senator Novosiltsev, who was in charge of the Wilno investigation, and the Polish Prince Czartoryski, then curator of the Wilno school district. The case against them was trumped up and their lives were indeed disrupted by the harsh sentences imposed on them. The facts speak for themselves. But whatever the harassment and dislocation suffered by the Wilno youths, the only way in which they can be viewed as the first victims of a Russian policy of *genocide* against the Poles – the undeniable accusation made by *Fore-fathers' Eve* not only in the prose Foreword to the play but in the long narrative passages in the first and seventh scenes – is in the metaphoric sense necessary to Mickiewicz's mythopoeic purposes in his drama.

Once we take notice of the political and psychic factors in the play's genesis, we can go on to appreciate those literary and dramatic qualities of *Forefathers' Eve* which establish it as one of the few unusual works of the European Romantic theatre of the first half of the nineteenth century.

Years after writing *Forefathers' Eve*, Part III, when he was lecturing as the first holder of a newly established chair of Slavic literature at the Collège de France in Paris, Mickiewicz expounded his views on the drama in his now famous sixteenth (or "theatrical") lecture of April 4, 1843.[11] Anticipating Wagner's concept of a theatre of the future in which the dramatic, choreographic, auditory, and visual arts are brought to-gether in an organic synthesis, Mickiewicz spoke of the need for the new drama "to play all the most varied strings, to run up and down all the rungs of poetry from the simple song to the epos".[12] This drama also had to be national in the sense of uniting all elements of a truly national poetic tradition.

Although these ideas were not developed enough to constitute a concrete program for a national theatre, they were imbued with a remarkable spirit of the visionary and monumental.[13] It was in this spirit that Mickiewicz pleaded for a vibrant drama capable of striking respon-sive chords in the innermost beings of mass audiences and urged Slavic poets in particular to ignore the contemporary stage in their playwrit-ing because of its physical limitations, opining that a great Slavic drama

---

[11] Tymon Terlecki gives a brief account in "A Critical Appraisal of Mickiewicz's Lecture about the Theater", in *Studies in Polish Civilization*. On Mickiewicz's lectures at the Collège de France in general, see Wiktor Weintraub's *Literature as Prophecy: Scholarship and Martinist Poetics in Mickiewicz's Parisian Lectures* (The Hague, 1959).

[12] Adam Mickiewicz, *Dzieła*, XI, Literatura słowiańska, Kurs trzeci i czwarty, trans. Leon Płoszewski (Warsaw, 1955), p. 120.

[13] For an interesting critique of Mickiewicz's lecture, see also Maja Zawadzka, "Lekcja XVI Mickiewicza jako program narodowego dramatu romantycznego", *Poezja*, XI, Nos. 120–121 (Warsaw, 1975), 124–136.

and theatre awaited new developments in architecture, painting, and lighting.

The principal sources for Mickiewicz's attempt to create a national drama in the *Forefathers' Eve* cycle – long before the articulation of his theoretical views in the Parisian lectures – were classical Greek tragedy, the Christian drama and theatre of the Middle Ages, the Catholic rites of confession, repentance, and sacrifice, and folklore. From classical antiquity the poet derived not so much specific techniques as the model of a great and universal Greek tragic drama developed integrally out of popular myth and ritual. The Belorussian folk rite of ancestor celebration was to serve as the same raw material for fashioning an exemplary new Polish and, indeed, Slavic drama.

The attraction of medieval drama was considerable. Its supernaturalism and looseness of form accorded with Romantic metaphysics and Romantic aesthetics. But Mickiewicz also saw medieval drama as especially relevant to his purpose in the third part of *Forefathers' Eve*. By welding medieval mystery form, Catholic rite, and actual events and people of his own time, he was, in effect, creating a modern Passion play celebrating the martyrdom of Poland as exemplified by the persecution of the Wilno youths.[14] From Catholic tradition and the techniques of the mystery Mickiewicz derived the entire supernatural structure of *Forefathers' Eve*. This incorporates the conflict between Good and Evil – the axis on which the play turns – the inner spiritual drama of the central character Konrad, and such motifs as the Guardian Angel who keeps vigil over Gustav-Konrad, the good and bad spirits who urge Konrad in one direction or another (Heaven or Hell) as his high-soaring transport brings him ever closer to the damnation of blasphemy, the devils who fight among themselves on stage as they struggle to take possession of the soul of the exhausted Konrad, the exorcism of the chief devil by the pious and humble Father Peter who serves as Konrad's spiritual mentor in the play, Senator Novosiltsev's troubled dreams, and the divine retribution visited upon one of his henchmen.

The contribution of folklore to *Forefathers' Eve*, Part III, is minor. The twice-yearly rite of the graveyard banquet to which the souls of departed ancestors are invited serves as the setting of the earlier parts of the drama in which more extensive use of folk materials is made. In the later third part, the folk rite appears only in the ninth and last scene. The reintroduction of the folk motif at this point seems to have been motivated solely by Mickiewicz's desire to forge an obvious link between the play he

---

[14] Weintraub, *The Poetry of Adam Mickiewicz*, p. 179.

wrote in 1832 and the *Forefathers' Eve* of 1823. The later play clearly is an entirely different work. If so, then why did the poet call it *Forefathers' Eve* and then designate it as the third part of a multipartite drama begun ten years earlier?

The answer to this question again touches on both the poet's personal drama and his literary ambitions. By designating the play of 1832 as the third part of a much earlier work and giving it the same general title as that work, Mickiewicz plainly signaled his intention to trace the spiritual evolution of Gustav and to suggest, moreover, that the metamorphosis of Gustav into Konrad is that of Mickiewicz himself. From the Romantic singer of Wertherian love in the second and fourth parts of *Forefathers' Eve*, Mickiewicz has become transformed by the personal and political events of the period from 1823 to 1832 into the poet-*vates* whose voice is now that of the entire Polish nation, whose very soul has become one with that of his people.

Mickiewicz's career after *Forefathers' Eve*, Part III, bears out this view. Following in rapid succession after the play were the last of the poet's major works, *The Books of the Polish Nation and Pilgrimage* and *Pan Tadeusz* (*Master Thaddeus*, 1834).[15] Both lend themselves to interpretation as the creations of a poet-seer intent on serving a given community as its spiritual leader. The first, as we have seen earlier, is essentially a messianic reading of Polish history and a plea for the émigrés to perceive the Great Emigration as a Great Pilgrimage. The biblical prose style of *The Books* and the extensive use of parable leave no doubt concerning Mickiewicz's conception of the nature and significance of his own "holy" undertaking.

Master Thaddeus, on the other hand, is a superb evocation of a past Polish way of life. Its purpose was to enable the émigrés of the 1830s to understand that their common heritage should be a unifying factor in their lives and in the collective existence of the emigration as a whole, strong enough to hold them together as a community despite the divisive pull of dissension and frustration. Blending epic and pastoral, its style deceptively simple and even homey despite its classical epic meter, *Master Thaddeus* so transforms the everyday into the mythic that it deservedly ranks as one of the great books of world literature.

Although Mickiewicz's literary career virtually ended with *Master Thaddeus*, he tried in one way or another to fulfill himself as poet-seer and spiritual guide until his death in Constantinople in 1855. Even his

---

[15] Of the three available translations of *Pan Tadeusz* into English, the best is by Kenneth Mackenzie, in the Everyman's Library series (London and New York, 1966).

appearance in Turkey was informed with the mystique of his reputation as poet and *wieszcz*. Polish volunteer forces had come to Turkey to fight with the Allies against the Russians during the Crimean War. By assisting the Allies, the Poles hoped to gain support for a restoration of even partial Polish independence following the anticipated defeat of the Russians. When divergent political attitudes brought rivalry and conflict to the different volunteer organizations and the entire operation seemed in jeopardy, Mickiewicz was prevailed upon because of his immense prestige to use his influence while in Turkey to restore harmony among them. At the very end of his life, Mickiewicz was still trying, as *wieszcz*, to maintain the unity of the emigration to which he so passionately and totally committed himself from the conception in 1832 of *Forefathers' Eve*, Part III, in Dresden.

While Mickiewicz's reputation as the foremost poet of the Polish language went unchallenged in his lifetime (and is still unquestioned today), his spiritual authority in the emigration did not. Much of the career of Poland's second greatest poet, Juliusz Słowacki, had the character of a contest for supremacy with Mickiewicz.[16] Słowacki regarded himself as a superior poet, a "purer" talent, but convinced few of even his peer status until the end of the nineteenth century. His reputation since then has grown so rapidly that today he plays the Shelley to Mickiewicz's Byron.

Słowacki's resentment and even envy of Mickiewicz fed not only on the latter's preeminence as a poet but on his self-appointed role as a spiritual leader of the emigration. If Słowacki held himself to be the superior poetic talent, he also disagreed profoundly with Mickiewicz's views on the emigration and its future and, above all, on Mickiewicz's concept of the poet as seer and national leader. Through a series of works Słowacki conducted a running polemic with Mickiewicz about the poet and poetry, on the one hand, and the emigration and Polish destiny, on the other.

To Mickiewicz's belief in the emergence of a *wieszcz* who would conduct the émigrés from the hell of the emigration to the Promised Land

---

[16] For an introductory account in English of Słowacki's life and work, see Stefan Treugutt's *Juliusz Słowacki: Romantic Poet* (Warsaw, 1959). Two good, mainly biographical works on the poet in Polish are Eugeniusz Sawrymowicz's *Kalendarz życia i twórczości Juliusza Słowackiego* (Wrocław, 1960), and his *Juliusz Słowacki* (Warsaw, 1973). Of a more specialized nature, an interesting discussion of one of Słowacki's more curious plays, *Mazepa* (1839), appears in Hubert F. Babinski, *The Mazeppa Legend in European Romanticism* (New York and London, 1974).

of a resurrected Poland, Słowacki opposed the vision (especially in his biblical prose poem *Anhelli*, 1838) of an emigration fragmented by internal dissension and incapable of achieving anything positive in its own time. Mickiewicz's by no means uncritical but still warm embrace (in *Master Thaddeus*, for example) of the traditional Polish ruling class, the landowning gentry (*szlachta*), was categorically rejected by Słowacki. The younger poet, anticipating a major current in later nineteenth-century Polish historiography, held the gentry's conservatism and narrow self-concern largely responsible for the disasters that had befallen Poland. Unlike Mickiewicz, Słowacki assigns the gentry virtually no role in the reestablishment of Polish independence. In a familiar Romantic gesture, he directs his gaze instead to the people, the folk or *lud* in Polish. It will be only in a general uprising of the people – everywhere – that Poland will be reborn in the context of a new European social order. Advocating social revolution as the only sure path to Polish emancipation, Słowacki repudiates the mysticomessianic philosophy of Mickiewicz. It follows, then, that if Mickiewicz's messianism and mysticism have little or no validity, the idea of the *wieszcz* or poet-seer as conceptualized by Mickiewicz in *Forefathers' Eve*, Part III, and embodied in a work such as *The Books of the Polish Nation and Pilgrimage* is equally invalid. In *Anhelli* and elsewhere Słowacki plays havoc with the very notion of a spiritual leader emerging from within the generation whose ineffectuality, according to the poet, was nowhere more apparent than in the failure of the November Insurrection. In an even stronger indictment, Słowacki lays the blame for the ineffectuality and even spiritual weakness of his own generation at the doorstep of romanticism itself. The generation of 1830 failed in its attempt to translate the poetry of abstract ideals into concrete action because it was a *Romantic* generation. The point is made unequivocally in Słowacki's best known dramatic work, *Kordian* (1834).[17]

Słowacki's first major play and serious attempt at political drama, *Kordian*, was conceived as a direct response to Mickiewicz's *Forefathers' Eve*, Part III. The evidence for such an assertion is abundant, but suffice it to mention the title of the drama, which is the name of the "hero". Kordian is obviously an anagram of Konrad and the character represents a refutation of everything symbolized by the central figure of the third part of Mickiewicz's *Forefathers' Eve*.

Słowacki's Kordian is a dreamer, a Romantic dreamer, to be precise, who yearns to find meaning in life. The Polish cause seems to offer the

---

[17] The play is unavailable in English. For discussions of it, see the studies by Miłosz and Treugutt.

best possibility for this, and accordingly he identifies with it by joining a conspiracy plotting to assassinate the Russian tsar during a state visit to Warsaw. Kordian personally assumes responsibility for the deed, already intoxicated with the image of himself as a national avenger and deliverer. But when the decisive moment comes and Kordian stands poised, bayonet in hand, above the sleeping body of the tsar he falters. Imagination and Fear, presented as actual characters in the play, take hold of him and he proves incapable of the assassination.

What Słowacki is trying to show through Kordian is the impossibility of a great avenger and deliverer, such as delineated on different levels by Mickiewicz in *Konrad Wallenrod* and the third part of *Forefathers' Eve*, appearing in his own time. And the reason for this – apart from an ethical tradition unequivocally opposed to violence, whatever the motivation – is the heavy burden of romanticism borne by his generation. Because of this burden, Słowacki sees his generation condemned to ineffectuality through its fondness for the (ill-conceived) Romantic gesture and for brilliant words and poetic images of no substance. In line with this attitude, Mickiewicz's conception of Konrad as *vates* and deliverer is nothing more than another example of Romantic image-making and self-delusion – worse in the case of Mickiewicz because his mysticomessianic vision is a projection of the poet himself.

An immature work in some respects, *Kordian* still delivers a forceful message. If it did not endear Słowacki to the many Polish émigrés who were happier with the palliatives profered by Mickiewicz, it did establish the poet as a major dramatic talent. The play has since become a classic of the Polish theatre and is performed regularly. Before considering Słowacki's later and patently more satirical broadside against romanticism, *Fantazy*, let us turn our attention to the last member of the trinity of great Polish Romantic playwrights, Count Zygmunt Krasiński.[18]

Krasiński's career followed very different lines than that of Mickiewicz and Słowacki and his reputation as a writer has fluctuated more than that of any other major figure of Polish literature. Although identified with the Great Emigration, Krasiński was no émigré like Mickiewicz or Słowacki and never lost physical contact with his homeland. Mickiewicz, we recall, left Russia after his exile in 1829, settled in the West, became a part of the emigration, and never returned to Poland. A graduate of the University of Wilno, like Mickiewicz, Słowacki left Poland not long before the

---

[18] The most useful general work on Krasiński in English is the book of essays *Zygmunt Krasiński, Romantic Universalist: An International Tribute*, ed. Wacław Lednicki (New York, 1964). See also Monica M. Gardner's now outdated *The Anonymous Poet of Poland: Zygmunt Krasiński* (Cambridge, England, 1919).

suppression of the November Insurrection; after a sojourn in London, where he carried out an assignment as diplomatic courier for the revolutionary government in Warsaw, he, too, settled in Paris with the majority of the émigrés. Never entirely comfortable in the French capital, however – in part because of his sense of rivalry with Mickiewicz – he traveled a great deal, a journey to Greece and the Holy Land from 1836 to 1839 being of particular importance for his development as a writer. During the European uprisings of 1848, Słowacki was able to make a short visit to Wrocław, in Prussian Poland, where he was briefly reunited with his mother whom he had not seen in eighteen years.

Unlike Mickiewicz and Słowacki, Krasiński could come and go virtually as he chose. He was the son of a Polish general who had distinguished himself in Napoleon's service. When what remained of the Polish army that had fought for Napoleon was delivered over to the command of the Russian tsar after the French defeat, Genral Wincenty Krasiński, obedient soldier that he was, thereupon became a general in the imperial Russian army. This opened many doors in St. Petersburg but created deep psychological problems for young Zygmunt. To a great many Poles at the time, above all his school fellows, he was the son of a traitor – or of an opportunist. As a submissive son who worshiped as well as feared his father, Zygmunt was incapable of doing anything of which his father might disapprove. This meant that however strong his feelings for the cause of Polish independence, he could not make any display of them.

Because of his failing vision and the need for frequent medical treatment in the West, Krasiński spent much time outside Poland and Russia. Though circumstances prohibited his physical relocation in the emigration, he identified with it spiritually and turned to Polish national problems increasingly as his literary career developed. Desiring to become at least a spiritual émigré and to be heard by his fellow Poles in the West as a voice addressing their deepest aspirations, Krasiński published his works in Paris. But because of his sensitivity concerning his father and his own position, he insisted on publishing his works anonymously, for which he became known as the "anonymous poet".

Ambivalent feelings about Krasiński lingered long among the émigrés even when it was common knowledge that he was the "anonymous poet". His father's defection, the poet's subservience to him, his ease of movement in and out of Poland, and his family's wealth aroused resentment and envy. Yet Krasiński's dedication to Poland, his spiritual union with the Great Emigration were beyond dispute.

Despite sometimes acrimonious polemics with other Polish writers, notably Słowacki (who definitely had a penchant for acrimony and polemics), Krasiński was admired in his own time for his poetry and his philosophical writings. Much of his work was of a prophetically visionary and messianic character reminiscent of the ideology of Mickiewicz's *Books of the Polish Nation and Pilgrimage.*

When writers of the fin-de-siècle generation known as Young Poland (Młoda Polska) made their far-reaching reassessment of every aspect of the Romantic period, the reputations of the great Romantic trinity underwent extensive modification. Critical of Romantic mysticism and messianism, Young Poland insisted on the primacy of artistic values in literature as opposed to ideological engagement. Judged by these standards, Mickiewicz was faulted for so blatantly tendentious a piece of writing (or preachment) as *The Books* and looked upon with pity for the misfortune of his later involvement with Towianski and the futile efforts of the 1840s and 1850s to combine spiritual and political leadership. To the writers of Young Poland, the wasteland that was Mickiewicz's literary career after *Master Thaddeus* was the most grievous loss of all. But despite some reservations, they were generous in their recognition of Mickiewicz's genius in transforming national content into universal art in *Forefathers' Eve* and *Master Thaddeus.*

Because of his personal distaste for a "committed art", his aloofness from Polish Romantic émigré politics, and the sheer brilliance of his poetic gifts, Słowacki finally came into his own in the time of Young Poland. Not only was he the focus of new studies and appreciations, he was hailed by the poets of Young Poland as the most kindred spirit among the Romantics. So great was the admiration for him, and so extensive his influence, that Słowacki was considered by many not only the equal of Mickiewicz but indeed his superior. If he did not, finally, succeed in dislodging Mickiewicz from his position as Poland's greatest poet, his reputation as second greatest is by now secure.

Krasiński's reputation suffered the most in the late nineteenth and early twentieth centuries. His poetry came to be regarded as little more than a pedestrian vehicle for an embarrassing messianism. Much of his other writing was neglected because of its reflection of Krasiński's extremely conservative social views and what came to be regarded as his amateur and shallow Romantic philosophizing. The only works of Krasiński that survived the general depreciation of his talent were his two plays, *Irydion* (begun in 1832, completed 1836)[19] and *Nie-Boska komedia* (*The UnDivine Comedy*, 1833).

---

[19] There is an older, somewhat dated translation of the play into English: *Irdyion* by Count Zygmunt Krasiński, translated from the Polish by Florence Noyes and edited with an introduction by George Rapall Noyes (London, 1927).

With the establishment of a Communist regime after World War II, Krasiński was all but relegated to oblivion. His messianism, Catholicism, and social conservatism were totally repugnant to Poland's new leadership and for some years no new editions of his works could be published. The situation changed in the early 1960s owing to a more liberal cultural policy. Studies of the poet, supplemented by new editions of his works, started to appear after a long hiatus. As Krasiński came to be better known, a rehabilitation of his reputation as a writer ensued. The results are curious. The very early Romantic tales and most of his poetry are still considered weak, but his voluminous correspondence has at last been fully brought to light and reveals him as a superb prose stylist and easily the outstanding epistolary artist of Polish romanticism. Of his two dramatic works, *Irydion* attracts no great attention though it is staged from time to time. Apart from its markedly Christian ending, the play is yet another Romantic study in the psychology of vengeance much like Mickiewicz's *Konrad Wallenrod*. The main protagonist this time is a Greek burning with desire to avenge his native country for its subjugation by Rome. Like Konrad Wallenrod he enters the service of the enemy to destroy him from within. Despite their trappings of antique history, both *Konrad Wallenrod* and *Irydion* spoke directly to the Polish situation in relation to Russia in the nineteenth century and thus became irrelevant once Poland regained its independence after World War I. If *Konrad Wallenrod* is remembered more kindly than *Irydion*, this is only because of its pivotal importance in understanding Mickiewicz's later development as writer and *wieszcz* in the émigré period. *Irydion* has no such significance in any study of Krasiński's evolution and has less claim on our interest today.

The Un-Divine Comedy is an entirely different matter, however. The play has steadily gained prestige in the twentieth century and is widely regarded in contemporary Poland as one of the greatest dramatic works to emerge from the Romantic period. Enhancing its position in the history of modern Polish drama is the growing awareness of the play outside Poland. It has been successfully staged in other languages (including English) and enjoys the distinction of being the Polish Romantic drama to have attracted the most serious attention abroad thus far.

Setting *The Un-Divine Comedy* apart from most other Polish Romantic drama is its immediacy and its particular relevance for the twentieth century. The play deals with revolution, social upheaval, class war, political morality, and the historical process. The importance of such themes to the present century needs no commentary. Its composition in prose, albeit often a highly sylized prose, also helps its international career; it is easier to translate than the plays of Mickiewicz and especially

Słowacki, almost all of which were written in verse. The play also demands no special initiation on the part of the foreign audience. Unlike the more obtrusive "Polishness" of Mickiewicz's *Forefathers' Eve*, Part III, or Słowacki's *Kordian* and *Fantazy*, its setting is indeterminate. Yet like these other masterworks of Polish Romantic drama, its genesis can be traced to the political predicament of Poland in the first half of the nineteenth century.

Krasiński reflected deeply on his age and on such specific Polish concerns as the partitions, the November Insurrection, the role of the emigration, and the future of the nation. His views conformed only partially to those of Mickiewicz and not at all to those of Słowacki. With Mickiewicz, he shared a mysticomessianic vision of Poland as the Christ of nations destined to be resurrected and, through its martyrdom and resurrection, to serve as the agency for the salvation of European Christendom. It was, however, in his social and political thought that Krasiński differed from his peers.

Mickiewicz accorded the gentry the political direction of a reborn Poland because of their heritage of leadership and their preservation of what were regarded in the emigration as the meaningful and authentically Polish traditions of the past. But the gentry Mickiewicz envisaged for the future was one firmly set on the path of a democratic evolution by the calamitous events of the period 1772 to 1831. A reconstitution of prepartition Poland was out of the question, as he suggests in *Master Thaddeus*. Mickiewicz was also very sympathetic throughout his life to the problems of the peasant and the minority group, especially the Jews, and fully appreciated that unless they were brought into the mainstream of Polish life as well as into the political process eventually, a newly independent Poland would have small hope for survival. His later participation in an international Socialist paper published in Paris only capped the development of his progressive social views.

Greatly influenced by Romantic providential and catastrophist philosophy (Ballanche, in particular), Krasiński could not accept Mickiewicz's vision of the future, and even less Słowacki's contempt for the gentry and his espousal of social revolution. To Krasiński – whatever his aristocratic biases – the political order of the past and the nobility who shaped that order were doomed to oblivion. Wherever he looked around him in the Europe of the 1830s Krasiński discerned the unmistakable signs of social unrest and political turmoil: the Russian Decembrist Revolt of 1825, the November Insurrection in Poland in 1830, the Belgian and French uprisings of the same year, the Lyons textile workers' riots of 1831, and so on. As a conservative, Krasiński recoiled in horror at the specter of revolution but resigned himself to what he regarded as the inevitable by interpreting the historical process in a curious mixture of Hegelian dialectical and Romantic providential terms.[20]

It is this particular view of history that Krasiński propounds in *The Un-Divine Comedy*, which in its own way can be read as a refutation of ideas presented in both Mickiewicz's *Forefathers' Eve*, Part III, and Słowacki's *Kordian*. Working outward from the microcosm of the emigration with its internal stresses and divisions to the macrocosm of European civilization as a whole, Krasiński prophetically foresaw imminent social and political warfare. The great – and final – contest would pit the old order of the nobility and conservatives (represented in the play by Count Henry and the Holy Trinity Castle) against the revolutionary progressives (led by Pancras and Leonard) made up of all the disfranchised and oppressed. It was to be, essentially, a struggle to the death between master and servant, haves and have-nots. The outcome was a foregone conclusion: the old order was doomed; the handwriting was already on the wall of Europe.

Krasiński was hardly enthuasiastic about his conception of the future even though he could not intellectually reach any other conclusion about the direction of history. His animosity toward the social revolutionaries is manifest in the play. Their leader, Pancras, is portrayed as a cynic hungry for absolute power, to achieve which he is willing to sacrifice any principle. Lacking Mickiewicz's sympathy for Jews, Krasiński reveals an obvious bias in assigning baptized Jews an especially sinister role in Pancras' revolution. The Jews merely pretend to be Christians in order to identify themselves with the revolutionary camp. Secretly, however, they remain faithful to Judaism, like many of the converts in Inquisition Spain, and use the revolution of Pancras and his followers for their own purpose. Continuing Krasiński's line of thought – and without doing him injustice – the only conclusion possible is that in the poet's personal vision of the future the Jews would assist the social revolution until it became successful, whereupon they would subvert it from within to emerge finally as the dominant element. If Krasiński's play prophetically anticipates the Russian Revolution of 1917, as some critics have maintained (G. K. Chesterton, for example, in England),[21] it also looks forward

---

[20] The introduction by Maria Janion, the leading Polish Krasiński specialist, to the ninth revised edition of *The Un-Divine Comedy*, in the excellent Biblioteka Narodowa series (Wrocław, Warsaw, and Cracow, 1969), has been of particular value to me in the formulation of my own views of the work.

[21] Chesterton's remarks on the play appear in the Preface to the translation by Harriette E. Kennedy and Zofia Umińska (London and Warsaw, 1924). A notorious anti-Semite, Chesterton admires *The Un-Divine Comedy* not only for its

to the vicious anti-Semitism of a decade or so earlier in Russia, largely nourished by the "discovery" of the so-called *Protocols of the Elders of Zion*.

As a Hegelian, Krasiński could not have been expected to conclude *The Un-Divine Comedy* with the triumph of the revolution; otherwise how would the requisite synthesis be accommodated? Besides, if Krasiński's interpretation of history led him to the ascendancy of the new order over the old, his profound sense of Christian morality could not accept the triumph of godless materialism as definitive. Hence the ending of *The Un-Divine Comedy*.

In the play's final battlefield scene, as Pancras is about to exult in his decisive victory over Count Henry and the rest of the aristocracy collected together for the last scene in the Holy Trinity Castle, the sky darkens above him and in the clouds he beholds a vision so terrifying that he pales, becomes incoherent, falls into Leonard's arms, and expires. The vision is of the Day of Judgment. This is reinforced by the words Pancras utters as he breathes his last in Leonard's arms: "Galilaee, vicisti!" ("Galilean, Thou hast conquered"). The Galilean, of course, is Christ.

The play's conclusion is wholly consistent with Krasiński's world view: *Irydion* also concludes with the triumph of the Christian order even

---

prophecy of the Bolshevik Revolution but also for its prophecy of the Jewish "role" in it. He writes (p. 51):

In a political sense the prophesy is even more startling. Any uninformed Englishman, merely dipping into the scenes of social revolt in Eastern Europe, would take it for granted that it had been written after those lands had been overshadowed by the Babel tower of Bolshevism. In one particular the point will strike him as singularly significant. It is evidently taken for granted that, whatever the real excuses for the revolution, at the earlier stage when the revolution is a conspiracy, it must be a conspiracy of the Jews. It is notable that it is especially a conspiracy of the Jews who do not call themselves Jews; or, as the poet puts it, of the baptised Jews. The whole story of the popular revolt begins in a sort of secret sanhedrin, in which these Jews plot the destruction of our society almost in the exact terms which have since been attributed to the Elders of Zion. To an average Englishman this notion was quite new when the newspapers first began to hint at it a year or two ago. But the Polish poet positively takes it for granted in the early days of the great liberal century. This is a curiosity of literature and history that is really illuminating. There was not a word of either Semitism or Anti-Semitism in the French Revolution or the first liberal movements of the West. Krasiński must have perceived this element of Bolshevism, either because it was quite obvious even then in Eastern Europe, or because he was a man of extraordinary penetration and prevision.

though Irydion's hatred of Rome and desire for vengeance were passionate enough to lead him into a pact with Satan. To Krasiński, it could not be otherwise. Human history, as he perceived it, whatever the mechanism operating it, was moving along a frightening path of disintegration and destruction. It was a path that led inevitably to chaos. If the old order with values and traditions dear to Krasiński was doomed to disappear, Krasiński may have been saddened by the thought but hardly blind to the contribution of the old order to its own demise. This is established clearly in *The Un-Divine Comedy*. Krasiński, however, was repelled by the forces emerging triumphant over the old order. He saw them only as those of darkness and evil. Anarchic, atheistic, amoral, and materialistic, they were capable only of destruction. In the end, nothing but chaos would remain. But precisely at this moment – the dissolution into chaos – Krasiński's vision turns optimistic. When human history runs its course and mankind has finally been brought to the very edge of the abyss, God's order will be established. A new era in the life of man on earth will dawn, an era founded on true Christian love and morality. Krasiński's Hegelianism thus acquires a Christian providential – and metaphysical – coloration. When antagonistic social forces (human history, the "un-divine comedy" of man) ultimately exhaust themselves in mortal combat, the void of chaos will be filled by the synthesis heralding the millennium, the coming of the divine order.

Krasiński's approach to the restoration of Polish independence was rooted in the same premises. If the destructive forces of human history could eliminate the once great Polish Commonwealth, then its reappearance would come only when the order of Christian love and morality was imposed. Had this order existed previously, had love and morality reigned supreme on earth, then no partitions, no rape of one Christian nation by another, could have been possible.

The first title of *The Un-Divine Comedy* – "Mąż" ("The Husband", or "The Man") – suggests the smaller dimensions of the original conception. In its final form, the play develops along two parallel lines which eventually merge. One is political, the drama of the revolution. The other is private, the drama of the family.

In what must have been the original nucleus of the play, the family drama, Krasiński approached Słowacki's perception of their own age. The domestic drama of *The Un-Divine Comedy* – the drama of Count Henry, his wife, and his son George – is a powerful indictment of what Krasiński regarded as the malady of "false" romanticism. Perhaps we may refer to it as the Kordian syndrome. If the indictment does not embrace, as indeed it might, the whole of romanticism, it does address itself to that aspect or dimension of the Romantic mind and world view that encourages a self-delusive intoxication with word and gesture. Instead of becoming the means through which man can be uplifted and society transformed, poetry (or art, in general), in a Romantic sense, becomes rather the narcotic from which the myth of the self is created. The greater the recognition of poetic endowment, the more ardent the elaboration of image for the sake of image and the making of gesture for the sake of gesture. As poetry creates an ever greater distance between art and life, vision becomes distorted and all that can be seen is self. Słowacki's Kordian is so beguiled by the image he constructs of himself as an avenging angel that he loses contact with reality. So overripe is his imagination that when at last he is able to act decisively, to translate into life the poetic image he has of himself, this imagination cripples his will and makes action impossible.

The ramifications of the syndrome are wider in *The Un-Divine Comedy*. In Słowacki's play Kordian destroys only himself in his failure to assassinate the tsar when he has the chance. The plan itself is hardly more than a romantic gesture, for how efficacious can the tsar's murder really be? Count Henry's romantic madness, in *The Un-Divine Comedy*, dooms not only his family but the social order which he represents and which he finally leads into a hopeless battle. Poetry so distorts Count Henry's perception that it functions only as a destructive force. In the play's domes- tic drama it is through poetry that Count Henry brings about the insanity and premature death of his wife and the madness of his son George. In the larger dimensions of the sociopolitical drama, Count Henry's poetic vision of the conflict and his personal role in it results in his own death and in the total destruction of the society he leads and struggles to preserve. Given the contiguity of Słowacki's and Krasiński's views in this area, the social drama could not have been resolved differently. The old order is doomed to disappear because it has proven itself incapable of change, of keeping pace with history; it has become an anachronism as surely as the world of Ranevskaya in Chekhov's *The Cherry Orchard*. Appropriately, in the play, this old order is ushered to defeat by a leader who is so blinded to surrounding reality by poetic romanticization that he becomes the perfect symbol for the order, and the age, that must perish.

If Count Henry represents an extreme form of Słowacki's Kordian, then his son George appears as truly a *reductio ad absurdum* of the type. George's world is only poetic vision. This is intensified by the boy's blindness, a probable autobiographical motif in view of Krasiński's own weak eyesight. Because he cannot see the outer world George lives only the inner life, which is composed exclusively of the poetic. In a grotesque distortion, he is the fulfillment of Count Henry's ambition that his son be

31

a poet, but by his madness he becomes the means by which the count finally can glimpse the folly of his entire life.

After the grandiose historiophilosophical and Christian drama of *The Un-Divine Comedy*, with its interwoven themes of the human and divine and its "open", epico-lyrical structure, Słowacki's later debunking of romanticism, *Fantazy*, comes as a pleasant change of pace. As a realistic comedy and social satire, it is an unusual item in Słowacki's dramatic oeuvre and an altogether rare type of play for Polish émigré romanticism of the 1830s and 1840s.

Fantazy was among Słowacki's posthumously published works. It was discovered untitled and not quite finished among the poet's effects. For its first printing in 1866, its editor gave it the title *Niepoprawni* ("The Incorrrigible") with reference doubtless to the social types represented by Count and Countess Respekt, on the one hand, and the incurable Romantics Fantazy and Idalia, on the other. This title was later dropped in favor of *Nowa Dejanira* ("The New Deianira"), which alluded to the play's burlesque of a classical myth – the violation of Heracles' bride Deianira by the Centaur Nessus. The Słowacki revival in the late nineteenth and early twentieth centuries engendered voluminous new research on the poet which resulted, among other things, in still another change of title, from "The New Deianira" to *Fantazy*, after the name of the play's main character. Although some scholars have since argued that the comedy should have the double title *Fantazy, or The New Deianira* as conforming more to Słowacki's intentions, and it has occasionally been published with this title, equally convincing arguments contend that such double titles were not the fashion in the 1840s when the work was written and that *Fantazy* is the best possible choice.[22] The play is known today only by this title.

Establishing a precise chronology for the composition of *Fantazy* has also created controversy. The most reasonable opinion favors late 1843 or early 1844, not long after Słowacki had broken away from Towiański's influence.[23] The departure from the Circle did not mark an end to the poet's interest in mysticism itself. Quite the contrary. In 1843, he began writing a series of works that one cannot comprehend fully without

---

[22] My account of the publishing history of the play and the problems involved with its title follows Mieczysław Inglot's introduction to the second revised edition of *Fantazy*, in the Biblioteka Narodowa series (Wrocław, Warsaw, and Cracow, 1966).

[23] Inglot argues for a somewhat later date, about 1845, in the Biblioteka Narodowa edition of 1966. My preference for the early date is based on the more convincing views of Sawrymowicz, pp. 324–325.

reference to mystic thought. The richest fruit of this period are the plays *Ksiądz Marek* ("Father Marek") and *Sen srebrny Salomei* ("The Silver Dream of Salome"), both of which deal with political events in the Polish Ukraine (the region in which Słowacki was born) during the eighteenth century, and *Książe niezłomny* ("The Constant Prince"), a poetically brilliant adaptation of Calderón's play *El Principe Constante*.[24] In a curious footnote to literary history, the Calderón adaptation began in 1842 as a project of the Towiański Circle; Towiański greatly esteemed the Spaniard's spiritual thought and initiated a group translation program of which Słowacki's contribution was the sole completed effort.

The plays of 1843 were followed by mysticomessianic and visionary poems of great scope, such as *Genezis z ducha* ("Genesis from the Spirit", written 1844) and the unfinished *Król Duch* ("The King-Spirit", the first part of which was published in 1847). Here Słowacki examines the whole course of human history in terms of the metempsychic migration of several great spirits.

As a comedy, *Fantazy* may indeed seem an odd work for Słowacki to have written when he had only recently parted company with the Towiański Circle and was deep in mystic contemplation. When the play is viewed, however, as a reflection of the poet's new intellectual and spiritual values, it appears more natural for this strange period in his life.

Older studies of Słowacki used to make a strong point of *Fantazy's* putative autobiographical elements. In 1840 and 1841 the poet had a romantic liaison with Joanna Bobrowa (1807–1889), with whom Zygmunt Krasiński had once been in love. Słowacki's affair with the beauty was doomed to failure, but when the romance faded they remained good friends. Presumably, this did not prevent the poet, perhaps out of a kind of playful malice directed chiefly against Krasiński, from using her and Krasiński as the prototypes for the exaggeratedly Romantic lovers in *Fantazy*, Fantazy himself and the Countess Idalia. This biographical interpretation still enjoys some currency but is of limited use in any serious analysis of the play.

Like *The Un-Divine Comedy*, *Fantazy* is a multifaceted work. In its combination of a domestic and political drama it recalls Krasiński's play. But *Fantazy* brings together the comic and tragic as well.

On the level of the comic, *Fantazy* mocks Romantic posturing and narcissism. By the 1840s, Słowacki's ironic disposition toward romanticism

---

[24] Słowacki's version of the Calderón play has been one of the major items in the repertory of the contemporary Polish director Jerzy Grotowski's Laboratory Theatre. See the remarks on it by Grotowski's close collaborator, Ludwik Flaszen, in Jerzy Grotowski, *Towards a Poor Theatre* (New York, 1969), pp. 97–99.

had so colored his vision that he could no longer approach it with the same intensity and seriousness as before. The Romantic fondness for the exalted word and gesture and the Romantic concept of ideal love now seemed so preposterous to him that he could treat them only as subjects for comedy. Anything even resembling the solemnity of *Kordian* was out of the question – hence the exuberant ridicule of *Fantazy*.

Interwoven with the comic satire of Fantazy and Idalia, two of the most absurd creations in Romantic literature, is the family drama, involving the Respekts, and the political drama centered on the Russian Major and the exiled Polish patriot and revolutionary Jan. For all the ludicrousness of their portrayal, the Respekts represent a very real socioeconomic condition of the time: the uprooting of Polish gentry families for political reasons and their subsequent impoverishment. To Słowacki, the situation has a moral dimension as well. So desperate is the financial plight of the Respekts that they are even prepared to barter their daughter Diana to Fantazy in exchange for a sizable cash settlement.

Through the Major and Jan the earlier Siberian exile of the Respekts is revealed and with it the whole political tragedy of postpartition revolutionary Poland. Even granting the contrived nature of Jan's reappearance just at the time Fantazy is negotiating his suit of Diana's hand and the play's resolution which reunites the former lovers Jan and Diana and provides them, moreover, with a handsome wedding present, Jan and the Major assume a highly important ideological role in the drama. The real world they represent is juxtaposed both to the unreality and absurdity of Fantazy and Idalia and to the moral hypocrisy of the Respekts for whom existence and appearance are one. What Słowacki implies unmistakably is that the real world of Jan and the Major, a world of courage, heroism, and self-sacrifice, constitutes true romanticism, in comparison to which the posturing and flirting with death of Fantazy and Idalia are mere sham. The play's marital intrigue itself is nothing more than conventional plot material – separated lovers, impoverished parents, a wealthy suitor, the *deus ex machina* acquisition of a fortune, the eventual reunion of the lovers – which Słowacki uses merely as a convenient structure within which to reexamine the entire Romantic ethos against the background of concrete social and political conditions.

The Major is perhaps Słowacki's most intriguing character in *Fantazy* and a significant point of contact with the poet's contemporary mysticism. If the character is viewed only in dramatic terms, he seems scarcely believable – a symbolic projection, an idealized version of a new order of Russo-Polish relations. In this sense, analogues to the type are to be found elsewhere in nineteenth-century and early twentieth-century Polish literature which often sought to draw a distinction between the Russian as an individual worthy of esteem and the Russian as an agent of imperial tsarist policy.[25]

But the Major embodies far more importantly the ideas of Christian self-sacrifice and love that so strongly attracted Słowacki at the time to the plays of Calderón. What the Polish poet, dramatist, and mystic admired above all in *The Constant Prince*, in particular, is the noble figure of the Prince who staunchly refuses to compromise moral principle even when faced with death. The Prince's fidelity, devotion, suffering, and self-sacrifice ultimately gain him a spiritual triumph, and it was this triumph that Słowacki saw as the true salvation of mankind. By sacrificing himself out of love for Jan, the Major at the same time atones for his burdensome indecision during the Russian Decembrist Revolt of 1825. Faced with a second opportunity in his lifetime to act decisively for a cause dear to him, he does not fail. Through the Major's willingness to lay down his life so that Jan and Diana may find happiness, self-sacrifice for love becomes the supreme act of redemption.

Polish Romantic Drama on Stage

The stage history of the major, postinsurrectionary dramatic writings of Mickiewicz, Krasiński, and Słowacki is fascinating in itself.[26] The plays were written and published outside Poland. Since the Polish émigrés had no theatre, the poet-dramatists could not consider writing for the stage. As Romantics they shared the general interest of romanticism in the art of drama and sought, like their counterparts elsewhere in Europe, to evolve new dramatic forms. But the plays they wrote could be only read. Does this mean that Polish Romantic drama is essentially "closet" drama, meant primarily for the reader rather than the theatre-goer? Strictly speaking, the answer would have to be yes, since the plays were not written with foreseeable production in mind. On the other hand, the plays of Mickiewicz, Krasiński, and Słowacki manifest an undeniable theatrical consciousness despite such nontheatrical elements as the following: Słowacki's stage direction at one point in *Kordian* calling for the appearance of ten thousand devils on the stage; the long narrative passages in *Forefathers' Eve, Part III*; the introductions to all the acts of *The Un-Divine Comedy*, which are clearly intended for reading (though these can be delivered quite effectively by an on-stage or off-stage narrator); or some of the very lengthy

---

[25] Compare, for example, Mickiewicz's *Master Thaddeus*.

[26] A useful survey of the Polish theatre in English is Edward Csato's *The Polish Theatre* (Warsaw, 1963). See also Konstanty Puzyna's introduction to *Theatre in Modern Poland* (Warsaw, 1963).

monologues in *Fantazy* (which do, to be sure, "illuminate" the speakers and represent an acceptable theatrical convention of the time).

The political situation in partitioned Poland itself would have made production of the Romantic plays impossible there in the first half of the nineteenth century. Conditions were somewhat more favorable in the second half of the century, and then productions began to be mounted. *Fantazy*, for example, was first staged (as "The Incorrigible") as early as May 1867.[27] The literary climate, however, militated against any extensive commitment to the Romantic drama of the great émigré poets. After the unsuccessful January Insurrection of 1863 brought even greater repression, a wave of anti-Romantic sentiment swept across Poland. Romanticism and especially the writings of the émigré poets of the 1830s and 1840s were held responsible for misleading Poles by their appeals to revolutions doomed to failure from the very outset and by their mystic dreams of a great messianic national destiny. The ideology of positivism, which came to supplant romanticism, preached an evolutionary regeneration through toil, education, and the gradual improvement of every facet of Polish life within the context of partition.

Given the hostility of the Positivists to the Romantic movement, it is easy to appreciate that in the hegemony of positivism in the 1860s, 1870s, and early 1880s there was no real interest in bringing the literary drama of the émigré Romantics to the stage. One obvious reason why *Fantazy* was mounted so early, despite the unfinished form in which it was found, was the patent appeal to the Positivists of the play's mockery of Romantic posturing.

The situation changed considerably in Poland at the turn of the century. The poets especially of Young Poland felt deep affinities with the Romantics of the first half of the nineteenth century – notwithstanding a critical reassessment of the Romantic ideology – and actively propagated their works. The geographical factor was also of some importance at the time. Because of the relatively more liberal political and cultural conditions prevailing in Austrian Poland, writers and artists gravitated toward Cracow, in the southern part of the country. Thus the ancient Polish capital, the most important Polish city in the Austrian partition, became the center of a new florescence of the arts in Poland in the late nineteenth and early twentieth centuries.

In this setting Polish Romantic drama began its remarkable stage career. The foremost dramatist of Young Poland, Stanisław Wyspiański

---

[27] On stage productions of Słowacki's plays, see Tadeusz Sivert, ed., *Słowacki na scenach polskich* (Wrocław, Warsaw, and Cracow, 1963).

(1869–1907), who was deeply influenced by Romantic drama, played a decisive role in furthering the cause of Romantic drama in the theatre. In addition to writing several major plays about the outstanding events and personalities of the Romantic period,[28] plays in which Wyspiański clearly manifests his indebtedness to Romantic play form and technique, he approached the stage mounting of the Romantics' dramatic works with a keen sense of mission. His major achievement in this respect was his own production at the Cracow Theatre (then directed by Józef Kotarbiński) of all four parts of Mickiewicz's *Forefathers* merged and shortened to a seven-scene drama that could be performed in one evening.[29] The landmark premiere took place on October 31, 1901. It was the first time that more than single scenes of the work had been mounted. Encouraged by Wyspiański's successful demonstration of the feasibility of bringing not just Part III but the whole of *Forefathers' Eve* to the stage, other Polish directors soon undertook their own productions for which Wyspiański's version – with only minor variations – became the accepted norm.

Wyspiański's outstanding successor as an interpreter of Polish Romantic drama was the distinguished director of the pre-World War II Polish theatre, Leon Schiller (1887–1954). Schiller began his career in Warsaw's first modern private theatre, the Teatr Polski (Polish Theatre), founded in 1913 by Arnold Szyfman. Indicative of the preeminent place the Romantic drama had come to occupy in the minds of twentieth-century Polish theatrical entrepreneurs, the inaugural play at the Teatr Polski was Krasiński's *Irydion*. This was a little over a decade after the first staging of *The Un-Divine Comedy* by Kotarbiński in Cracow on November 29, 1902.

In 1924, in cooperation with the prominent actor Aleksander Zelwerowicz and the critic and later producer Wilam Horzyca, Schiller opened his own theatre in Warsaw, the Bogusławski Theatre, named after

---

[28] The most provocative and, in some respects, enigmatic is *Wyzwolenie* ("Liberation", 1901), a polemic with the ideology of Mickiewicz' *Forefathers' Eve*, Part III. Mickiewicz's Konrad reappears as the principal character in Wyspiański's drama. The play's use of masks and the play-within-a-play device make it one of the structurally most interesting and advanced Polish dramatic works of the period.

[29] On stage productions of Mickiewicz's plays, see Tadeusz Pacewicz, ed., *Mickiewicz na scenach polskich* (Wrocław, 1959). There is a good analysis of the Wyspiański production of *Forefathers' Eve* – its strengths and weaknesses – in Zenobiusz Strzelecki's *Polska plastyka teatralna*, I (Warsaw, 1963), 201–202. The complete text of Wyspiański's version of *Forefathers' Eve* appears in Stanisław Wyspiański, *Dzieła wybrane*, XII. Leon Płoszewski, general ed. (Cracow, 1961).

the founder of Poland's first national theatre, Wojciech Bogusławski (1757–1829). Although the theatre's politically liberal orientation soon aroused the wrath of Warsaw officialdom, who succeeded in closing it in 1926, Schiller had already attracted considerable attention with productions notable for their spectacular, "monumental" qualities. In translating his conceptualization of the production into the language of the stage he was ably assisted by two talented stage designers of the period, the brothers Andrzej and Zbigniew Pronaszko. With their help, the theatre's last year was made more memorable by a brilliant production of *The Un-Divine Comedy*.[30]

After the closing of the Bogusławski Theatre, Schiller moved to Lwów, where with Horzyca he opened another theatre. Splendid productions of Słowacki and Shakespeare (in whom Wyspiański himself had been keenly interested) were mounted, but the most sensational production of all was of *Forefathers' Eve* as a modern national mystery play with decor by Andrzej Pronaszko in 1932.[31] This production, which surpassed Wyspiański's in its grandiosity of structure, style, and range, and which Schiller repeated two years later in Warsaw, was regarded as the most exciting theatrical event of interwar Poland. Schiller's production of Słowacki's *Kordian* at the Teatr Polski in Warsaw in 1935 was his next triumph with a Romantic drama.

Another major directorial talent of pre-World War II Poland was Juliusz Osterwa (1885–1947), the cofounder with Mieczysław Limanowski (1876–1948) of the famous Reduta (Redoubt) Theatre in Warsaw in 1919. Osterwa favored social and psychological realism and was much influenced by Stanislavsky, whose work he became acquainted with in Russia during World War I. But he also recognized the challenge of Romantic drama and achieved noteworthy results with Romantic productions in which the plays' poetic and monumental qualities were treated in a muted, low-key manner contrasting sharply with Schiller's conceptions. One of the more interesting was Słowacki's version of Calderón's *The Constant Prince* as a spectacle for open-air theatre, a tradition which Osterwa's Reduta revived on tours of the Polish provinces.[32]

---

[30] On Schiller's production of *The Un-Divine Comedy*, see Stefania Skwarczyńska, *Leona Schillera trzy opracowania teatralne "Nieboskiej komedii" w dziejach jej inscenizacji w Polsce* (Warsaw, 1959).

[31] For detailed analyses of the 1932 and 1934 Schiller productions of *Forefathers' Eve* and the play text used, see Jerzy Timosewicz, *"Dziady" w inscenizacji Leona Schillera: partytura i jej wykonanie* (Warsaw, 1970)

[32] *Theatre in Modern Poland*, p. 11.

Osterwa had a particular liking for Słowacki's *Fantazy* as well as for Romantic comedy in general (Musset, for example) and was responsible for some of the most attractive productions of the play in this century. After its theatrical debut in Stanisławów in then eastern Poland in 1867 and subsequent stagings in Lwów in 1868, Poznań in 1870, and Cracow in 1878, *Fantazy* was first staged in the twentieth century in December 1900 at the Teatr Miejski (Town Theatre) in Lwów under the directorship of Tadeusz Pawlikowski (1862–1915). The brilliant actress Helena Modrzejewska (later known in America as Helena Modjeska) particularly liked the role of Idalia, appearing in it (at the age of sixty-two) for the first time in 1902, in Lwów. She created the role again in Cracow in January 1903 in a performance that featured two other popular actors – Michał Tarasiewicz, as Fantazy, and Józef Kotarbiński, as the Major.

Osterwa did a production of *Fantazy* as early as 1916, while he was in Moscow, but his most spectacular version of it was staged by the Teatr Narodowy (National Theatre) in Warsaw on February 13, 1929. A fine actor himself, Osterwa played the role of Fantazy while Idalia and Rzecznicki were played by two superb Warsaw artists, Irena Solska and Ludwik Solski, respectively.

Polish Romantic drama has had a curious stage history in post-World War II Poland. Because of the repressive political situation from 1945 to 1953, when the death of Stalin was followed by a liberalizing trend in the arts in Communist Europe, the Romantic drama was virtually impossible to stage. Plays such as *Forefathers' Eve*, Part III, and *Kordian* raise unhappy (and, in the context of post-World War II Poland, embarrassing) memories of Russian oppression in Poland, while plays such as Słowacki's version of Calderón's *The Constant Prince* and Krasiński's *The Un-Divine Comedy* either reflect Christian idealism or, in the case of Krasiński, depict an ultimate Christian triumph over social revolution and materialism.

From the political point of view, just as in the time of positivism, Słowacki's *Fantazy* seemed the least objectionable. The political reality of the Siberian exile of the Respekts and Jan is still inescapable, but the play is "redeemed" by the attractive portrait of the Russian Major. Moreover, in the warm personal relationship between Jan and the Major, both of whom share an enthusiasm for democratic social revolution, a model of Russo-Polish amity can be seen. Not surprisingly, therefore, *Fantazy* was the first Romantic play staged after the war. It was produced by Osterwa at the Teatr Wojska Polskiego (The Theatre of the Polish Army) in Łódź on June 19, 1945.

When the political climate became more favorable after the death of Stalin, *Forefathers' Eve* was staged for the first time since the war in 1955 at the Teatr Polski in Warsaw under the direction of Alexander Bardini.

Jan Kott, who was in the audience the first night, vividly recalls the occasion and its significance:

> The production of Mickiewicz's *Forefathers' Eve* ... was the most important event in the Polish theatre for ten years. We all felt this on the first night in the tightly packed auditorium of the Teatr Polski. The greatness of poetry and the presence of poetry are not one and the same thing...
>
> At the first night of *Forefathers' Eve* people cried – in the orchestra as well as in the balcony. Government ministers were crying, the hands of the technical crew were shaking, the cloakroom attendants were wiping their eyes. *Forefathers' Eve* moved and shocked and became the subject of discussions going on long into the night. I know of no other drama in the whole of world literature that could move an audience after a hundred and twenty-five years as *Forefathers' Eve* did. *Forefathers' Eve* struck home with greater force than any play written since the war, in its historical aspect as well as in its contemporary relevance... Time did not consume the play's modern spirit, and it still haunts us today. There is dynamite in *Forefathers' Eve*, and it exploded on the first night.[33]

Other productions of Romantic drama followed in rapid succession. The one of *Kordian* in 1956 at the Teatr Narodowy by a major postwar director, Erwin Axer, in particular attracted very favorable notice.

Throughout the twentieth century, from Wyspiański's production of *Forefathers' Eve* to the present, the Romantic drama has represented a continuing challenge to Polish directors and actors. To the actor, the Romantic characters are classic roles approached in much the same way that an English or American actor approaches a Shakespearean performance. To the director, on the other hand, the Romantic drama usually serves as a point of departure for experimentation. Beginning with Wyspiański and continuing through Schiller, Osterwa, Axer, Kazimierz Dejmek, Konrad Swinarski, and Jerzy Grotowski, producing Romantic drama has become the foundation on which the modern Polish theatre, especially the theatre of the avantgarde, has been built. Or, to view the phenomenon from another perspective: perhaps just because the great Romantic plays were not conceived for the stage and usually require some modification to make them suitable for theatrical production, the director's creative energies are constantly tempted by visions of ever new configurations of text and setting. How provocative the Romantic drama continues to be from precisely the view of the experimentalist can be judged from such an unusual event as the staging in 1962 in four different Polish theatres of *Forefathers Eve*, with each theatre presenting the play in a wholly different interpretation and style.

---

[33] Jan Kott, *Theatre Notebook*, 1947–1967, translated from the Polish by Bolesław Taborski (Garden City, N.Y., 1968), pp. 50–51

1. The stage director Konrad Swinarski (1929–1975), whose productions of Polish Romantic drama at the Stary Teatr in Cracow from 1965 to 1975 have been among the most successful and controversial in the history of the twentieth-century Polish theatre. Shown here (center) with actors from his production of Shakespeare's *Midsummer Night's Dream*. (Photograph: Wojciech Plewiński)

But the provocative power of Polish Romantic drama has also attracted attention in another sense. In the years after the Poznań riots of October 1956 the theatre became more of an outlet for pent-up emotions in Communist Poland than virtually any other institution of Polish life, including the university. This was vividly demonstrated by the *Forefathers' Eve* affair of 1968. A new production of the play was mounted at the Teatr Narodowy in late 1967 by the highly respected director Dejmek.[34] The political situation was tense. A regrettable anti-Semitic campaign, which resulted in the expulsion of many Jews from Poland, was instituted in the wake of the Six Day War in the Middle East. Accompanying this campaign were signs of renewed cultural repression.

Dejmek's production may well have been intended as a form of oblique protest. Whatever the underlying factors, the play as staged by him at the Narodowy seemed to highlight its anti-Russian elements. The audience reaction was electric. People applauded at the recitation of the passages depicting Russian tyranny. To the authorities, the production became increasingly discomforting. They chose to view it as a manifestation against the regime and an embarrassment to Soviet-Polish relations. On January 30, 1968, all further performances of *Forefathers' Eve* at the Narodowy were banned.

Forefathers' Eve has since been revived. The much praised production at the Stary Teatr (Old Theatre) in Cracow in 1973 by Swinarski inaugurated, in fact, what the Polish theatre journal *Le Théâtre en Pologne/The Theatre in Poland* refers to in its December 1974 issue as "a new wave of productions of the great national stage classics which made an impact on the theatre life of the last two seasons in Poland".[35] Once again, Polish

---

[34] See Harold B. Segel, "The Polish Spark", *New Leader*, March 25, 1968, pp. 12–15.

[35] *Le Théâtre en Pologne/The Theatre in Poland*, XII, No. 195 (1974), 13. On the Swinarski production of *Forefathers' Eve*, see Elżbieta Morawiec, "Adam Mickiewicz's *Forefathers* Produced by Konrad Swinarski in the Cracow Teatr Stary", *Le Théâtre en Pologne/The Theatre in Poland*, VIII, No. 180 (1973), 17–23.

As further evidence of the vitality of Polish Romantic drama in the contemporary Polish theatre, another entirely new stage concept involving Mickiewicz and *Forefathers' Eve* became the sensation of the Warsaw stage in 1976. On February 21 that year, the premiere took place at the Teatr Narodowy of the play (the Poles themselves refer to it as a "theatrical spectacle") *Mickiewicz – młodość* ("Mickiewicz – The Young Years"), devised and directed by Adam Hanuszkiewicz, who had several provocative productions of Romantic drama to his credit. Based on a variety of Mickiewicz's nontheatrical writings, "Mickiewicz – The Young Years" deals primarily with the period of the poet's involvement in the Wilno student organizations for which he was eventually

INTRODUCTION

Romantic drama reasserts its inexhaustible vitality as creative catalyst, as living theatre, and, most important of all, as myth. No other tradition of Romantic drama in Europe can lay claim to such a place in art or national consciousness.

---

exiled to Russia. What is most interesting, however, is that the play was just the first part of a more grandiose undertaking – a theatrical triptych on Mickiewicz's poetic and political career of which the central part was to be a version of *Forefathers' Eve*.

Forefathers' Eve, Part III

by Adam Mickiewicz

Translated by various hands
and edited by George Rapall Noyes,
with revisions by
Harold B. Segel

To the Holy Memory of
JAN SOBOLEWSKI,
CYPRIAN DASZKIEWICZ,
and
FELIX KOLAKOWSKI,
fellow students, fellow prisoners, and fellow exiles,
who were persecuted because of love for their country
and died of longing for their country
in Archangel, in Moscow, and in St. Petersburg,
MARTYRS OF THE NATIONAL CAUSE,
the author dedicates his poem.

PREFACE

Poland for the last fifty years has presented a picture of such continual, unwearied, and inexorable cruelty on the part of tyrants, and of such boundless devotion and obstinate endurance on the part of the people, as are unparalleled since the times of the persecution of Christianity. It is evident that the kings, like Herod, have a premonition of the appearance of a new light upon earth and of their own imminent destruction, and that the Polish people believes more and more fervently in its own regeneration and resurrection.

The annals of Polish martyrdom include many generations and countless victims; bloody scenes are being enacted in every part of our own country and in foreign lands as well. The poem here published contains a few minor features of that immense picture, a few events from the period of persecution inaugurated by the Emperor Alexander.

About the year 1822 the policy of the Emperor Alexander, which was opposed to liberty of every sort, began to declare itself, to adopt a firm and definite course of action. There was then inaugurated against the whole Polish race a general persecution, which, as time went on, became more and more violent and bloody. Senator Novosiltsev, memorable in our history, came upon the scene. He was the first man to give a rational basis to the Russian government's brutal and instinctive hatred of the Poles, regarding it as salutary and politic; he made it the foundation of all his work and aimed at the annihilation of Polish nationality. Thereupon all the lands from the Prosna to the Dnieper and from Galicia to the Baltic Sea were locked up and administered as a vast prison. The whole administrative machinery was transformed into a single great engine for torturing the Poles – an engine the wheels of which were turned by the Tsarevich Constantine and Senator Novosiltsev. The systematic Novosiltsev applied himself first to the torture of children and youths, in order to exterminate in the very germ the hopes of future generations. He established his headquarters as executioner at Wilno, the intellectual capital of the Lithuanian-Russian provinces. Among the young men of the university there existed at that time various literary societies aiming to maintain the Polish language and nationality, which had been secured to the Poles by the Congress of Vienna and by imperial charters. These societies, seeing that the suspicions of the government were increasing, disbanded even before an ukase forbade their existence. But Novosiltsev, although he did not arrive in Wilno until the year after their disbanding, pretended to the emperor that he had found them still active. Their literary occupations he represented as an open rebellion against the government; he imprisoned several hundred young men and set up under his own influence military courts for the trial of the schoolboys. According to the secret Russian procedure the accused have no means of defense, for they are often ignorant of the charges against them. Even their confessions, according to the caprice of the examining commission, may either be accepted and entered in the report, or may be entirely rejected. Novosiltsev, who was sent as plenipotentiary by the Tsarevich Constantine, was accuser, judge, and executioner. He abolished several schools in Lithuania, with orders that the lads enrolled in them should be regarded as civilly dead, that they should be debarred from holding any office or public employment, and that they should be refused permission to complete their studies in any public or private institution. Such an edict, forbidding young men to study, is without precedent in history, and is a peculiar invention of the Russian intellect. Aside from the closure of the schools, dozens of their pupils were sentenced to the mines of Siberia; to forced labor, chained to wheelbarrows; to service in Asiatic garrisons: among their number were lads not yet of age, members of noted Lithuanian families. More than twenty young men, some already teachers, others students of the university, were banished for life to the interior of Russia, as persons suspected of Polish national aspirations. Of these many exiles only one has yet succeeded in escaping from Russia.

All writers who have mentioned the persecution in Lithuania during that period agree that in the case of the Wilno students there was something mystical and mysterious. The mystical, gentle, yet inflexible character of Thomas Zan, the leader of the young men; the religious resignation, the brotherly love and harmony of the young prisoners; the divine punishment that visibly overtook their persecutors, made a deep impression on the minds of those who were witnesses of the events or who shared in them. The story of this episode seems to carry the reader back to ancient times – times of faith and of miracles.

Anyone who is familiar with the occurrences of that period will bear witness to the author that he has portrayed conscientiously both the historic scenes and the characters of the persons acting in them, adding nothing and never exaggerating. Why should he add or exaggerate? To quicken in the hearts of his fellow countrymen their hatred for their enemies? Or to arouse pity in Europe? What are all the barbarities of that time in comparison with those which the Polish nation is now suffering and on which Europe is now gazing with indifference? The author has merely desired to preserve for his nation a faithful memorial of Lithuanian history of a few years ago. He did not need to make odious in the eyes of his fellow countrymen enemies whom they have known for ages; and to the compassionate nations of Europe, who have wept over

Poland as the feeble women of Jerusalem over Christ, our nation will speak only with the words of the Savior: "Daughters of Jerusalem, weep not for me, but weep for yourselves."

Forefathers' Eve

PART III

PROLOGUE

(Lithuania. Wilno, in Ostrobramska Street in the cloister of the Basilian Fathers, which has been made over into a prison of state. A prisoner's cell.)

But beware of men; for they will deliver you up to the councils, and they will scourge you in their synagogues. – Matthew 10: 17.

And ye shall be brought before governors and kings for my sake, for a testimony against them and the Gentiles. – 10: 18.

And ye shall be hated of all men for my name's sake, but he that endureth to the end shall be saved. – 10: 22.

GUARDIAN ANGEL:
  Naughty and unfeeling child!
  Your mother's earthly merits here,
  Her suppliance in heaven's sphere,
  Long have guarded your young days
  From sinful thoughts and evil ways.
  So the daylight-flowering rose,
  Angel of the garden close,
  Breathes a perfumed power by night
  Banishing all plague and blight
  Harmful to a sleeping child.
    Often when your mother pled
  And if heaven's law allowed,
  Speeding down a shaft of light,
  Silent in the silent night,
  In your cottage, o'er your bed,
  I kept vigil with wings bowed.
    Through the night I stood attending
  To the passions of your dream,
  Like a lily pale and bending
  O'er a muddied, rushing stream.
  Often did that evil press
  Give my spirit sick offense,
  Yet I sought, though it were weak,
  Just one gleam of righteousness,

As in anthills people seek
Tiny grains of frankincense.
   When at last a good thought shone,
I took your spirit by the hand,
Led it upward to the land
Where eternity holds throne.
There a chant did I intone
Which the earthborn rarely ever
Hear in sleep, and waking never.
I revealed the path before you,
In my arms to heaven bore you.
But you heard the sounds celestial
As no more than drunken revel.
   I, a son of deathless glory,
Then assumed the foul disguise
Of a beast from purgatory,
You to frighten and chastise;
But to you God's scourging blow
Seemed the torture of a foe.
Still in pride and unregretting
You awoke, though ill at ease,
As if the fountain of forgetting
You had drunk down to the lees.
Dreams of worlds more high than ours
Drowned in you as whirling waves,
Dragging with them leaves and flowers,
Sunk in subterranean caves.
   Then I hid my face and wept
Long and bitterly, not even
Daring to go back to heaven
Lest I meet your mother there,
Lest she ask how do you fare,
If above her son I'd kept
Faithful vigil while he slept.
PRISONER: (*Awakens, wearied, and looks through the window. Dawn.*)
   O silent night, you fall, and who will ask
From whence you come? We see you at your task
Of scattering star points as a sower seed,
Yet who therein your future course will read!
"The sun has set!" So from the towers high
The gray astronomers boom gravely forth.
Why has it set? They grant us no reply.

51

The shadows come and cover all the earth,
Men fall asleep and no one questions why;
They wake, unmarveling, when darkness lifts,
To see the daily marvel of the sun;
Shadow and splendor change like sentry-shifts –
But what great ruler thus commands the sky,
What captain orders his high bidding done?
   And sleep? Ah, that dim, deaf, and silent shore
Where spirits wake, why do men not explore
Its bounds, its times, and their signification?
The sleeper, waking, mocks his own creation.
And wise men say, dreams are but memory!
   Curst be their chill decision!
Are then my recollection and my vision
All one? These prison walls I see,
   Are they but memory?

The joys and punishments of sleep, they say,
   Are only fancy's play.
Dullards, whom fancy ever disregards,
   Prate of her to us bards!
I who have dwelt in her and measured her domain,
I know, beyond her farthest edge lies dream;
Sooner will day be night and pleasure pain
Than dreams and visions a remembered gleam.

(*Lies down and rises again. Goes to the window.*)

Sleep comes with visions now magnificent,
Now terrible, but always leaves me spent.

(*He dozes.*)

SPIRITS OF NIGHT:
   Lay him on eiderdown, shadow his brows,
   Sing to him, softly now, let him not rouse.
SPIRIT FROM THE LEFT SIDE:
   Here in the prison but darkness and gloom;
     There in the town all is bright.
   Minstrels are singing, dispelling all doom;
     Comets are roving the night;
   Their tresses are trailing, their shining eyes beam;

(The Prisoner sleeps.)

    Who steers by their guidance to land,
  Falling asleep in a ravishing dream,
    Will awaken on our strand.
ANGEL:
  We have prayed the Lord on high
  Yield you to your enemy.
  In a lonely prison placed
  Like a prophet in the waste,
  Think upon your destiny:
  Solitude is wisdom's key.
CHORUS OF NIGHT SPIRITS:
  God frets us by day, but when dark we carouse,
    All sluggards grow fat with the moon;
  Throwing caution aside, singers passions arouse,
    For the devils are calling the tune.
  Who leaves morning mass with pure thoughts in his head
    And the taste of good words on his tongue,
  By night the bloodsucker of thoughts will be bled
    And his taste by night's venom be stung.
  Fellow sons of the night, come sing o'er his bed,
    Let us serve him until he serves us;
  Let us crawl in his heart, dance around in his head;
    Let him sleep – he'll be ours with no fuss!
ANGEL:
  In heaven and on earth they pray for you,
  The tyrants soon must grant you liberty.
PRISONER: *(Wakes and meditates.)*
  O you who prison, scourge, and slay your own,
  Who night and day in carefree revels spend,
  Do you recall one single dream at dawn,
  Or, recollecting, do you comprehend?

(He slumbers.)

ANGEL:
  We come to say, you shall be free once more.
PRISONER: *(Awakens)*
  Free! Ah, one bade me yesterday rejoice.
  Was it a dream or was it God's own voice?

(*He falls asleep.*)

ANGELS:
   Tend him, protect him now, watch every thought,
   'Twixt good and evil the battle is fought.
SPIRITS FROM THE LEFT SIDE: Double the onset!
SPIRITS FROM THE RIGHT: Redouble the guard!
Whether forces of good or of evil have scored,
Tomorrow shall show us in deed and in word.
One moment of battle, the tiniest span,
Determines forever the fate of a man.
PRISONER:
   I shall be free – yes, and full well I know
   The sort of grace the Muscovite will show,
   Striking the fetters from my feet and hands
   To rivet on my spirit heavier bands!
   An exiled singer, now condemned to go
   Where foreign and inimicable throngs
   Will take for rude and idle sounds my songs.
   Wretches! They leave me with my sword, 'tis true,
   But first they break its shining blade in two;
   Alive, I shall be dead to these dear lands,
   And all I think shall lie within my soul,
   A diamond locked within its shell of coal.

(*Rises and writes with charcoal on one side.*)

D. O. M.
GUSTAVUS
OBIIT M. D. CCC. XXIII.
CALENDIS NOVEMBRIS.

(*On the other side.*)

HIC NATUS EST
CONRADUS
M. D. CCC. XXIII.
CALENDIS NOVEMBRIS

(*Leans against the window. Falls asleep.*)

SPIRIT:
    O man, if you but knew how great your power!
    One thought of yours, like hidden lightning flashing,
    Through gathered clouds can send the thunder crashing
    In wasteful storm or pour down fruitful shower.
    If you but knew that hardly thoughts arise
    When there await, as elements the thunder,
    Demons and angels in expectant wonder –
    Will you plunge down to hell or light the skies?
    You glow like errant clouds that wander high
    Yet know not what they do nor where they fly.
    Men! One of you, in chains, by thought alone
    Can overturn or raise the loftiest throne.

ACT I

Scene i

(*A corridor. In the distance stand guards armed with rifles. Some young prisoners come out of their cells with candles. Midnight.*)

JACOB: Can this be true? We meet again?
ADOLF: The guard,
            Our corporal, is at his whiskey now.
JACOB: And what's the time?
ADOLF: Midnight, or nearly so.
JACOB:
    If the patrol should catch us on their round
    Our corporal would be done for, that's for sure.
ADOLF:
    Put out your candle; see, it strikes the pane.

(*They put out the candle.*)

    The round! Pooh! First they hammer at the door,
    Give and receive the password, hunt their keys –
    Before they're halfway down the corridor
    We'll scatter, reach our rooms, drop down, and snore.

(*Other prisoners, who have been called, come out of their cells.*)

ZEGOTA: Good evening!
KONRAD: You!
FATHER LWOWICZ: And you!
JAN SOBOLEWSKI: And I am here.
FREYEND:
    We'll all go to your cell, Zegota. Come,
    Our brother enters his novitiate
    Today, so we will light a fire and tell
    The news. It's always good to see fresh walls.
JAN:
    Zegota! Ah, dear fellow, you here too!
ZEGOTA:
    My cell is three steps wide and you're a crowd.
FREYEND:
    Yes, Konrad's cell is better; we'll go there –

It's farthest off, and next the chapel wall,
And none could hear were we to sing and shout.
Today I'd like to talk aloud and sing;
The town will think they're singing in the church;
Tomorrow's Christmas, after all. Eh, friends,
I have some bottles.
JACOB: Does the corporal know?
FREYEND:
He'll get his share and he's an honest soul,
A Pole himself, a former legionnaire,*
Made over to a Muscovite by force;
And a good Catholic like him will let
Poor prisoners celebrate on Christmas Eve.
JACOB:
If they find out, he won't come off unscathed.

(*They go into Konrad's cell, lay a fire in the fireplace and light a candle. Konrad's cell as in the Prologue.*)

FATHER LWOWICZ:
And whence, Zegota, came you here, old friend?
ZEGOTA:
Today they dragged me off from house and barn.
FATHER LWOWICZ: Were you a farmer too?
ZEGOTA: And how! Renowned!
If you could see my oxen and my sheep!
At first I couldn't tell the oats from straw,
But now all Lithuania sings my praise.
JACOB:
They took you by surprise, then?
ZEGOTA: I had heard
About the Wilno inquest. Past my house
I'd seen kibitkas † gallop and at night
The ominous clatter of the post alarmed us.
And when we sat at supper, if in jest
Some one should make a glass ring with his knife,
The women trembled, the old men grew pale,
Thinking they heard the bell of the gendarme;

* A Pole who served in the Polish legions that fought with Napoleon. – Ed.
† A Russian covered wagon, used for transporting prisoners. – Ed.

But whom or what they sought I never knew,
I've had no part in any plot or plan.
I think the government is after bribes –
They'll make us all pay dearly, I dare say,
And send us home.
THOMAS ZAN:
And you can hope for that?
ZEGOTA:
They can't send people to Siberia
For nothing, can they? And what is our crime?
You're silent – tell me, what is happening here?
Why would they punish us – upon what ground?
THOMAS:
The ground that Novosiltsev has arrived
From Warsaw. Well, you know the Senator –
He'd fallen out of favor with the tsar
And drunk away and spent the thieving gains
From former days and had no credit left,
And yet despite his wishes and his pains
He could not ferret out a Polish plot;
And so he thought to visit a new land,
For which he honors Lithuania
With staff of spies, to plunder as he likes
And crawl back in the autocrat's good will;
And from our student clubs he must deduce
Some weighty thing as offering to the tsar.
ZEGOTA: But we are innocent –
THOMAS: It would be vain
To try to prove it, for the inquest holds
Its sessions secret; no one knows his crime,
The judge who sentences heeds no defense,
He longs to find us guilty and he will.
One last unhappy course remains for us:
To choose some few men for the sacrifice,
Who'll take upon themselves the blame for all.
I was the leader of your comradeship,
So I'm the one to suffer for the rest.
Choose out some brothers who will go with me,
Orphaned or older or unmarried men,
Whose death will cause the fewest hearts to bleed.
Our best shall thus escape the enemy's hands.
ZEGOTA: It's come to this!

JACOB:

He grieves. He did not know
That he might never see his home again.
FREYEND:

Our Jackie left his wife in childbed, yet
He does not weep.
FELIX KOLAKOWSKI:

Weep? Why, he should praise God.
If she brings forth a son, I'll prophesy
His future for you. Let me read your hand:
I'm something of a chiromant; I'll trace
What fortune will be that of your infante.

(*Looking at his hand*)

If he be honest, under Moscow's rule
Courts and kibitkas will bestrew his path.
Who knows but some day he may find us here?
I see our future comrades in all sons.
ZEGOTA: You've been here long?
FREYEND:

How should we know the date?
We get no letters, we've no calendar,
Nor can we tell how long we are to stay.
SUZIN:

My window's barred by heavy wooden blinds;
I cannot tell the daytime from the night.
FREYEND:

Ask Thomas, he's the patriarch of woe;
The biggest fish fell first into the net.
He met us all and will go out the last,
He knows of each, from where he came and when.
SUZIN:

Thomas! I did not know you, let me take
Your hand. You knew me only briefly once;
Your friendship then was dear to every one
And many more intimate surrounded you;
You scarcely saw me then, but I knew you
And know what you have suffered for our sakes,
And I shall boast of your acquaintance when
I die, and say, "I wept with Thomas once."

59

FREYEND:
  In heaven's name, why all these sighs and tears!
  Why, when our Thomas walked at liberty,
  "Prison" was written large upon his brow,
  And now, confined, he lives as if at home,
  In his own element. In freedom he
  Was like a mushroom that will waste away
  Beneath the sun, but, planted in a cave
  Where we gay sunflowers lose our gold and droop,
  Will bud and blossom and grow big and stout.
  For Thomas took the fashionable cure –
  The hunger cure has come to be the rage.
ZEGOTA: (*To Thomas*) They starved you then?
FREYEND: Oh no, they gave him food!
  You should have seen it, what a curious sight!
  Its fragrance in a room was quite enough
  To kill the crickets and to choke the mice.
ZEGOTA: You ate it?
THOMAS: I ate nothing for a week,
  And then I tried it, then I lost all strength,
  Then as if poisoned I felt cramping pains,
  Then lay for weeks again as in a faint.
  I do not know what sickness I passed through;
  There was no doctor, so it had no name.
  I rose at last and ate and found new strength:
  I feel as if they'd reared me on such food.
FREYEND: (*With forced gaiety*)
  Outside the prison it's no life at all,
  But here you learn what living really is;
  Evil or good, it's habit makes it so.
  They asked the devil or a man from Pinsk,
  I don't know which, "Why always in the mud?"
  – "Because it is my habit," he replied.
JACOB: But, friends, to get the habit!
FREYEND: That's the trick.
JACOB:
  It must be nearly eight months since I came;
  I yearn for home no less.
FREYEND: But still, no more?
  Our Thomas is so used to it, fresh air
  Would make him giddy, weigh upon his breast.
  He hardly needs to breathe. If he got free,

His life in jail would pay him his reward;
He'd never need to spend a cent for wine
But get drunk from a single draught of air.
THOMAS:
Oh, I would choose the mines, and sickness, hunger;
I'd bear the lash – the inquest, worst of all –
Rather than see you fellow prisoners here.
Villains, they'll bury us in one huge grave!
FREYEND:
How's this? You weep for us? We're no great loss.
What profit was my life to me, I ask?
I had some little talent in a fight
And still could spit some Cossacks of the Don,
But during times of peace what is the gain
If I should live a hundred years to curse
The Muscovite, and die at last – and rot?
I'd be a good-for-nothing were I free,
For I'm like powder or indifferent wine:
Now while the wine is sealed, the powder plugged –
While I'm locked up, I've value, but at large
I'd be as flat as wine in open jugs,
Or flash like powder in an open pan.
But if they send me forth to exile, chained,
All Lithuania will look on and think:
"See, there is noble blood, *so* our youth dies!"
Wait, murdering tsar; wait, wicked Muscovite!
Why, Thomas, such as I would gladly hang
If you might live a moment more on earth.
It's only by my death I serve my land
And I would die ten times to save you once,
You or our gloomy poet Konrad here,
Who tells the future like a Gypsy king.

(*To Konrad*)

Our Thomas says you are a poet, so
I love you. You are like a flask of wine:
You pour forth song, you breathe out feeling, fire:
We drink it, feel it – and we leave you drained.

(*Takes Konrad's hand and wipes away his tears. To Thomas and Konrad*)

61

You know I love you, but a man can love
And yet not weep. So, brothers, dry your tears –
For once I start to melt away in sobs,
I make no tea – and I put out the fire.

(*He makes the tea. A moment of silence.*)

FATHER LWOWICZ:
We make a poor reception for our guest.

(*Pointing to Zegota*)

We Lithuanians hold it a bad sign
To weep upon the day of housewarming.
Our tongues are sealed by day, so let's chat now.
JACOB: Is there no news from town?
ALL: News?
FATHER LWOWICZ: Any news?
ADOLF:
Jan went out to the inquest for an hour
But came back still and gloomy and, you see,
Has no desire to talk.
SEVERAL PRISONERS: Well, Jan, no news?
JAN: (*Gloomily*)
Unpleasant: the kibitkas, twenty loads,
Have started for Siberia today.
ZEGOTA: What, not our men?
JAN: Those young school boys from Zmudz.
ALL: Siberia!
JAN:
Just like some state affair,
Such crowds had gathered.
SEVERAL: They are really gone!
JAN: I saw it all.
JACKIE:
You saw it! Did they take
My brother, too?
JAN: They took all, every one.
It was as I returned. I begged the guard
To stop a moment, so he let me stand
Concealed behind the pillars of the church
While mass went on; and there were many folk –

62

But suddenly they tumbled forth and left
The service for the prison. At the door
I stood and saw the nave stripped bare. The priest
Alone remained beyond the chancel rail
With chalice raised, and his boy acolyte.
Outside, the people thronged in silent watch.
From prison gates to square, as on some feast,
Soldiers with arms and drums formed two long files;
And in between, kibitkas. From the square
The captain of police came riding up –
He looked a great man holding triumph here,
The triumph of the tsar o'er – little boys!
A drum beat, and the jail doors opened wide.
I saw them then. Behind each one walked guards
With bayonets, behind these wasted lads,
Sickly and small and all like new recruits
With shaven heads and chains upon their legs.
Poor boys! The youngest, only ten years old,
Complained he couldn't lift his heavy chains
And showed his foot all flecked with blood and bare.
The captain then rode up to see to this –
So kind and just, himself would test the chains!
"Ten pounds, quite right; that is the weight prescribed."
   They brought Janczewski out: I saw him there,
Disfigured, black, but strangely noble, too.
A year before a gay, engaging boy,
Today he gazed from the kibitka as
That emperor from his island rock. His eyes
Were proud and dry and calm; and now he seemed
To cheer the comrades of his slavery,
And now he smiled upon the crowd, a smile
Gracious and kind for all its bitterness,
As if to say, "The pain is not too much."
And then it seemed to me he met my eyes,
Not seeing that the corporal held my coat,
And thought that I was freed; he kissed his hand,
Nodding that he rejoiced at my good luck –
And instantly all eyes were turned on me.
The corporal pulled at me to hide myself;
I only pressed the nearer to the church
And watched each slightest stir the prisoners made.
He saw the people weeping at his chains –

He shook them, showing he could bear the weight;
And then they lashed the horse, the wagon rolled
Along; he rose and waved his cap, and thrice
He shouted, "Poland has not perished yet!"
They vanished in the crowd, but long that hand
Against the sky, that cap like funeral plume,
That head which shameless tyranny had shaved,
A head unshamed and proud, were seen afar,
Telling of innocence and infamy;
And rising from the huddle of black heads
Like dolphin from the sea, that tells of storm,
That head and hand are printed on my heart
And shall be while I walk my way in life,
A compass pointing me where virtue leads.
If I forget them, then may God forget
Me too!

FATHER LWOWICZ: Amen for you.

ALL THE PRISONERS: And for ourselves.

JAN:

Meanwhile the rest of the kibitkas, ranged
In one long gloomy file, were moving off.
I cast a look about the close-packed crowd,
Then on the army – all were white as death,
And such dark stillness lay upon the throng
That I could hear each step, each clank of chains.
How strange, that though all feel such punishment
Inhuman, common folk and soldiery
Alike are silent, they so fear the tsar!
They led the last one out; he seemed to be
Resisting them – but, no, he could not walk.
Poor lad! he swayed, he started down the steps,
And fell full length. 'Twas Wasilewski, he
Who was our neighbor but two days ago.
They'd flogged him at the inquest so that not
One drop of blood remained to flush his face.
A soldier raised his body from the ground
And bore it to its place, while he himself
With furtive gestures wiped away his tears.
'Twas not a faint, the prisoner did not hang
All limp, but just as he had fallen, straight,
Stark, like a column being borne along,

His arms outstretched across the soldier's back
As if he had been taken from the cross.
His eyes were dreadful, white and staring wide.
Then all the people opened up their lips
And from a thousand breasts one sigh was torn,
A deep and subterranean sound of dread,
As if the graves beneath the church had groaned.
Swiftly an order drowned it with the drum:
"To arms!" and "March!" They started. Down the road
Like lightning flashes the kibitkas flew.
In one we did not see the prisoner; but
His hand, stretched deathlike toward us from the straw,
Shook in the jostling cart as in farewell.
They passed, but, caught a moment in the crowd
Before the whips had quite dispersed the throng,
The dead man stopped before the empty church.
I heard the bell and glanced inside and saw
The priest about to elevate the host,
And then I cried: "Lord, who to save the world
Did shed by Pilate's judgment guiltless blood,
Accept this sacrifice of children from
The judgment of the tsar: it's not so great
Nor holy, but it is as innocent."

(*A long silence.*)

JOSEPH:
  I've read of wars in ancient, heathen days.
  They say that then they waged such monstrous strife,
  They did not spare the foe his forest trees
  And burned the grain still ripening in the ear.
  The tsar is still more clever and he bleeds
  Poland more deep: he crushes out the seed.
  Satan himself has taught him to destroy.
FELIX:
  And will reward his pupil with first prize.

(*A momentary silence.*)

FATHER LWOWICZ:
  Brothers, it's possible the prisoner lives;

God will reveal it all in his good time.
I'll pray for him as priest, and counsel you
To say a prayer to rest the martyr's soul.
Who knows what fate tomorrow holds for us!
ADOLF:
  And say a prayer for Xavier too. You know,
  Before he could be jailed, he shot himself.
FREYEND:
  Stout lad! He shared our feasts, but when 'twas time
  To share our woes, he took leave of the world.
FATHER LWOWICZ:
  Yes, we will pray for him; it would be well.
JANKOWSKI:
  Your faith, my priest, will prove a mockery:
  Though I were worse than Tatars or than Turks,
  Though I turned robber, cutthroat, or base spy,
  Held office under Prussia, Austria, or
  The tsar himself, what then? I do not fear
  God's overhasty judgment. We are here,
  And Wasilewski's slain – the tsars still live.
FREYEND:
  That's what I'd meant to say myself; I'm glad
  You took the sin of uttering it from me.
  But let me get my breath, I've been struck dumb
  By all these tales – a man grows dazed and weeps.
  Eh, Felix, cheer us up a bit, for you
  Could make the very devils laugh in hell.
SEVERAL OF THE PRISONERS:
  Ah, that's the thing, let Felix sing and talk;
  He has a voice. Come, Freyend, start the wine.
ZEGOTA:
  Hold on! I have a Diet seat like you,
  So, though the last arrival, hear my say!
  Joseph has talked of grain – a farming man
  Is duty-bound to state his point of view.
  Although the tsar may plunder all our grain
  And bury it in his empire, in his ground,
  There may be scarcity, but we'll not starve.
  That's what Gorecki * tells us in his tale.

---

* Antoni Gorecki (1787–1861), a minor writer of the period. – Ed.

SEVERAL OF THE PRISONERS: Antoni?
ZEGOTA:
Yes, you know, his fable, or
Not fable – truth.
SEVERAL VOICES: What is it? Tell us, lad.
ZEGOTA:
When God drove Adam out of Paradise
He would not see him die for lack of food,
And so he bade his angels gather grain
And strew the kernels on the path man took.
So Adam came and found them, looked askance,
And went his way – he knew no use for grain.
But in the night sly Satan came, and thought:
"God does not scatter rye for nothing here;
Some hidden virtue must be in these seeds;
I'll bury them ere man finds out their worth."
So with his horn he made a furrow in
The earth, poured in the rye, spat, covered it,
And with his hoof tramped firmly down the ground.
Proud to have circumvented God's designs,
He nearly burst with laughter and made off;
But in the spring, the devil was amazed,
Came forth blade, blossom, ear, and finally grain.
O you who only walk the world by night,
Who think craft wisdom and call malice power,
Who find and bury liberty and faith,
You think to cheat the Lord, and cheat yourselves.
JACOB:
Bravo, Gorecki! He'll see Warsaw yet
And sit his year in prison for that tale.
FREYEND:
Well told – but let's go back to Felix now.
Fables! What sort of poetry are they!
You have to rack your brains to find the sense.
Now long live Felix, Felix of the songs!

(*He pours him out some wine.*)

JANKOWSKI:
What's Lwowicz doing? Praying for the dead!
Listen, I'll sing the priest a little hymn.

(*Sings.*)
  Call upon him, those who will,
    Jesus, Son of Mary!
  I won't believe in him until
    Jesus, Son of Mary,
  These vile miscreants shall kill –
    Jesus, Son of Mary!
  For the tsar is lusting still,
    Jesus, Son of Mary!

  Novosiltsev plots us ill,
    Jesus, Son of Mary!
  While the tsar may glut his fill,
    Jesus, Son of Mary,
  Novosiltsev drink and swill,
    Jesus, Son of Mary,
  I won't believe in your good will,
    Jesus, Son of Mary!
KONRAD:
  Beware those names before me, in your cups!
  I lost my faith long since: go on, blaspheme
  The saints throughout the litany and I'll
  Not care, but let the name of Mary be.
CORPORAL: (*Coming up to Konrad*)
  It's good one name is sacred to you yet.
  Although the gambler plays away his stakes,
  He hasn't lost while he has one piece left.
  He'll find it in his pouch some lucky day,
  Put it at interest, God will give him gain,
  And at his death he'll leave more than before.
  That's not a name to jest on. So I found
  One night in Spain, oh, many years ago,
  Before I donned this Russky uniform.
  I first served with Dombrowski's legions, then
  In Sobolewski's famous regiment.
JAN: My brother!
CORPORAL: God! May his soul rest in peace!
  He was a gallant soldier, aye, and died
  Struck by five bullets in a single blast.
  You're like him, sir. Well – once when I had gone
  With orders from your brother to a town,
  Lamego – I recall it well – I found

The place was full of Frenchies – there they were
Playing at dice or cards, or hugging tarts.
Such yelling! When the French get drunk, they roar!
They all were howling out some silly stuff,
Gray-bearded tipplers, singing dirty songs,
Till I, a young man, was ashamed. It went
From bad to worse, till they dragged in the saints
And finally the Blessed Virgin cursed.
Now you must know that I once took the vows
Of a sodality, to shield that name,
And so, since I am duty bound, I told
Them shut their traps, or else they'll pay for it!
They stopped – they didn't want to deal with me.

(*Konrad falls into a fit of musing. The others begin to chat.*)

But hear what happened: After the carouse
We went to sleep, all pretty fairly soused;
Some time at night they called to horse, the camp
Began to stir, the Frenchies stretched their hands
Out for their caps – they couldn't manage it,
For there was nothing now to put them on –
Each head was cleanly snapped off like a poppy!
It was the knavish landlord did them in;
He sliced their necks as though they had been hens.
I looked to see if still I had my head
And in my cap I found some Latin words:
Vivat Polonus, unus defensor Mariae.
You see, I owe my life to Mary's name.
ONE OF THE PRISONERS:
  Felix, come sing! Let's pour him out some tea
  Or wine.
FELIX:
  The brothers vote with one accord
  That I be merry. Though my heart may break,
  I will be gay, and you shall have your song.

(*He sings.*)

Mines, Siberia, and fetters,
  All the punishments that are –
Yet I'll be a faithful subject,
  Always working for the tsar.

In the mines my mallet, knocking,
  Shall find iron for a bar
And a later man shall forge it
  To an axe to slay the tsar.

If I must, I'll stay forever
  In that wilderness afar,
With a Tatar wife to bear me
  A new Pahlen * for the tsar.

If I'm on an army farmstead,
  Then with hoe and plough and axe
I'll plant garden and sow furrow
  Just with hemp and silken flax.

From the hemp thread will be woven –
  And a sash with silver sewn.
It may sometime have the honor
  Round the tsar's neck to be thrown.

CHORUS: (*Sings.*)
  A new Pahlen for the tsar –
  Zah, zah, zah! zah, zah, zah!

SUZIN:
  But why does Konrad sit so still and brooding,
  As if he were counting over all his sins
  Before confession? And he did not hear
  A word of Felix' singing. Konrad! Look,
  He pales and glows by turns. Is he not well?

FELIX:
  Sh! Quiet now! I guessed it would be so.
  Oh, we know Konrad and what this may mean.
  His hour is midnight. Felix will be dumb,
  For, brothers, now we'll hear a better song;
  But it needs music. Freyend, you've a flute,
  Play his old tune and we'll keep silent till
  He needs the chorus; then we'll all join in.

JOSEPH: (*Gazing at Konrad*)
  Brothers! His spirit wanders far, unbodied,
  And maybe reads the future in the stars,
  Companioned on its way by kindred spirits

---

 * Pahlen was a Russian minister involved in the assassination of Tsar Paul I in 1801. – Ed.

That tell to his the secrets of the skies.
How strange his glance! His eyes are flashing fire
And yet their gleam betrays no soul within;
They shine like campfires of a mighty army
That has departed silently by night
And stolen on some distant expedition,
To come again before the glow dies out.

(*Freyend tries one or two airs.*)

KONRAD: (*Sings.*)
  Song lay cold within the grave;
    Blood it sniffed from underground.
  Up it rose, as vampires crave
    Blood of any victims found.
    Vengeance, vengeance on the foe,
    God upon our side or no!

(*The chorus repeats the refrain.*)

Then spoke Song: "I'll walk by night.
    First I'll gnaw each brother worm;
  Whomsoever my fangs bite
    Shall, like me, take vampire's form."
    Vengeance, vengeance on the foe,
    God upon our side or no!

Then we'll seek the foe at last,
    Suck his blood, and body hew
Into bits and nail it fast
    Lest he rise a vampire too.
Then we'll take his soul to hell,
    Stamp on it with all our might,
Squeeze its last immortal yell;
    As it groans, we'll scratch and bite.
    Vengeance, vengeance on the foe,
    God upon our side or no!

FATHER LWOWICZ: In God's name, Konrad, cease that pagan song!
CORPORAL: How horribly he stares – 'twas Satan singing!

(*They stop singing.*)

71

KONRAD: (*To the accompaniment of the flute.*)
  I rise and to the mountain crest I fly
    Till far and high
  Above mankind's dominions I have soared,
    And now amid the seers
  I pierce the clouds that veil the coming years
  With eye as keen as a descending sword.
  My arms are spreading whirlwinds to disperse
    The veiling mists; through crystal air I look
    On men; I gaze into the Sibyl's book
  Where lie the secrets of the universe.
  And now I see below down vast descents
  The shaping years and yet unborn events;
  And they, like little birds that suddenly
    Behold an eagle sailing high,
    Gaze on me, the eagle of their sky.
  Look, how they drop to earth and flee,
  The whole flock burrowing within the sand!
    After them, my falcon eyes!
    After them, my lightning eyes!
  My talons seize them, they are in my hand!

  What is this bird of sable plume, that swings
    Across the heavens and with haughty eye
  Defies me? Broad as rainbows are its wings,
  And like a rising hurricane it flings
    Dark clouds across the sky.
  Who are you, monstrous raven? It is I,
  The eagle, ask! My senses are o'ershrouded –
  Who are you, bird? The thunder lord am I! –
  Then suddenly it puffs into my eye
    A ball of vapor, and my mind grows clouded –
SEVERAL OF THE PRISONERS:
  What is he saying? Look how pale he grows!

(*They seize Konrad.*)

KONRAD:
  Stop! With the raven I have matched my strength,
  And I must know the end. On with the song!

(*He staggers.*)

FATHER LWOWICZ: Have done with singing!
OTHERS: It's enough!
CORPORAL: Lord God!
  The bell! You hear! The watch is at the gate.
  Put out the light and to your cells!
ONE OF THE PRISONERS:

(*Looking out the window*)

                                    They come!
  Konrad has swooned – we'll leave him here alone.

(*They all flee.*)

Scene ii

The Improvisation

KONRAD: (*After a long silence*)
        Alone! Ah, men! And who of you, divining
        My spirit, grasps the meaning of its song?
        Whose eye will see the radiance of its shining?
        Alas, who toils to sing for men, toils long!
        The tongue belies all sound, and sound all thought,
        While thoughts fly hence ere by slow phrases caught;
        Words but engulf our thoughts and o'er them quiver
        As does the earth where streams flow underground,
        Yet from that trembling who will know the river,
        How deep it lie, or where its source be found?

        My feeling surges through my heart; it glows
        Like blood that sings deep down within the veins,
        And so much crimson as my pale face shows,
        So much men comprehend of my heart strains.
        My song, you are a star beyond the bourne
        Of earth; and human eyes,
        Seeking to track you through the skies,
        Will reach you not though they take wings of glass.
        They only strike against the Milky Way,
        Behold the suns that turn
        Through space, yet may
        Not measure them, nor count them as they pass.

What need have you, my song, of human ears?
Flow in the secret places of my heart,
Gleam on its heights, inviolate, apart,
Like sunken streams, like stars beyond the spheres.

Then heed me, God and nature, for my song
Is worthy you, worthy to echo long.
　　A master I!
I stretch my hands on high
And touch the stars. Ah, see!
Now forth there peels
As from the crystal wheels
Of some harmonica,* a melody;
And as the circles roll
I tune the turning planets to my soul.
　　A million notes stream on;
　　I catch each one,
I braid them into rainbow-colored chords,
And out they flow and flash like lightning swords.

I take my hands away: each starry circle
Of that harmonica its turning stays;
Through spaces far beyond the planets' sparkle,
Beyond all confines now, my arms I raise.
I sing alone; and, long
And wailing like the tempest's breath, my song
Searches the ocean of humanity;
It moans with grief, it roars with storm,
And listening centuries transform
The echoes to a vast antiphony.
I hear it as I hear the wind that rocks
The rushing waters, whistling loud;
I see it as I see the wind that walks
Appareled in a robe of cloud.
My song is worthy God and nature; great
It is, for with it I create!
Such song is power and deathless energy,
Such song is immortality!
Yes, I have made this immortality I feel;

---

*A reference to the glass harmonica, a popular instrument of the period. – Ed.

What greater deed, O God, can you reveal?
I body forth my songs in words; they fly,
They scatter over all the sky,
They whirl on high, they play, they shine;
I touch them still though they are far,
Their tender graces I caress
And their rounded forms I press:
Their every movement I divine.
I love you, children of my poetry,
I love my thoughts, my songs, each one a star;
My feelings, tempests swirling high and far.
Amid the lot of you I stand, the sovereign
And loving father of his progeny,
For you are mine, all mine!

Poets and prophets, wise men of past days
On whom the wide world heaps abundant praise,
I hold you all in scorn!
Though you yet walked among the children born
Of your own spirits, and yet heard the bright air riven
With hymns and plaudits that you knew were rightly given;
Though round your brows there shone
Fair coronets enwoven of the gleams
Of daily homage and melodious themes
Sung you by generations past and gone,
Still never would you feel your happiness and might
As I feel mine, here in the lonely night,
Singing unheard, alone,
Singing unto myself alone.

Yes, I have wisdom now, and love, and power!
Oh, never have I felt as at this hour!
This is my zenith, and my strength tonight
Has reached its height;
Now I shall know
If I be one supreme, or only proud.
This is the destined moment; lo,
I strain my spirit's shoulders broad!
It is the moment that was Samson's when a prisoner,
    blind,
He brooded by the pillars. Now my mind
Casts off its body; through the air's expanse
It soars, and far and fleet,

On past the mazy planets' dance
I take my course where God and nature meet.

My wings! I have them now, and they suffice!
I stretch them to the east and to the west,
The right wing strikes the future and the left the past,
And higher, higher, on the beams of love I rise
And peer into your breast.
O you! of whom they say that you still feel –
I'm here, I've come, you see my power is real!
My wings reach even here to you!
But I am human yet, and there where lies
My body, in the land I loved, my heart lies too.

And yet my love has never found repose
In selfish joy with any single man,
Like the poor insect, living in the rose;
Nor in one generation nor one clan.
I love a nation, and my wide embrace
Presses the past and future of the race
    To my deep breast.
Both friend and lover, spouse and father, I;
And I would raise my country high
    Upon the crest
Of joy, for all the world to glorify.
But I have not the means; this lack has brought
Me here, armed with the power of thought,
Of thought that snatched your lightnings from the sky,
That followed where the planets go,
That opened up the ocean's floor
By its great strength. And I have more,
A power that men cannot bestow:
Feeling, that oftentimes must choke
Within itself, and yet sometimes does pour
Forth words as the volcano smoke.

Nor have I plucked this strength from Eden's tree:
'Twas not the fruit of knowledge gave it me;
Not from books and tales it springs,
Not from magic questionings,
Nor unriddling secret things,
For I am a creator born;
My power has its source

Whence yours draws no greater force.
You did not seek it and you do not fear
That of that power you shall e'er be shorn.
So I, who have my strength, from you or otherwhere,
My swift and potent eye,
Fear not, and when the time is on me, high,
Scarce visible along a cloudy trail,
I see the distant birds of passage sail:
Then I send forth my wish, and my swift sight
Holds them as in a snare;
And, till I loose them, they may cry in mournful tone,
But cannot move in flight,
Although to drive them on
You sent forth gusts of air.
I gaze upon a comet's track to prove
My power – and the comet cannot move.
   Only men, corrupt of heart,
    Yet with an immortal part,
Obey me not and know not You nor Me.
In heaven, here, I seek such mastery,
And with the power I have o'er nature, bind
   The human mind.
As I rule birds and planets with my nod,
So will I rule my fellow man, my rod
No sword – that calls forth sword; no song –
For it must germinate too long;
Not learning – it will soon decay;
Not miracles – too loud are they;
But I will rule men by the love in me,
As you rule all, forever, secretly.
What I desire, at once let all
Divine, and joyously fulfill;
And if they shall oppose my will,
Let them suffer, let them fall!
Let men be unto me as speech and thought,
From whom at will the house of song is wrought;
No different is your rule, they say.
You know that I have never twisted thought
Nor stinted speech. If given equal sway
O'er souls, I would then make my nation's lot
A living song, and do a greater thing
Than you – a song of happiness I'd sing!

Give me the rule of souls! This lifeless building
That common people call the world, and praise,
I so despise that I have never tested
Whether my word has not the power to raze
And ruin it. But well I know if through the portal
Of air I shot my will in one swift bound,
Its power compressed and centered, that it might
Put out a hundred stars and then might light
Another hundred, for I am immortal!
I know that in creation's round
Are other deathless ones, but higher than I
I know none yet, and so I seek you here
   Within the sky,
I, highest of the sentient of earth's sphere.
I have not seen you yet, but that you are I guess;
Give me the power I seek, or tell me how
To gain it. I have heard of prophets who
Could reign o'er spirits, and so can I, too.
I would have power o'er souls no less
Than you in heaven here possess,
To rule them as you do so now.

(*A long silence.*)

(*With irony.*)

Still silent! Ha! At last I have the key
To who and what you are, your sovereignty:
He lied who called you love; your name
Is wisdom, therein lies your fame.
Not to the heart, but to the mind alone
Are your ways and your arsenal made known.
He who has delved in books alone,
In numbers, corpses, metals, stone,
'Tis he and only he who may approach
You and upon your power encroach.
He shall find poison, dust, and steam,
Uproar and smoke and tinsel gleam,
And empty laws, to teach again
To would-be wise or witless men.
You granted all the fruits of earth
To mind, but left the heart in dearth;

To me, you gave life's shortest span,
Yet power to feel beyond each man.

(*Silence.*)

What is the feeling that I feel?
  A spark, no more!
What is my life's ordeal?
  A moment's time!
And the lightnings of tomorrow, what are they today?
  A spark, no more!
And the storied ages coursing on their endless way?
  A moment's time!
Whence came this little world and all mankind?
  From just a spark!
And what is death that wastes the riches of the mind?
  A moment's time!
What was He while the worlds yet lay within his breast?
  A spark, no more!
And eternity, when He shall swallow it at last?
  A moment's time!

VOICE FROM THE LEFT SIDE:	VOICE FROM THE RIGHT:
Saddle his soul!	How he does rave!
Mount it and gallop,	Wrap our wide wings
On, on to our goal!	round him,
	Shelter and save!

The moment and the spark, as they expand and burn,
  Can make and overturn.
Then stretch and lengthen out the fleeting time,
Blow up the flickering flame to fire sublime.
Now – and I challenge you – come forth! Once more,
Baring my soul to you as to a friend,
I call upon you solemnly, attend!
No answer? Yet in person you waged war
With Satan. Spurn me not: although alone
  I call you out,
I and a nation's mighty heart are one;
Thrones, powers, armies follow after me.
If I am to blaspheme, a bloodier bout
Than that with Satan shall you have with me.
For Satan sought dominion for the mind,
I battle for the heart of all mankind!

I have grown up in suffering and love,
And though of my own happiness dispossessed,
I beat my hands upon my bleeding breast,
But never raised them against heaven above.

VOICE:

The steed is a bird,
And, onward spurred,
Let it mount the height
In eagle flight.

VOICE:

A falling star. Alas,
It sinks in the abyss!

Now is my soul incarnate in my country
And in my body dwells her soul;
My fatherland and I are one great whole.
My name is million, for I love as millions:
Their pain and suffering I feel;
I gaze upon my country fallen on days
Of torment, as a son would gaze
Upon his father broken on the wheel.
I feel within myself my country's massacre
Just as a mother feels within her womb
The labor of the children whom
She bears. Yet you, still wise and cool,
Reigning in bliss, do rule,
And men will say that you can never err!
Hear me if that be true which once I heard
With filial faith, that you do love the earth
    To which you once gave birth:
    Hear me, if once your word
Saved from the flood within the sheltering ark,
With man and each original beast, the spark
Of love: if love be no monstrosity,
Whose nature is impermanence,
That cannot ripen to maturity:
If in your rule love is not anarchy:
If on the millions crying, "Save us, Lord!"
You do not gaze with an unmoved regard,
As you would gaze on the confusion wrought
By some false reckoning: if in creation,
As you have planned and made it, love is naught
But a wrong figure in your calculation,
    Then hear me, Lord!

VOICE:

Now like a hydra

VOICE:

From the brightest sun

The eagle shall rise;	The comet strays;
Outward and upward,	When will its race be run,
Pluck out his eyes!	Whither its ways?

Silent! Yet I have opened all my heart!
I beg you, give me power! The smallest part
Of that which here on earth pride arrogates.
From that one part what joy I would create!
Silent! If not the heart, give for the mind!
Foremost am I of angels and mankind,
And know you better than your seraphs must;
By right, you should share half your power with me.
If I have erred, then say! Why silent be?
I lie not! You stay silent and still trust
In your strong arm. But know, for your own sake,
That love can burn what mind can never break.
My fire is love, and I
Will heap it up till it burn high.
Then, as with powder, I will fill
With it the cannon of my will.

VOICE: VOICE:
Ready! Aim! Fire!   Mercy! Grace!
Speak, or I loose my charge, and if I can
Not shatter nature into shards, yet all your plan
Of wheeling worlds and planets, every star,
Shall rock, as my voice shot throughout creation
From generation unto generation
Shouts you are not the father...

VOICE OF THE DEVIL: But the tsar!

(Konrad stands for a moment, then totters and falls.)

SPIRITS FROM THE LEFT SIDE:
FIRST SPIRIT: Trample him, catch him!
SECOND SPIRIT: He is breathing still.
FIRST SPIRIT:
He faints. Before he wakes, we'll smother him.
SPIRIT FROM THE RIGHT SIDE:
Begone, for some still pray for him!
SPIRIT FROM THE LEFT: You see,
They'll drive us off.
FIRST SPIRIT FROM THE LEFT:
You stupid beast, could not

81

2. Adam Mickiewicz's *Forefathers' Eve*, Scene ii. Presented at the Stary Teatr, Cracow, in 1973. Directed by Konrad Swinarski. Devils and angels fighting for the soul of Konrad at the end of The Improvisation. (Photograph: Wojciech Plewiński)

You wring from him the final, fatal word,
Puff him up only one step more in pride!
A moment, and he would have been a corpse.
To be so near and yet not to be able
To trample on him! To behold the blood
Reddening his lips and not to lap it up!
Most foolish devil, you dropped him just halfway!
SECOND SPIRIT: He'll come again!
FIRST SPIRIT: Off, or I'll take you on
My horns and carry you a thousand years,
Then ram you into Satan's jaws.
SECOND SPIRIT: Ha ha!
Mama and auntie want to frighten me!
I'll cry. (*Cries*) Take that!

(*Strikes him with his horn.*)

          Well now, did I aim well?
Be off to the infernal pit! He's struck
The bottom. Bravo! Bravo!
FIRST SPIRIT: *Sacrédieu!*
SECOND SPIRIT: Here's one for you! (*Strikes him.*)
FIRST SPIRIT: Take to your heels!

(*There is a noise at the door and the sound of a key in the lock.*)

SECOND SPIRIT: A priest
Is coming! Quiet, draw your horns in, beast!

Scene iii

(*The Corporal, Father Peter [a Bernardine], and a prisoner come in.*)

FATHER PETER:
In the name of the Father, Son, and Holy Ghost!
PRISONER:
He's fainted – Konrad! No, he does not hear.
FATHER PETER:
Peace to this house and peace unto the sinner!
PRISONER:
God help us! He has swooned – he frowns and tosses,
He's very ill! See how he bites his lips!

(*Father Peter prays.*)

CORPORAL: (*To the Prisoner.*)
  Good sir, please go and leave us here alone!
PRISONER:
  In Heaven's name, don't prattle idle prayers,
  But lift him up and lay him on the bed,
  Father!
FATHER PETER: No, leave him.
PRISONER:
  Here's a pillow. (*Places Konrad upon it.*) Ah!
  I know what all this means! Sometimes there falls
  A frenzy on him and he sings and talks
  For long, but when the morrow comes, he'll be
  Sound as a fish. Who told you he passed out?
CORPORAL:
  Be quiet, sir, and let good Brother Peter
  Pray for your comrade's soul, because I know
  That there was something – something evil – here;
  No sooner had the watch departed when
  I heard a babel coming from this cell.
  I glued my eyes up to the keyhole then –
  And what I saw, I saw! I dashed away
  To Brother Peter – he's a man of God –
  But see the sick man: things go ill with him!
PRISONER:
  In God's name, what's all this? It drives me mad!
CORPORAL:
  Mad? Aye, you gentlefolk had best beware!
  You've eloquent lips, much learning in your heads,
  But see, the learned head rolls in the dust,
  And on these eloquent lips the froth is white!
  I heard his song, although the words I could
  Not comprehend; but on his brow and in
  His eyes was something, something... Take my word,
  An evil thing has hold upon this man.
  I've stormed redoubts and many a cloister wall,
  First in the legions, later as recruit,
  And I have seen more souls departing hence
  Than you've read books, good sir, in all your life.
  It's no small thing to see the way men die.
  In Praga * I have seen them hew down priests;

In Spain beheld men hurled alive from towers;
I have seen mothers with their breasts pierced through,
And children dying upon Cossack pikes,
Frenchmen upon the snow, and Turks impaled;
I know the aspect dying martyrs wear,
And that of murderers, Turks, and Muscovites.
I've looked on men condemned and seen them gaze
Boldly into the barrels of the guns,
Their eyes unblindfolded; but when they dropped
To earth, forth from each corpse came fear,
Imprisoned while alive by shame and pride,
And crawled off from the bodies like a worm –
Fear horrider than that which strikes the coward
In battle, so that one need only look
Upon a dead man's brow, and know his soul
Suffers and fears, while it despises, pain,
And so will suffer on eternally.
And therefore, sir, I think a dead man's face
His army patent for the world beyond;
You know at once how he will be received –
Among the blest or curst, and in what rank.
Thus this man's singing and his sickness now,
His brow and glances, I don't like at all.
So go, sir, to your own cell, quietly,
While I and Brother Peter stay with him.

(*The Prisoner goes out.*)

KONRAD:
　The abyss – a thousand years – the void, ah, more,
　I will hold out ten thousand thousand years –
　And shall I pray? No, prayer cannot avail –
　I did not know there was an abyss so deep,
　So bottomless as this.
CORPORAL: Hear how he sobs!
FATHER PETER:
　My son, you are upon a heart that loves you.

---

*A district of Warsaw. The scene of a massacre of Poles by Russian troops
under the command of General Suvorov in 1794. – Ed.

(*To the Corporal*)

Go out and see that no one enters here
To hinder me, till I come forth myself.

(*The Corporal goes out.*)

KONRAD: (*Starts up.*)
    No, it was not plucked out, my potent eye;
    I still can pierce the dark and depth; I try
    And you, my brother, Rollison, see there.
    But why in prison, scourged, with bloody stains?
    God has not listened to you; in despair
    You seek a knife, try to beat out your brains
    Against the walls, or cry on God to save.
    He will not and I cannot: still I have
    My potent glance – and with it I can slay
    You. No, it fails – but it can point the way
    To death. Leap to the window, burst it through,
    And dash yourself below – I'll fly with you
    Down, down to the abyss – 'tis better far
    Within the pit than earthly valleys are;
    There are no brothers, mothers, nations there –
    There are no tyrants. Come!
FATHER PETER: You unclean sprite,
    I know you by the venom of your bite.
    Once more, you wily Satan, do appear
    In this deserted dwelling, horrid snake,
    And now come crawling through his lips, to make
    His ruin? In the name of God on high
    I've caught and bound you. *Exorciso* –
SPIRIT: No,
    Don't curse me. Leave the threshold and I'll go.
FATHER PETER:
    You shall not leave until you make reply!
    The Lion of Judah's tribe is master here –
    You slyly laid a snare for him, and lo!
    Are caught therein yourself. You shall not jeer –
    God has entrapped you in this sinning youth
    And here I strike you the most bitter blow,
    Liar, and charge you now to speak the truth!

SPIRIT:

Parle-moi donc français, mon pauvre capucin;
J'ai pu dans le grand monde oublier mon latin.
Mais étant saint, tu dois avoir le don des langues –
Vielleicht sprechen Sie deutsch? Was murmeln Sie so bang?
What is it? Caballeros, risponderò io.

FATHER PETER:

Hundred-tongued snake, 'tis you speaks through him so.

SPIRIT:

C'est juste. Dans ce jeu nous sommes de moitié;
Il est savant, et moi, diable de mon métier.
J'étais son précepteur et je m'en glorifie.
En sais-tu plus que nous? Parle – je te défie!

FATHER PETER:

In the name of Father, Son, and Holy Ghost!

SPIRIT:

Enough of that, my priest, leave off your ban!
Torment me not as if you were a host
Of imps, or Satan's self!

FATHER PETER: Who are you, come!

SPIRIT:

I am Lucretius and Leviathan, Voltaire, *der alte* Fritz,
    Legio sum.

FATHER PETER: Tell me what you have seen.

SPIRIT: I saw a beast.

FATHER PETER: And where?

SPIRIT: In Rome.

FATHER PETER:

He still does not obey!
I'll pray again. (*He prays.*)

SPIRIT: But I will mind you, priest.

FATHER PETER: Where was the prisoner?

SPIRIT: In Rome, I say.

FATHER PETER: Still lying.

SPIRIT: By my honor, by my bride,
My coal-black love who ever sighs for me –
You know her name that I thus swear by? Pride!
How void you are of curiosity!

FATHER PETER: (*To himself*)

The demons are perverse. I will abase
Myself before the Lord and seek his grace.

(He prays.)

SPIRIT:
 Why bother? Off I go, and I confess:
 In crawling in this soul I made a mess;
 I donned it inside out, and now it cuts,
 Like hedgehog's skin – its quills right in my guts.

(The priest prays.)

 But you're a master, though a simple friar.
 Asses! They'd make you Pope if they were bright.
 Instead, the Church stupidity thrusts higher
 But you hides in a corner, star of light!
FATHER PETER:
 Tyrant and flatterer, both base and proud,
 To stab the heart, you crawl in sand, head bowed.
SPIRIT: *(Laughing)*
 Aha! You're angry and have ceased your prayer.
 Da capo! Could you see how droll the air
 With which you twist your paws, like some great bear
 That strikes at gnats! And still you babble on.
 But now enough of jesting, let's have done.
 I know your power and would confess to you;
 I'll tell you of the past and future, too.
 You'd like to know the talk of you that's spread,

(The priest prays.)

 And Poland's fate two hundred years ahead?
 And why your prior works for your eclipse,
 And what the beast in the Apocalypse
 May mean? He answers nothing, only prays,
 And fixes on me still his awful gaze.
 But tell me, priest, how is it that you chose
 To strike at me? Have I deserved your blows?
 I am no king of devils. On my word,
 I think you whip the servant for his lord.
 I came here but at Satan's own command –
 It would be hard to make him understand –
 We're not on equal terms – I'd come to grief.
 I'm but *Kreishauptmann, Landrat,* district chief:
 They say: "Arrest this soul." I do, and throw
 It forth to darkness. If some little woe

Befall the soul, I'm but a tool, you know;
'Twas the ukase that ordered matters so.
Do I love torturing them? It hurts me worst.
Alas for those who feel! (*He sighs.*) My heart will burst!
Yes, while my talons make the sinner quail,
I have to wipe my own eyes with my tail.

(*The priest prays.*)

Tomorrow like Haman you shall meet death.
FATHER PETER:
In nomine Patris et Filii et Spiritus Sancti, Amen.
Ego te exorciso, spiritus immunde –
SPIRIT:
Stop, priest – I'll mind. I'll speak – wait but a breath!
FATHER PETER:
Where is the unhappy prisoner who would slay
His soul? You're silent. *Exorciso te –*
SPIRIT: I'll speak – I'll speak – I must.
FATHER PETER: Whom did you see?
SPIRIT: A prisoner.
FATHER PETER: Of what sort?
SPIRIT: A sinning man.
FATHER PETER: Where?
SPIRIT: In that convent, in captivity.
FATHER PETER: In which one?
SPIRIT: Yonder, the Dominican.
   He's damned, and is already mine by right.
FATHER PETER: You lie.
SPIRIT: He's dead.
FATHER PETER: You lie.
SPIRIT: He's ill.
FATHER PETER: Spite
   Me! *Exorciso te!*
SPIRIT: I'll speak – I'll sing,
   I'll dance. You choke me. Cease your conjuring.
FATHER PETER: Then speak the truth.
SPIRIT: The prisoner's wits are gone;
   Beyond a doubt he'll break his neck at dawn.
FATHER PETER: You lie.
SPIRIT: Beelzebub will swear 'tis so;
   Plague him, and let my guiltless spirit go.

PETER: How can I save the sinner?
SPIRIT: Go to hell.
FATHER PETER: *Exorciso te . . .*
SPIRIT: Console – no more I'll tell.
FATHER PETER:
  Fine! Now speak plain – what has he need of most?
SPIRIT:
  My throat is sore; I'm no good as a host.
FATHER PETER: Speak!
SPIRIT: O my king!
  Unless I rest I'm dead.
FATHER PETER: His needs . . .
SPIRIT: I cannot say.
FATHER PETER: Speak!
SPIRIT: Wine and bread.
FATHER PETER:
  I understand. Thy bread and wine, O Lord!
  I go, and grant me to fulfill thy word!

(To the Spirit.)

  Away! and take your wickedness and sin
  Along the road on which you came herein.

(The Spirit departs.)

KONRAD:
  Who raises me? You too shall fall – beware!
  He stretches forth his hand! And like a bird,
  I fly where glory streams through fragrant air.
  Who is it, man or guardian angel, stirred
  With pity, stoops to where I lie unmourned?
  Angels I never knew and men I scorned.
FATHER PETER:
  The hand of God is heavy on you. Pray!
  The lips that have denied his majesty
  An evil spirit soiled with blasphemy –
  Such spoken folly makes our bitterest pain.
  May your words be forgotten wholly, may
  They purge you!
KONRAD:
  They are hammered on my brain.

FATHER PETER:

That you may never more decipher them,
That God ask not their meaning to condemn
You, sinner, pray! Your thought, decked out in mean
And evil words, is like a sinning queen
Cast from her throne, in sackcloth and in ashes,
Who must wait thus until her penance washes
Her clean; then in her regal robes once more
She mounts her throne, more glorious than before.
He sleeps. (*Kneels.*) Thy mercies, Lord, are manifold!

(*He falls to the floor in the form of a cross.*)

Lo, here am I, thy servant long, an old
And sinning servant, worn and good for naught:
O make this youth the bearer of thy thought!
And let me take upon my head his blame;
He will amend, and glorify thy name.
Accept the sacrifice that we have brought!

(*He prays.*)

(*In the church nearby, beyond the wall, the Christmas hymn is begun. Above
Father Peter is heard the singing of a choir of angels to the air, "The Angel spake
unto the Shepherds."*)

CHOIR OF ANGELS: (*Children's voices*)
    Peace be on this dwelling,
    The sinner's grief dispelling;
  Thou, servant, humble, quiet-eyed
  Hast filled with peace the house of pride.
    Peace be on this dwelling!
FIRST ARCHANGEL: (*To the air, "God Our Refuge"*)
  Lord, he hath sinned against thee, greatly sinned.
SECOND ARCHANGEL:
  But yet thine angels weep o'er him and pray.
FIRST ARCHANGEL:
  Slay thy contemners with thy wrathful wind.
SECOND ARCHANGEL:
  Forgive, O Lord, those who know not thy way!
ANGEL:
    When bright the star of hope
    Shone o'er Judea's slope,

91

The angels sang on high the Christmas hymn;
Kings did not hear, nor wise men see
   The angelic jubilee,
But shepherds saw and ran to Bethlehem.
   The lowly of the earth,
   Rejoicing at the birth,
Acknowledged deathless power and good in him.
FIRST ARCHANGEL:
   When in his angels' hearts the Lord beheld
   How prying craft and proud presumption swelled,
   He pardoned not those spirits, bright, immortal,
   But in a starry rain from heaven's portal
   They fell; and so the wise men of today
   Follow those lost ones on destruction's way.
CHOIR OF ANGELS:
   What unto earthly pride
   The Lord our God denied,
He granted to the humble of the earth.
   Oh, pity on thy son
   Whose greatness is undone,
Pity upon this fallen son of earth!
SECOND ARCHANGEL:
   He did not search the secrets of thy name
   From curiosity or love of fame.
FIRST ARCHANGEL:
   He knew thee not, nor honored thee, great Lord;
   He loved thee not, our Savior, nor thy word!
SECOND ARCHANGEL:
   And yet the Virgin's name his heart could touch.
   He loved his country and he loved it much.
ANGEL:
   A richly-fashioned cross
   Of goldwork doth emboss
The crowns of kings and gleameth like a gem
   On wise men, but imparts
   No softness to their hearts.
Enlighten them, O Lord, enlighten them!
CHOIR OF ANGELS:
   We so have loved mankind
   That with them we would find
A dwelling. When the wise man and the king
   Refused us, then the poor

Did welcome us and o'er
Him night and day our carols we will sing.
CHOIR OF ARCHANGELS:
Lift him, and he will rise up from the dust
To heaven and freely worship at the cross;
Then may the whole world know its gold for dross
And praise thee, Lord, the merciful and just.
BOTH CHOIRS:
Oh, peace unto the lowly,
To virtue calm and holy!
Thou servant, humble, quiet-eyed,
Hast filled with peace the house of pride;
Peace to the sinner lowly!

Scene iv

(*A country house near Lwów. A bedroom. Eve, a young girl, runs in, arranges some flowers before the image of the Most Holy Virgin, kneels, and prays. Marcelina comes in.*)

MARCELINA:
Still praying! It is midnight, time for sleep.
EVE:
I have just prayed a moment for my country
As I was taught, for father, and for mother.
Now for those others let us likewise pray.
Although they are so far, they too are children
Of Poland, of one country of one mother.
The Lithuanian who arrived today
Escaped the Russians; it is horrible
To hear how terribly they treat them there;
The wicked tsar has put them all in dungeons:
Like Herod, he would wipe the whole race out.
The stranger made our father very sad:
He walked abroad and has not yet returned;
And mother sent an offering for a mass,
A funeral mass, for many of them have died.
And I will say a special prayer for him
Who is the author of this book of songs.

(*Showing a little book*)

He is in prison, too, the stranger said.
I've read the verses, some are beautiful.
I'll kneel once more before the Holy Mother
And pray for him. Who knows, perhaps this moment
His parents, too, are saying prayers for him.

(*Marcelina goes out. Eve prays and falls asleep.*)

ANGEL:
  Light and soft as a dream we fly.
CHOIR OF ANGELS:
  To gladden the sleep of our darling one,
    Under her head
    Our wings we spread;
  Our starry glances lightly lie
  On her face as we sing her our benison.
  A dancing wreath, we fly above
  Our pure, our tranquil slumbering love;
  Our lily hands we plait like leaves,
  Our brows are like the petaled rose;
  From underneath its starry bands
  Our hair in fragrant, falling sheaves
  Of golden streaming glory flows.
  A flowering garland with clasped hands
  We circle o'er our darling's breast
  To guard her in her sleeping nest,
  And sing while wreathing close above
  Our pure, our tranquil slumbering love.
EVE: (*In a vision*)
  A rain as gentle and as still as dew –
  Whence comes it? All the heaven is so blue,
    So clear and blue!
  The drops are rainbow-bright! And nosegays wound
  Of roses and lilies wreathe me round!
    Sweet dream,
  Flow on forever like a sleeping stream!
    O roses filled with light,
    Pure lilies, milky-white,
     You never knew
  This earth, beyond the fleecy clouds you grew!
  Narcissus, with your snowy glance,
  And you, blue flowers of memory,

Like eyes of innocence,
I know you all; but yesterday
I watered you in my garden there
And plucked of you a sweet bouquet
And crowned the Holy Mother where
She gleams above my bed, so mild!
O miracle, O Virgin! She
Bends and gazes downward. See,
Now she gives the holy child
The wreath, and Jesus, smilingly,
Throws the flowers down to me.
They have grown more fresh and fair
And multiplied a thousandfold;
Floating, flying on, they find
One another in the air.
Of themselves a wreath they wind,
       Of every bloom!
Lord, how good you are and kind!
'Tis heaven in my room.
Rose, narcissus, eyes of snow,
Hovering ever o'er me, so
Gazing on your hearts, may I
       Fall asleep and die!

       A spirit is alight
              Within this rose:
       It stirs its head, and bright
              As flame it glows!
A living blush like dawn-fire in the sky!
It laughs, and 'mid its lovely leaves unrolled
In smiles, two lips of coral pink unfold;
And decorously, softly as a sigh,
       They speak. But why
       This voice of pain?
       Dear rose, do you complain
Because I broke you from your parent tree?

I did not pluck you for my own delight
But crowned with you our Lady bright,
And after I confessed last night
       I watered you with tears.
Now from those coral lips there flows
A line of sparks that floats along:

Oh, is this radiance your song?
    What do you wish, dear rose?
ROSE:
  Lay me upon your heart!
ANGELS:
  Let us weave our wreath apart.
ROSE:
  I'll loose my wings, I'll free my brow.
ANGELS:
  We will fly home to heaven now.
ROSE:
  But I will gladden her till day,
  Lay my head on hers till dawn,
  As the beloved apostle John
  Upon his Master's bosom lay.

Scene v

(*The cell of Father Peter.*)

FATHER PETER: (*Prays, lying in the form of a cross.*)
  Lord, what am I before thy countenance?
    Dust and naught.
  But when I have confessed my nothingness to thee,
  I, dust, may yet hold converse with my Lord.

(*He beholds a vision.*)

A tyrant has arisen, Herod! Lord, the youth of Poland
Is all delivered into Herod's hands.
What do I see? Long snowy ways, with many crossroads,
White roads that stretch through wastes too distant to descry!
All running to the north, that far, far country,
  As rivers flow;
On, on they stream, and one leads straight to iron portals,
That other, like a stream that vanishes beneath the ground,
Drops into unseen caverns, lost to view;
And this one finds its outlet in the sea.
Over the roads they fly, a mass of wagons
Like clouds driven onward by the winds.
All to the north they go. O Lord,

They are our children, and is such their fate,
   Exile, great Lord?
Dost thou destroy them all, so young, so young?
And wilt thou wipe our race out utterly?
But see – a child escapes, grows up – he is our savior,
   The restorer of our land!
Born of a foreign mother,* in his veins
The blood of ancient warriors – and his name
   Shall be forty and four.†

O Lord, wilt thou not deign to speed his coming,
   My people to console?
No, they must suffer to the end – I see a rabble:
Tyrants and murderers run and catch at him –
I see my nation bound, all Europe drags him on
   And mocks at him:
"To the judgment hall!" The multitude leads in the guiltless man.
Mouths, without hearts or hands, are judges here,
And all shout, "Gaul! Let Gaul be judge!"
Gaul found no fault in him – and washed his hands;
And yet the kings shout, "Judge him! Punish him!
His blood shall be on us and on our children;
Crucify Mary's son and loose Barabbas!
He scorns great Caesar's crown: crucify him,
Or we will say, you are not Caesar's friend."
And Gaul delivered him unto the people –
They led him forth – and then his innocent head
Grew bloodstained from the mocking crown of thorns;
They raised him up in sight of all the world –
The people thronged to see – and Gaul cried out,
"Behold the free and independent nation!"

I see the cross. O Lord, how long, how long
Must he still bear it? Lord, be merciful!
Strengthen thy servant lest he fall and die!
The cross has arms that shadow all of Europe,
Made of three withered peoples, like dead trees.

---

*Perhaps a reference to Mickiewicz's possible Jewish ancestry on his mother's side. – Ed.

†Possibly the numerical value of the letters in the Hebrew alphabet which spell out Mickiewicz's first name, Adam. A prophetic numerology typical of the Cabala. – Ed.

Now is my nation on the martyr's throne.
He speaks and says, "I thirst," and Rakus gives him
To drink of vinegar, and Borus, gall,
While Mother Freedom stands below and weeps.
And now a soldier hired in Muscovy
Comes forward with his pike and pierces him,
And from my guiltless nation blood has gushed.
What have you done, most stupid myrmidon,
Most heartless! Yet he only shall repent –
And God will pardon him his sins at last.

O my beloved! He droops his dying head
And now in a loud voice he calls, "My God,
My God, and why hast thou forsaken me?"
    And he is dead.

(*Choirs of angels are heard in the distance, singing the Easter hymn. At the end come the words, "Alleluia, alleluia."*)

    My belovèd has risen,
    And ascended into heaven.
    His garment white as snow
      Floats down below,
      And wide unfurled
Wraps in its spreading raiment all the world.
    He has gone up on high
Yet is not vanished from our sight,
    And from his triple eye
Shines as from triple suns a radiant light,
And he displays his piercèd hands to all.

Who is this man? He is the viceroy upon earth.
I knew him as a child. But ah, since then
How have his soul and body blossomed forth!
An angel boy is leading him – the man of dread
Is blind – he has a threefold countenance
And threefold brow. And like a baldachin outspread,
The book of mysteries above his head
    Veils him from nearer glance.
Three cities are his footstool – when he calls,
Three ends of earth must tremble.* Now there falls

---

  *Possibly an allusion to the three nations responsible for the partitions of Poland – Prussia, Russia, and Austria. – Ed.

A voice from heaven like a thunderpeal,
"Lo, here is Freedom's Viceroy in sight!"
On glory he will build his temple's might;
Before him peoples, kings must finally kneel.
Upon three crowns he stands, himself uncrowned;
His life – the toil of toils; his appellation –
Of nations, the one nation –
Of warrior blood, a foreign mother bore
The man; his name, that shall resound
For ages unto ages, shall be forty-four!
   Glory! glory! glory!

(*He falls asleep.*)

ANGELS: (*Descending in visible form*)
  He sleeps. We'll take his spirit from his body
  As from its golden crib a sleeping child,
  Lightly lay off the clothing of his senses
  And robe his soul in radiance undefiled.
  To the third heaven swiftly we will bear him
  And place him sleeping on his father's knees:
  Sanctified by those fatherly caresses
  He shall have taste of heaven's hallowed ease.
  Ere morning mass we will return his spirit
  And in the wrappings of his senses fold
  Him once again, and lay him in his body
  As a pure infant in its crib of gold.

Scene vi

(*A sumptuous sleeping chamber. The Senator turns on his bed and sighs. Two devils above his bed.*)

FIRST DEVIL:
  He's drunk and just can't sleep,
  How long a watch I keep.
  The scoundrel won't lie still,
  Were bristles in his swill?
SECOND DEVIL:
  Try poppy in his eyes.

FIRST DEVIL:

Asleep, I'll make the kill.

SECOND DEVIL:

The hawk's prey swiftly dies.

BOTH DEVILS:

We'll drag his soul to hell,

Flog him with serpents well,

And roast him to a glow!

BEELZEBUB: Take care!

BOTH DEVILS: And what's your name?

BEELZEBUB: Beelzebub.

BOTH DEVILS: And so?

BEELZEBUB:

Don't frighten off my game!

FIRST DEVIL:

But when he sleeps, the swine,

Is not his slumber mine?

BEELZEBUB:

When fire and pitch he sees,

The woes and miseries,

He'll fear these awful pains,

Recall the dream next day,

Perhaps pull in his reins –

His end's still far away!

SECOND DEVIL: (*Extending his talons*)

Come, let me have my fun –

Don't fret for such a one!

If he reforms his way,

I'll call a holiday

And take the cross – and pray!

BEELZEBUB:

But carry fright too far,

His memory you'll jar;

He'll make our scheme collapse

And slip right from our traps.

FIRST DEVIL: (*Pointing to the sleeping man*)

But shall our brotherkin,

My dearest kith and kin,

Sleep like a babe this night?

I'd give him quite a fright!

BEELZEBUB:

Recall my rank, imp! I

Am Caesar's deputy!
FIRST DEVIL:
  Ah, pardon! Your commands?
BEELZEBUB:
  His soul is in your hands.
  You can puff it with pride,
  Then thrust it down to shame,
  Heap it with scorn and blame,
  Sow it with mockery.
  But not a glimpse of hell!
  We're off and away! Farewell!

(*Flies off.*)

FIRST DEVIL:
  I'll at him in a trice!
  You're trembling, knave, I see!
SECOND DEVIL:
  Don't let your claws get free,
  Play as cats do with mice.

The Senator's Vision

SENATOR: (*In his sleep*)
  A message from the tsar's own hand – to me!
  A hundred thousand rubles. Ah, and far
  Greater, the princely title! And a star!
  Here, lackey, pin it on! Ah, when they see!
  The marshal! Ah, they'll burst with jealousy!

(*He turns on his other side.*)

  The imperial antechamber – all are here!
  And how they hate me, but they bow, from fear.
  Marshal and grand controller, in this mask
  You'd hardly know them. Hear the whispers! Bliss!
  How rapturous to bask
  In whisperings like this:
  "The Senator's in favor, in favor, in favor,
  The Senator's in favor with the tsar!"
  Ah, let me die amid such murmured bliss,

Sweeter than mistresses' caresses are!
  And see them bow to me
  The soul of all the company,
    While I
    Toss my head high!
Such ecstasy – I die of joy, I die!

(*He turns on his other side.*)

His Imperial Majesty the tsar has come!
He does not see me. What! He looks askance
At me, now with a frowning glance!
Your Gracious Highness! Oh, I'm stricken dumb,
My voice has died within me – a cold chill,
An icy sweat is on me. I am ill!
Ah, marshal! Hateful man, he turns his back,
And senators and courtiers too! Alack!
I'll die, I'm dead and buried in the ground
And rotting, and the worms are crawling round!
What taunts – what sneers – and all about me flee,
They will have nothing more to do with me!
The chamberlain, the villain, see him gloat!
His grin leaps like a spider down my throat.

(*He spits.*)

Such din – such jibes – this nasty fly, it goes
And buzzes like a wasp around my nose.

(*He brushes something away from his nose.*)

And epigrams and biting jests and jeers,
Singing like crickets, crawl into my ears,
    My ears, my ears!

(*He shakes his ears with his fingers.*)

Such noises! Kammerjunkers hoot like owls,
The ladies' dresses hiss like snakes, and far
Their acid laughter echoes, bitter howls,
    Like gall and vinegar:

"The Senator has fallen, has fallen, has fallen,
Has fallen out of favor with the tsar!"

(*He drops from his bed to the ground.*)

DEVILS: (*Come down in visible form.*)
His spirit from his senses we will peel
As we'd unchain a hound, but muzzle him
So half his body still has power to feel.
Now half of him we'll drag to the world's brim
Where time leaves off and where eternity
Begins, and conscience touches hell. And we
Will bind the brute upon the borders there.
Then labor, hand! and whistle, whip! For ere
The cock crows thrice we must return the soul,
Besmirched and worn from its ignoble pain,
And fetter it upon its senses' chain
Within its body, like a foul beast's hole.

Scene vii

Warsaw Salon

(*A few high officials, a few distinguished men of letters, a few society ladies, a few generals and staff officers, all incognito, are drinking tea around a small table. Nearer the door are several young men and two elderly Poles. The persons standing are conversing in a lively fashion. Those around the table speak French, those at the door Polish.*)

(*At the door*)

ZENON NIEMOJEWSKI: (*To Adolf*)
So in Lithuania it's much the same as here?
ADOLF:
Still worse, to shed blood they no longer fear.
NIEMOJEWSKI: Blood?
ADOLF:
Not in fight, but by the headsman's hand.
By knout and cudgel, not the warrior's brand.

(*They converse in a lower tone.*)

(*At the table*)

COUNT:
  The ball was splendid? Many soldiers there?
FRENCHMAN:
  As empty as a church, I've heard declare.
LADY: Rather, 'twas full –
COUNT: And fine?
LADY: A long, sad story!
GENTLEMAN OF THE BEDCHAMBER:
  Servants were many, but the service sorry!
  I got no glass of wine, no scrap of pasty:
  The crowd at the buffet was hot and hasty.
FIRST LADY:
  And at the ball, ungrouped they milled about,
  Trampling your toes, as at an English rout.
SECOND LADY:
  It was an evening for a private set.
CHAMBERLAIN:
  No, it was formal. I've my tickets yet.

(*Takes out the invitations and exhibits them; everybody is convinced.*)

FIRST LADY:
  So much the worse! The groups and gowns were muddled
  Until in judging them you'd grow befuddled.
SECOND LADY:
  Ever since Novosiltsev left the city,
  No one shows taste in parties, more's the pity!
  Since then I've seen no dances worth recall;
  But he could make a painting of a ball.

(*Laughter is heard among the men.*)

FIRST LADY:
  Go on and laugh, sirs; gossip as you please!
  He was essential in affairs like these.

(*At the door*)

ONE OF THE YOUNG MEN: And is Cichowski freed?
ADOLF: I know the man.

I called just now to see him; 'twas my plan
  To see the facts back home are brought to light.
NIEMOJEWSKl:
  We should support each other and unite
  Or, all divided, perish wretchedly.

(*They converse in a lower tone.*)

A YOUNG LADY: (*Standing near them*)
  What pain he suffered in captivity!

(*They converse.*)

(*At the table*)

GENERAL: (*To the Man of Letters*)
  Pray read the piece aloud – let me persuade you!
MAN OF LETTERS: I haven't it by heart.
GENERAL: No, but to aid you,
  You'll have it in your pocket. There it is!
  The ladies ask.
MAN OF LETTERS: These *femmes savantes* would quiz.
  They know by heart more verses out of France
  Than I myself.
GENERAL: (*Going over to speak to the ladies*)
                             Pray do not laugh, or glance.
LADY:
  You'll have a reading? Pardon me, I know
  Polish; but Polish verses – heavens no!
GENERAL: (*To an officer*)
  She's partly right, their dullness does not please.

(*He points to the Man of Letters*)

He chants a thousand lines on planting peas.

(*To the Man of Letters*)

Do read it! We must hear your verse betimes
  Or (*pointing to another man of letters*) yonder journalist
      will belch out rhymes.
  That were a service to set hearers blinking!

He seeks an invitation – laughing, winking:
His lips like a dead oyster open big;
He rolls a large eye sweet as any fig.
MAN OF LETTERS: (*To himself*)
  They're going out.

(*To the General*)

                    It's long. I'd strain my chest.
GENERAL: (*To the Officer*)
  He'd be a bore. His silence would be best.
YOUNG LADY: (*Leaving the younger group at the door and going to the table*)
  Gentlemen, listen! 'Tis a dreadful fate.

(*To Adolf*)

Pray tell these men about Cichowski's state.
OFFICER OF HIGH RANK:
  Cichowski free?
COUNT:
  So many years he gave to jail –
CHAMBERLAIN:
  I thought him lying in his gave.

(*To himself*)

The hearing of such themes I find too bold –
And rude to leave when tales are but half told.

(*Goes out.*)

COUNT:
  Released? That's very odd.
ADOLF:
  They found no crime.
MASTER OF CEREMONIES:
  That's not the point! More reasons mark our time:
  A man long prisoned sees and hears too much –
  Our governors have views, deep aims and such
  As must be hidden. Such affairs are set
  Deep in the projects of the cabinet.
  So is it ever – in a state affair.
  But you, from Lithuania – must stare!

Your rural gentry seek with simple charm
To know the empire as you would your farm.

(*Smiles.*)

GENTLEMAN OF THE BEDCHAMBER:
  You Lithuanians speak Polish right?
  I thought that all of you were Muscovite!
  I swear that on your country I'm a dunce:
  The *Constitutionnel* wrote of you once,
  The other French sheets gave no information.
A YOUNG LADY: (*To Adolf*)
  Please tell the story – it concerns our nation.
ELDERLY POLE:
  I knew the old Cichowskis – worthy folk,
  Come from Galicia. I have heard it spoke,
  Their son, my cousin, had been jailed and racked.
  'Tis long since I have seen him. Thus attacked,
  Three generations have known tyrants' chains:
  Our sons, as once our fathers, suffer pains!
ADOLF: (*All approach and listen.*)
  I knew him in my childhood: he was young,
  Famed for his beauty, witty and high-strung,
  The life of every party; where he came,
  He could keep all amused with tale and game;
  Children he loved. He'd take me on my knee.
  He was the "Jolly Gentleman" to me.
  I can recall his hair: I often twined
  My hands in the bright curls of one so kind.
  I can recall his look: so frank and gay
  That in our eyes he seemed a child at play;
  Caught by his charming glance, we children felt
  That with a playmate of our age we dealt.
  He planned a wedding soon and I recall
  He brought gifts from his bride and asked us all.
  Then he was absent long; at home they'd say
  That darkly, none knew where, he'd slipped away;
  The government had searched, without success.
  At last they said: "He's drowned himself, no less."
  Proof made conjectures by police seem sound:
  His cloak beside the Vistula was found;
  His wife had recognized it. All was clear.

The body was not found. So passed a year.
Why had he killed himself? Folk talked a lot,
Lamented, wept, and finally – forgot.
Two years passed by. One rainy night and drear,
Down from the abbey to the Belevedere
Some prisoners were being led. By chance,
Or purpose, someone saw that line advance –
One of those Warsaw youths, as bold as flames,
Who seek out dungeon cells and prisoners' names.
Watchmen patrolled the streets; the town was still;
Then, from behind a wall, a voice broke shrill:
"Prisoners, who are you?" And a hundred say
He was among them; and the following day
They told his wife, who wrote, begged, rushed about,
But not another shred did she find out.
Again three years passed by – no news or trace,
But someone spread vague stories through the place:
He was alive, but tortured to the hilt
Because as yet he'd not confessed his guilt;
For many nights they had not let him rest;
Had fed him on salt fish, all drink suppressed;
Dosed him with opium, with ghosts beset,
Tickled his soles and armpits to a sweat –
But soon men spoke of others, jailed for plot;
His wife lamented, but the rest forgot.
   At last, by night, they rang at his wife's door:
An officer, a gendarme, and one more –
Himself at last. They bade him take a pen
And sign himself as safe returned again.
They took his signature, and with a threat –
"If you betray . . . !" And grimly off they set.
I longed to see him; but a cautious friend
Said, "Do not go today, for spies attend!"
I went next day and found police on guard;
I went next week, and he returned my card.
At last I met him driving, vis-à-vis;
They told me who he was, so changed was he:
He had grown stout, with ghastly corpulence!
Bad food and rotten air had done offense;
His cheeks were swollen, yellowish and wan;
His brow was furrowed and his hair was gone.
I spoke; he did not know me; would not speak.

I told him who I was; his eyes were bleak.
When I recounted details from the past,
A fixed and searching glance was on me cast.
Ah, how the daily tortures he'd endured,
The thoughts of sleepless nights while long immured,
Showed in that single instant in his eye!
A dreadful veil obscured its agony:
His pupils were like dirty bits of glass
In grated prison windows, that surpass
The spider's web in gray, but viewed askance,
Shine like a sickly rainbow to the glance,
Mottled with sparks and spots of bloody rust;
We gaze, but cannot penetrate their dust.
They're clear no more; their surface shows they've lain
Where damp and empty dark and earth can stain.
Next month I called once more; and thought that he
Would have regained his poise and memory.
But many thousand days he'd stood the test,
And many thousand nights had marred his rest;
Tyrants had probed with torture all those years
And all that time the very walls had ears!
Silence had been his sole defense, you see;
Shadows had been his sole society;
So the gay city had not yet effaced
The teachings that a dozen years had traced.
The daylight seemed a rogue, the sun a spy,
His servants guards, his guest an enemy.
If someone came to call, at clink of latch
He'd think: "They're here, some new research to hatch."
Then he would turn away, head propped on hand,
As if to focus thought and will he planned;
Pressed his lips tight, lest random words might fall:
Lowered his eyes, keen guessing to forestall.
Ever he seemed still prisoned in his cell,
Fled to the room's rear, there in shadows fell,
And cried out always: "I don't know, won't speak!"
That was his constant saying, week by week.
His wife wept long before him on her knees,
Before his fear and horror seemed to ease.
　Prisoners are glad to tell of bondage past:
I thought that he'd be glad to talk at last,
And bring to light from earth and tyrant gloom

His tale, and Poland's heroes' daily doom.
For Poland lives and blossoms in the dark –
Siberian mines and torture-dungeons stark.
To all my questions, what was his reply?
Remembrance of his pangs was clean gone by.
His memory, though amply scrawled and jotted –
A book of Herculaneum, earth-rotted –
Baffles its author risen from the dead.
"Of that, I shall ask God," was all he said;
"He has recorded that, will tell me all."

(*Adolf wipes away his tears. A long silence.*)

YOUNG LADY: (*To the Man of Letters*)
   Why won't you gentlemen such tales recall?
COUNT:
   Let old Niemcewicz * put that in his *cache*
   Of memoirs, for I hear they're full of trash.
FIRST MAN OF LETTERS: Now there's a story!
SECOND MAN OF LETTERS: Dreadful.
GENTLEMAN OF THE BEDCHAMBER: Good, I swear!
FIRST MAN OF LETTERS:
   Though folk may listen, who will read the affair?
   What poet, too, can sing of our own time?
   Mythology, not truth, is fit for rhyme.
   Besides, it is Art's sacred edict still,
   Poets must wait until ... until ...
ONE OF THE YOUNG MEN: Until?
   In how few years are poets' themes matured,
   As figs grow candied or tobacco cured?
FIRST MAN OF LETTERS: No rules are fixed.
SECOND MAN OF LETTERS: A century.
FIRST MAN OF LETTERS: Oh, more!
THIRD MAN OF LETTERS: One or two thousand –
FOURTH MAN OF LETTERS: But what I deplore
   Is not that any subject may be new
   But that this theme in Poland rings not true.
   We like simplicity and heartiness,

---

*Julian Ursyn Niemcewicz (1757–1841), a major Polish writer, who is most highly regarded now for his voluminous memoirs. – Ed.

Not bloody scenes of violence and stress.
One should sing village courtships, peasant bridals,
Flocks, hillsides, shady trees. We Slavs love idylls.
FIRST MAN OF LETTERS:
  I surely hope that you will never wish
  To write in verse that someone ate salt fish!
  I say that polish must with verse consort,
  And there's no polish where there is no court.
  A court can judge of beauty, taste, and glory.
  Warsaw is courtless. That's poor Poland's story!
MASTER OF CEREMONIES:
  No court! You startle me, whom people call
  Master of Ceremonies, after all.
COUNT: (*In a low voice to the Master of Ceremonies*)
  Speak to the viceroy for my wife: she'll be
  Lady-in-waiting most assuredly.

(*Aloud*)

  High offices, alas, are not for us!
  Only aristocrats are honored thus.
SECOND COUNT: (*A townsman who has only recently received his title.*)
  Freedom depends on aristocracy:
  England, of that, gives ample guarantee.

(*A political wrangle begins. The young men start to leave the room.*)

FIRST OF THE YOUNG MEN:
  What rogues! They should be flogged!
ADAM GUROWSKI:
                              No, hanged in haste!
  I'd show them all the court; I'd teach 'em taste.
NABIELAK:
  Consider, friends, our chances of frustration!
  That is the sort of men who head our nation.
WYSOCKI:
  They're on its surface. We're a lava field,
  With surface cold and dirty, hard, congealed;
  But here are fires beneath, no years can end;
  Let's spit on this foul crust, and then descend.

(*They go out.*)

111

Scene viii

The Senator

(*In Wilno. An anteroom. On the right is the door to the Investigating Commission chamber, to which prisoners are taken, and in which huge bundles of papers can be seen. At the rear is the door to the Senator's rooms, whence music can be heard. Dinner is just over. At the window a secretary is sitting, busy with papers; somewhat farther to the left is a table at which a game of whist is in progress. Novosiltsev is drinking coffee; close to him are the Chamberlain Baykov, Pelikan, and the Doctor. At the door stand guards and some motionless footmen.*)

SENATOR: (*To Baykov*)
    Diable! quelle corvée! Why, dinner's through.
    La princesse has not come, the mocking shrew.
    En fait des dames, they're either old or fools:
    Official talk for soup course breaks all rules!
    Je jure, I'll have no *"patriotes" à ma table*,
    Avec franc parler et ton détestable.
    Figurez-vous, I talked of styles and games,
    And they of sons and fathers, damn these dames!
    "He is too old, he's young yet, Senator;
    He cannot bear confinement, Senator;
    He begs for a confessor, wants his wife,
    He" *Que sais-je!* Fine discourse, by my life!
    It drives one mad. I'll terminate this case,
    And make for Warsaw at a rapid pace.
    Monseigneur wrote me to return *bientôt.*
    He's bored without me; I with this rude show –
    Je n'en puis plus –
DOCTOR: (*Coming to him*)
                I have just told you, sir,
    The case is scarce begun; we now confer
    As if a doctor to a patient came
    To make his diagnosis. Toward this aim,
    Though students are in jail, we've still no proof;
    The center of the abcess lurks aloof.
    Verses we've found. *Ce sont des maux légers,*
    Ce sont, let's say, *accidents passagers*;
    But the plot's heart is still a mystery,
    And –

SENATOR: (*Offended*)
  Still a mystery? You're blind, I see!
  No wonder, after dinner. So, *dottore*,
  Addio, buona notte – to your story!
  A mystery! I've probed it on my own;
  And *vous osez* to tell me in that tone?
  When have we sought more carefully for taints?

(*Pointing to the papers*)

  Willing confessions, evidence, complaints,
  Everything's there; the whole conspiracy
  Stands written clear as any state decree –
  A mystery! That's all the thanks I've got!
DOCTOR:
  Excusez, sir! No person doubts the plot!
  In fact, they say . . .
FOOTMAN:
                   Merchant Kanissyn's man
  Is waiting with a bill he'd have you scan.
SENATOR: A bill? From whom?
FOOTMAN: Why, you know, sir, Kanissyn.
  You bade him call.
SENATOR: Get out, you stupid cretin!
  You see that I am busy.
DOCTOR: (*To the footmen*) Stupid brutes,
  Your master's at his coffee and cheroots!
SECRETARY: (*Rising from the table*)
  He says that if your payment still is slow,
  He'll seek the law.
SENATOR: Tell him to wait below.

(*After reflection*)

  A propos. We'll arrest this merchant's son.
  He's some sly bird!
SECRETARY: A boy, a little one.
SENATOR:
  They all are small, but look into their hearts!
  It's best to quench the fire as it starts.

SECRETARY: The lad's in Moscow.
SENATOR: Moscow? *Voyez-vous,*
  An agent of the clubs. Without ado
  We'll stop him.
SECRETARY: He's a soldier. A cadet.
SENATOR:
  Ha! In the army he'll breed treason yet.
SECRETARY: He left here as a child.
SCNATOR: *L'incendiaire!*
  They send him letters. (*To the Secretary*) *Ce n'est pas ton affaire!*
  Hey, officer! Tonight must end his capers.
  Send a kibitka out and seize his papers.
  The father has no reason for alarm
  If his son willingly admits his harm.
DOCTOR:
  I've had the honor to inform you, sir,
  In every class and age the plot's astir:
  That's the worst symptom of the cursèd thing,
  For all is managed by a hidden spring,
  Which ...
SENATOR: (*Indignantly*) Hidden?
DOCTOR: I mean cunningly concealed,
  But now, by your sagacity, revealed.

(*The Senator turns away.*)

DOCTOR: (*To himself*)
  He's an impatient devil, vile in pique!
  I've much to say, and he won't let me speak.
PELIKAN: (*To the Senator*)
  What will you have us do with Rollison?
SENATOR: With whom?
PELIKAN: The lad we flogged, the silent one.
SENATOR: *Eh bien?*
PELIKAN: He's ill.
SENATOR: How many blows were dealt?
PELIKAN:
  I witnessed it; they did not count each welt.
  Botvinko did the job.
BAYKOV: Botvinko, eh?
  He won't soon finish, once he starts to flay.

I'll warrant that his lash was warm to coax –
Parions that he gave three hundred strokes.
SENATOR: (*Amazed*)
Trois cents coups et vivant? Trois cents coups, le coquin!
Trois cents coups sans mourir – quel dos de jacobin!
I had thought that in Russia *la vertu cutannée*
Surpasse tout – that scamp has *une peau mieux tannée!*
Je n'y conçois rien! Laughter will burst my sides.

(*To one of the whist players, who is waiting for his partner*)

The Poles will surely rob us of our trade in hides.
Un honnête soldat en serait mort dix fois!
Quel rebelle! (*Going to the table*) For you I have *un homme de bois,*
A lad of wood. The blows master Botvinko gives!
A mere child gets three hundred lashes, and still lives!

(*To Pelikan*)

He confessed nothing?
PELIKAN: With clenched teeth he mews
 That he his harmless friends will not accuse.
 But much that little utterance portends –
 It's evident those students are his friends.
SENATOR: *C'est juste:* how stubborn!
DOCTOR: I have said with sadness,
 They are infecting our young men with madness
 By teaching history, things dull and hazy;
 It's clear that's why our lads are going crazy!
SENATOR: (*Gaily*)
Vous n'aimez pas l'histoire! Un satirique
 Would say you fear to *devenir historique.*
DOCTOR:
 Quite so: for history, I would teach my son
 What kings and ministers of state have done.
SENATOR: *C'est juste.*
DOCTOR: (*Consoled*)
 I say myself, as you will see,
 There is a way to teach youth history;
 But why keep talking of republicans
 In Athens, Sparta, Rome – suggesting plans?
PELIKAN: (*To one of his companions, pointing at the Doctor*)
 Look how the cursèd flatterer crawls and licks
 The senatorial spittle – what low tricks!

(*Going up to the Doctor*)

Why speak of this? For such a theme may bore,
At such a time as this, the Senator.
FOOTMAN: (*To the Senator*)
  Shall I admit those ladies, master, pray,
  Who call here in a carriage every day?
  The older one is blind –
SENATOR: Blind? Why this bother?
FOOTMAN: She's Mrs. Rollison.
PELIKAN: The flogged boy's mother.
FOOTMAN: Each day they come.
SENATOR: They should begone!
DOCTOR: Unheeded!
FOOTMAN:
  We sent her off, but she just sat and pleaded.
  We ordered her arrested; but she's blind.
  And folk beat up the soldier to be kind.
  Shall I admit her?
SENATOR: Bah! You've no finesse –
  Let her halfway upstairs – my point you'll guess –
  Then kick her down again so hard that she
  Won't bore us further with her beggary!

(*Another footman comes in and gives a letter to Baykov.*)

What do you stand there for?
BAYKOV: *Elle porte une lettre.*

(*Hands over the letter.*)

SENATOR: Who'd write to aid her?
BAYKOV: *La princesse peut-être.*
SENATOR: (*Reads.*)
  The princess? And she bids me help this creature
  Avec chaleur! Admit her, devil take her!

(*Two ladies and Father Peter come in.*)

PELIKAN: (*To Baykov*)
  It's the old witch, *mère de ce fripon.*
SENATOR: (*Courteously*)
  Welcome, now! Which is Mrs. Rollison?

MRS. ROLLISON:
　I am. My son! Your Excellency –
SENATOR:　　　　　　　　　　　　　　Please!
　Why have so many ladies come as these?
SECOND LADY: We are but two.
SENATOR: (*To the Second Lady*)
　And why are *you* here, pray?
SECOND LADY:
　Since Mrs. Rollison can't find her way.
　She's blind.
SENATOR:
　Aha! She's blind! But can't she smell?
　For she comes here each day.
SECOND LADY: She is not well –
　And old – so in a carriage come we two.
MRS. ROLLISON: In God's name!
SENATOR: Quiet!
　(*To the Second Lady*) Madam, who are you?
SECOND LADY: I'm Mrs. Kmita.
SENATOR: Stay home! Watch your sons!
　They are suspected.
MRS. KMITA: (*Turning pale*) What, my little ones!

(*The Senator laughs.*)

MRS. ROLLISON:
　I am a widow, sir! Ah, pity me!
　I hear they've killed my child. Can such things be!
　The good priest says that he is still alive:
　But they are beating him. What devils thrive!
　They flogged him! Oh, a flogging most inhuman!

(*She weeps.*)

SENATOR:
　Where? Whom? Speak like a human being, woman!
MRS. ROLLISON:
　Whom? Why, my son! I come a widow here –
　And many years it takes a child to rear!
　My boy was teaching others. All would say
　How good he was at school. He's all I've left;
　'Twas he maintained me from his meagre pay.
　I'm blind; he was my eyes. I'll starve to death!

117

SENATOR:
  Whoever said they beat him won't get clear!
  Who said so?
MRS. ROLLISON: Who? I have a mother's ear.
  I'm blind; and now my soul is in that sense,
  A mother's soul. Last night for evidence
  They took him.
SENATOR: Were you there?
MRS. ROLLISON: They thrust me out
  From threshold, gate, and yard. I sat about,
  By the thick corner wall. I listened there –
  From morn till midnight. In that silent square
  At midnight, from the wall – yes, I am sure;
  As sure as God in heaven must endure –
  With my own ears I heard his voice quite well,
  Soft, underground, as from the depths of hell.
  My hearing probed the wall, yes, very deep:
  Farther it went than swiftest eye could sweep.
  I heard them torture him!
SENATOR: A raving tale!
  But, madam, there are many in that jail!
MRS. ROLLISON:
  Not sure of my child's voice? Indeed I am!
  A sheep will know the bleating of its lamb
  Amid the biggest flock. Ah, such a cry!
  Had you but heard it once, good sir, as I,
  You'd never have another peaceful night.
SENATOR:
  Your son is well, to bellow with such might.
MRS. ROLLISON:
  (*Falling on her knees*) If you've a human heart –

(*The doors of the drawing room are opened. Music is heard. A young lady runs in, dressed as if for a ball.*)

YOUNG LADY: *Monsieur le Sénateur –*
  Oh! Je vous interromps! On va chanter le choeur
  de Don Giovanni: *et puis le concerto de Herz . . .*
SENATOR:
  Herz! choeur! Here, too, there has been talk of hearts.
  Vous venez à propos, vous belle comme un coeur.
  Moment sentimental. Il pleut ici des coeurs.

118

(*To Baykov*)

If *le grand-duc Michel* had heard that pun,
My place on the Grand Council would be won.

(*To the Young Lady*)

J'y suis – dans un moment.
MRS. ROLLISON: Sir, do not pass
  And leave us hopeless. (*Seizes his coat.*)
YOUNG LADY: *Faites-lui donc grâce!*
SENATOR:
  What the hag wants, I don't know in the least.
MRS. ROLLISON: To see my son.
SENATOR: (*With emphasis*) The tsar forbids!
FATHER PETER: A priest!
MRS. ROLLISON:
  Send him a priest; my son asks for a priest;
  Perhaps he's dying! As you fear God's toll,
  Torture the flesh but do not kill the soul!
SENATOR:
  C'est drôle! Who spreads this gossip through the city?
  Who told you that he asks now for a priest?
MRS. ROLLISON: (*Indicating Father Peter*)
  This honorable priest. For many weeks
  He has sought entrance, but in vain he seeks.
  Ask him; he'll tell you –
SENATOR: (*With a quick glance at Father Peter*)
          He knows that? He must –
  Oh, all right, very well. The tsar is just:
  He permits priests; sends them himself some days,
  That young men may turn back to moral ways.
  None loves the church and lauds it more than I.

(*Sighs.*)

How young men fall without morality!
Eh bien, I'll say farewell.
MRS. ROLLISON: (*To the Young Lady*)
                  Ah, dear young lady,
  I beg you, by God's wounds, once more to aid me!
  My little son! Imprisoned for a year,
  Starved, naked, in a dark, cold dungeon here . . .

119

YOUNG LADY: *Est-il possible?*
SENATOR: (*Embarrassed*)
      What's that? I did not know
That he'd been put in jail a year ago!

(*To Pelikan*)

We must look up this case without delay:
If this is true, my men will rue the day.

(*To Mrs. Rollison*)

Soyez tranquille, come here again at seven.
MRS. KMITA:
  Please, do not weep! The Senator, by heaven,
  Knew nothing of your son – perhaps will free him.
MRS. ROLLISON: (*Overjoyed*)
  Knew nothing? Now will know? God oversee him!
  I always said so: he's not bad clear through,
  As people say he is. God made him too,
  A man, fed with a mother's milk in youth –
  The people laughed: you see, I told the truth.

(*To the Senator*)

You did not know. They hide the facts, and flout you.
Believe me, sir, scoundrels are all about you!
Do not ask them, ask us: we'll tell you all
The whole truth.
SENATOR: (*Laughing*)
      Tell me that when next you call:
Today I have no time, *adieu*. And tell
The princess that I'll do her bidding well.

(*Courteously*)

Adieu, Madame Kmit, I'll do my best.

(*To Father Peter*)

Stay here, priest; I have something to suggest.

(*To the Young Lady*)

J'y suis dans un moment.

(*All go out except Father Peter and those present at the opening of the scene.*)

SENATOR: (After a pause, to the footmen)
                          You scoundrels! Knaves!
  You guard my doors, and let in those damned slaves!
  I'll flay you all, to teach you what's my due!

(*To one of the footmen*)

Follow the old hag –

(*To Pelikan*)

                   No, this job's for you:
  After she leaves the princess, you'll permit her
  To go and see her son – and there you'll sit her
  Safe in a separate cell, locked good and tight.
  C'en est trop – rogues! I'll teach you what is right!

(*Throws himself into a chair.*)

FOOTMAN: (*Trembling*)
  You bade us let her in.
SENATOR: (*Rising furiously*) You dare talk back?
  Have servants' tongues in Poland grown so slack?
  Wait, I'll soon cure you! To the cell he goes!
  Let the police deal out a hundred blows –
  Four weeks on bread and water.
PELIKAN: Senator,
  Think how despite all care, at wall and door,
  Regarding Rollison, vile go-betweens
  Are spreading news, perhaps will find the means
  To blacken to the tsar our pure desires,
  Unless our inquisition soon retires.
DOCTOR:
  I have been thinking, sir, upon that point.
  Rollison's brain is now quite out of joint;
  He shakes the windows, seeking suicide.
  But they are locked . . .

PELIKAN: His lungs are putrified;
  It is not right to smother him to death;
  I'll open wide his windows, give him breath.
  He's on the third floor – he'll enjoy the air.
  SENATOR: (*Absentmindedly*)
  While I was drinking coffee! I declare
  They won't give me an instant –
DOCTOR: You are right.
  Your health is much too paramount to slight.
  Just after dinner time, I always say,
  Postpone your business – *ça mine la santé.*
SENATOR: (*Calmly*)
  Eh, mon docteur, duty and order first!
  Besides, it helps me when my tummy hurts;
  It stirs the bile, and bile *fait la digestion.*
  When dinner's through, I could *voir donner la question,*
  If service bade... *En prenant son café*
  Is the best time to see autos-da-fé.
PELIKAN: (*Pushing the Doctor aside*)
  What's your decision as to Rollison
  In case he... dies ... today?
SENATOR: Have burial done!
  Embalm him, if you wish it. *A propos,*
  Balsam, my Baykov, well with you might go:
  You've such a corpselike body – yet you marry.
  You've heard? He is betrothed, and will not tarry.

(*The door on the left opens. A footman comes in. The Senator points to the door.*)

  Look at that young girl yonder, white and red...
  Baykov, *avec un teint si délabré*
  You should wed like Tiberius *à Capré.*
  I can't see how her lips a *yes* once said,
  Not if they forced her, to a man half-dead.
BAYKOV: Indeed! Why in a year I'll be divorced,
  And get a new wife yearly, quite unforced.
  I've only got to nod: she's at my side.
  A girl is thrilled to be a general's bride.
  Just ask the priest if marriage makes her cry.
SENATOR: *A propos –*

(*To Father Peter*)

      Here, black cherub, you're still by!
Look *quelle figure*! He has *l'air d'un poète*.
Who ever saw *un regard aussi bête*?
Let's rouse him up! Come, here's a glass of rum!
FATHER PETER: I don't –
SENATOR: Drink now!
FATHER PETER: I am a humble brother.
SENATOR:
  Brother or uncle, how now does it come
  You know what people's sons in jail express?
  Was it you brought a message to the mother?
FATHER PETER: Yes, I.
SENATOR: (*To the Secretary*)
  Note all. And those now here will witness.

(*To Father Peter*)

  How did you know it, eh? You're a fine bird!
  Start to take notes, and he won't say a word.
  Where dwells your Order?
FATHER PETER: With the Bernardines.
SENATOR:
  And the Dominicans are go-betweens?
  For Rollison is in a Blackfriar's cell.
  But go ahead and talk. Who told you? Tell!
  Don't whisper! I command you! Do you hear?
  In the tsar's name I bid you make this clear.
  Monk! Have you heard about the Russian rod?

(*To the Secretary*)

Note down that he won't speak.

(*To Father Peter*)

      But you serve God –
You'll know theology? Now hear me, clod,
All earthly power from the Lord must come –
And when they bid you speak, do not play dumb.

123

(*Father Peter is silent.*)

    Monk, I could hang you! And the prior, your head,
    Will have a chance to raise you from the dead.
FATHER PETER:
    A man who suffers force does not revere it;
    God may give power to an evil spirit.
SENATOR:
    If I should hang you, and the tsar should find
    I've gone too far, do you conceive he'll mind?
    "Eh, Senator," he'll say, "that's stern haranguing!"
    And you meanwhile, my monk, will keep on hanging!
    Come, for the last time, ere I have you smashed:
    Confess who told you that the boy was lashed.
    You're silent still? It's not from God you knew –
    Who told you? Angel? Devil?
FATHER PETER: It was you.
SENATOR (*Enraged*) Is that how you address *me*, monk?
DOCTOR: You wretch!
    A dignitary's rank its dues must fetch!

(*To Pelikan*)

    Teach him to talk, for pigs, not souls, he's tended.
    Hit him thus! (*Gestures with his hand.*)
PELIKAN: (*Giving Father Peter a slap in the face*)
                        Jackass, see, the lord's offended.
FATHER PETER:
    Forgive him, God, the evil of his way!

(*To the Doctor*)

    Ah, brother, you have slain yourself today;
    Today you die.
SENATOR: What's this?
BAYKOV: A monkish lie.
            Wallop his mug, and let him prophesy.

(*Gives him a rap on the nose.*)

FATHER PETER:
    Brother, you too have taken counsel black!
    Your days are spent; you follow in his track.

SENATOR:
  Hey, fetch Botvinko! Keep the shaveling here!
  I'll stay throughout the probe; we'll have good cheer.
  We'll see if he keeps obstinately mute.
  Someone has prompted this.
DOCTOR: I would impute
  All of these plots to one well-planned affair,
  Managed by Czartoryski, I declare!
SENATOR: (*Rising furiously from his chair.*)
  Que me dites-vous là, mon cher, of the prince?
  Impossible –

(*To himself*)

            Who knows? Ten years he'll wince
  And struggle if I once entangle him.

(*To the Doctor*)

  How do you know?
DOCTOR: The case has been my whim.
SENATOR: You told me nothing.
DOCTOR: You were all vexation.
  I told you *someone* lit this conflagration.
SENATOR: *Someone!* Is it the prince?
DOCTOR: I have sure clues;
  Complaints, and stolen letters that accuse.
SENATOR: The prince's letters?
DOCTOR: No, but this supplies
  The prince's guilt and all his enterprise.
  Professors are involved: behind the plot
  Is Lelewel,* who stirs the boiling pot.
SENATOR: (*To himself*)
  Oh, if there were some proof! The merest trace,
  The shadow of a shadow I'd embrace!
  Often already talk has reached my ear:
  "The prince gave Novosiltsev his career."
  Now we shall see which man can farther go –
  He who sets up, or I who overthrow.

---

  *Joachim Lelewel (1786–1861), a distinguished Polish historian of the period
and one of the key figures in the November Insurrection of 1830. – Ed.

(*To the Doctor*)

Come, *que je vous embrasse!* That's something rare!
I guessed at once this was no child's affair;
I guessed at once the prince was in this revel.
DOCTOR: (*Confidentially*)
You did? He who tricks *you* will eat the devil.
SENATOR: (*With dignity*)
Though I, state counsellor, know his offense,
Yet, if you have unearthed sure evidence,
Ecoutez, you've my word as senator,
I will increase your pay by half or more;
For ten years' service count this accusation,
Perhaps an Order? For our tsar is kind,
And I myself shall tell him of your find.
DOCTOR:
All this has greatly taxed my energies:
Out of my scanty pay I've hired spies;
Zeal for our blessèd tsar has made me wary.
SENATOR: (*Taking his arm*)
Mon cher, pray go, and take my secretary.

(*To the Secretary*)

Take all his documents and seal them straight.

(*To the Doctor*)

Tonight we'll sift the whole affair of state.

(*To himself*)

I've worked and carried out the whole inquiry:
Why should he win the praise at its expiry?

(*Reflects. Whispers in the Secretary's ear.*)

Arrest the doctor, seize his documents.

(*To Baykov, who comes in*)

This is important. We'll control events.

The doctor dropped some words of interest.
I've questioned him, we'll soon squeeze out the rest.

(*Pelikan, seeing the regard paid to the Doctor by the Senator, escorts the Doctor to the door and bows low to him.*)

DOCTOR: (*To himself*)
  Ho, ho, Pelikan! He was stiff before.
  I'll push him over, and he'll rise no more!

(*To the Senator*)

  I will return at once.
SENATOR: (*Carelessly*) I leave at eight.
DOCTOR: (*Looking at his watch*)
  What's this? My watch shows twelve. It's surely late.
SENATOR:
  It's five already.
DOCTOR: Five? My eyes must slumber:
  My minute hand's at twelve, right on the number.
  It stopped, and the hand's tip remained right there;
  It hasn't moved a second, not a hair!
FATHER PETER:
  Your clock has also stopped, beyond control,
  Until tomorrow noon. Think of your soul.
DOCTOR:
  What do you mean?
PELIKAN: He's rumbling prophecies.
  See his glance glitter; those are lizards' eyes!
FATHER PETER:
  By different signs God warns men they're to die.
PELIKAN:
  This little monk looks somehow like a spy.

(*The door opens on the left. A crowd of finely dressed ladies, officials, and guests come in. They are followed by musicians.*)

GOVERNOR'S WIFE: May we come in?
COUNCILLOR'S WIFE: *Indigne!*
GENERAL'S WIFE: *Ah, Sénateur!*
  We've waited long!
COUNCILLOR'S WIFE:
  Vraiment, c'est un malheur.

ALL: (*Together*) We've come to seek you ...
SENATOR: Gad!
What elegance!
LADY: Even this room will give us space to dance.

(*They arrange themselves for the dance.*)

SENATOR:
  Pardon, mille pardons, j'étais tres occupé;
  Que vois-je? Un menuet? Parfaitement groupé!
  Cela m'a rappelé les jours de ma jeunesse!
PRINCESS: *Ce n'est qu'une surprise.*
SENATOR: *Est-ce vous, ma déesse!*
  Que j'aime cette danse! Une surprise? Ah! dieux!
PRINCESS: *Vous danserez, j'espère?*
SENATOR: *Certes, et de mon mieux.*

(*The music plays the minuet from* Don Giovanni. *On the left stand officials and their wives; on the right a few young men, a few young Russian officers, a few elderly men dressed in Polish costume, and a few young ladies. In the center is the minuet. The Senator dances with Baykov's financée, Baykov with the Princess.*)

The Ball

(*This scene is sung, not recited.*)

LADY: (*On the right*)
  Look at the old man nod and beck
  And wheeze. I wish he'd break his neck!

(*To the Senator*)

  You dance divinely, graceful man!

(*Aside*)

  Il crèvera dans l'instant.
YOUNG MAN:
  He licks and cringes; yesterday
  He murdered, now of sport he thinks.
  See how he rolls his eyes for prey;
  He capers like a captured lynx.

3. The Cracow production of *Forefathers' Eve*, Scene viii. Senator Novosiltsev during the ball. (Photograph: Wojciech Plewiński)

LADY:

Ah, yesterday he did not pause
From murders most unmerciful;
Today he hides his wicked claws,
And makes himself agreeable.

(On the left)

COLLEGIATE REGISTRAR: (To the Councillor)
The Senator is tripping it:
Hey, Councillor, let's join the dance!
COUNCILLOR:
Consider whether it is fit
That you should partner me perchance.
REGISTRAR:
Some ladies here have not yet flown.
COUNCILLOR:
But that's not what I talk about;
I much prefer to dance alone
Rather than dance with you. Clear out!
REGISTRAR: Why so?
COUNCILLOR: I am a councillor.
REGISTRAR: Son of an officer am I.
COUNCILLOR:
My dear sir, dancing I abhor
With such low-ranking company.

(To the Colonel)

Come, Colonel, come and join the ball:
You see where all the gentry are.
COLONEL:
What dolt was gabbling with such gall?

(Pointing to the Registrar)

COUNCILLOR:
Just a collegiate registrar!
COLONEL:
That mob is mostly Jacobin!
LADY: (To the Senator)
You dance divinely, graceful man!

130

COUNCILLOR: (*Angrily*)
  How ranks are mixed here! What a sin!
LADY:
  Il crèvera dans l'instant.
LEFT SIDE: (*In chorus*)
LADIES:
  Ah, quelle beauté, quelle grâce!
MEN:
  What grace and pomp, there's nothing like them!
RIGHT SIDE: (*In chorus*)
MEN:
  What rogues and scoundrels these, alas!
  What villains, may thunder strike them!
SENATOR: (*Dancing, to the Governor's Wife*)
  There's the Starosta,* we've not met.
  He has a pretty wife and daughter,
  But envious.
GOVERNOR: (*Running after the Senator*)
                          Just dull, I'll bet.
  Trust us, and you've as good as caught her.

(*Going up to the Starosta*)

  Where is your wife?
STAROSTA: She's staying home.
GOVERNOR:
  Your daughters too?
STAROSTA: I've just one lass.
GOVERNOR'S WIFE:
  And to the ball she will not come?
STAROSTA: Oh, no!
GOVERNOR'S WIFE: You're here alone?
STAROSTA: Alas!
GOVERNOR:
  Your wife knows not the Senator?
STAROSTA:
  I have my wife for my own use.
GOVERNOR'S WIFE:
  I asked your daughter here before.

---

* A district official in old Poland. – Ed.

STAROSTA:

I thanked you, and I sent excuse.

GOVERNOR:

The minuet's a couple short:

The Senator needs ladies yonder.

STAROSTA:

Couples are not my daughter's forte;

I shall myself her nuptials ponder.

GOVERNOR'S WIFE:

They tell me that she plays and dances;

The Senator would like her here.

STAROSTA:

Indeed, I've seen him make advances

To several at once, it's clear.

LEFT SIDE: (*In chorus*)

What song! What music! In adorning,

This mansion is an easy winner!

RIGHT SIDE: (*In chorus*)

The scoundrels drink blood in the morning –

And swill their rum down after dinner.

COUNCILLOR: (*Pointing to the Senator*)

He flays them; but to hopes new risen

His flayings are not bad at all.

STAROSTA:

Our young men are confined in prison –

And we are bidden to a ball.

RUSSIAN OFFICER: (*To Bestuzhev*)

No wonder that they curse us here:

A generation now has past,

And still from Moscow every year

A sewer-stream of rogues runs fast.

STUDENT: (*To the Officer*)

See Baykov moving *à la mode*,

With airs and graces round about!

He dances like a dunghill toad.

See how he swells his belly out!

He bares his teeth, drunk as a boar –

Opens his yap amid the throng.

(*Baykov hums a song.*)

Just listen, Baykov starts to roar.

(To Baykov)

   Mon général, quelle chanson!
BAYKOV: (*Sings a song by Béranger.**)
   Quel honneur, quel bonheur!
   Ah, monsieur le sénateur!
   Je suis votre humble serviteur, etc.
STUDENT:
   Général, ce sont vos paroles?
BAYKOV: *Oui.*
STUDENT: *Je vous en fais mon compliment.*
ONE OF THE OFFICERS: (*Laughing*)
   Ces couplets sont vraiment fort drôles;
   Quel ton satirique et plaisant!
YOUNG MAN:
   Pour votre muse sans rivale,
   Je vous ferais académicien.
BAYKOV: (*Whispering in his ear, pointing to the Princess*)
   Horns will the Senator befall.
SENATOR: (*Whispers, pointing to Baykov's fiancée.*)
   Va, va, je te coifferai bien.
YOUNG LADY: (*Dancing, to her mother*)
   They are too hideous, too old.
MOTHER: (*On the right*)
   If he disgusts you, leave him, come!
COUNCILLOR'S WIFE: (*On the left*)
   Suits perfectly my daughter's mold!
STAROSTA:
   Disgusting, how they stink of rum!
SECOND COUNCILLOR'S WIFE: (*To her daughter, standing beside her*)
   My Zosia dear, just raise your eyes;
   The Senator may notice you.
STAROSTA:
   If *mine* he starts to compromise,
   I'll run His Excellency through.

(*Clutches his saber.*)

LEFT SIDE: (*In chorus*)

---

*Pierre Jean de Béranger (1780–1857), French lyric poet and author of many popular songs. – Ed.

133

Ah, quelle beauté, quelle grâce!
What grace and pomp, there's nothing like them!
RIGHT SIDE: (*In chorus*)
What rogues and scoundrels these, alas!
What villains, may thunder strike them!

(*On the right among the young men*)

JUSTYN POL: (*To Bestuzhev, pointing to the Senator*)
I'd like to stab him in the belly
Or pound his ugly features flat.
BESTUZHEV:
What use? You thrash him to a jelly
Or kill him, what's the help in that?
For such an act, some rogue begins
To sweep the colleges away –
To call the students Jacobins
And all your young men's hopes betray.
POL:
But he should pay a price quite dear
For all his torture, blood, and cries.
BESTUZHEV:
The tsar has many kennels here:
What difference, if this one dog dies?
POL: My knife is itching; let me slash him.
BESTUZHEV:
Once more I warn you, lest you fall.
POL: Permit me, anyway, to thrash him.
BESTUZHEV:
And be the ruin of you all!
POL: Ah, rascals scoundrels, criminals!
BESTUZHEV:
I must escort you out, roughshod.
POL: Will none chastise this thing that crawls?
Will none take vengeance for us?...

(*They go off toward the door.*)

FATHER PETER: God!

(*Suddenly the music changes, and plays the aria of the Commendatore.*)

DANCERS: What is it?
GUESTS: What a melancholy strain!
GUEST: (*Looking out of a window*)
  How dark it is! That black cloud looks like rain.

(*Closes the window. Thunder can be heard in the distance.*)

SENATOR: Why don't they play?
DIRECTOR OF THE ORCHESTRA: They made an error.
SENATOR: Flog them!
DIRECTOR:
  They were to play but part; with none to jog them,
  They did not understand, and grew confused.
SENATOR:
  Arrangez donc! Come, ladies, we're excused!

(*A loud cry is heard outside the door.*)

MRS. ROLLISON: (*Outside the door, in a frightful voice*)
  In!
SECRETARY: It's the blind dame!
FOOTMAN: (*Frightened*)
  She can see! She's rushing
  Up the stairs. Stop her!
OTHER FOOTMEN: Who can stop her pushing?
MRS. ROLLISON:
  I'll find him here, that drunken thing of evil!

(*A footman tries to check her; she overthrows one of them.*)

FOOTMAN:
  Look, how she threw him! Ah, she has a devil!

(*They flee.*)

MRS. ROLLISON:
  Out, tyrant, out! I'll smash your skull in two,
  As was my son's! He's dead because of you!
  Thrown from a window! Have all scruples flown?
  My son, down on the pavement, on cold stone . . .
  Ha, you old drunk, besmirched with guiltless blood,
  Where are you, crocodile who lives in mud?

4. The Cracow production of *Forefathers' Eve*, Scene viii. The blind mother's plea – Mrs. Rollison and Senator Novosiltsev. (Photograph: Wojciech Plewiński)

I'll tear you piecemeal, as my boy was torn –
They threw him from the window, and I mourn
My only child, sole source of life to me –
Is there a God, that leaves such monsters free?
FATHER PETER:
  Blaspheme not, woman! For your son breathes yet.
MRS. ROLLISON:
  He is alive? Who speaks? Whom have I met?
  Is that true, father? See, I came too late –
  "He fell," they shout. I ran. They did not wait.
  His corpse was gone! Alone, I'll lose my mind.
  I did not see my son's corpse. I am blind!
  But I smelt blood there. And by God I'm sure
  I smell it here, my son's blood; sprinkled, sir,
  On some one. Here's his executioner!

(*She walks straight toward the Senator. The Senator gets out of her way; Mrs. Rollison falls on the floor in a faint; Father Peter and the Starosta go up to her. A thunder clap is heard.*)

ALL: (*Terrified*)
  "The word made flesh!" 'Tis here!
OTHERS: Here, here!
FATHER PETER: Not here.
GUEST: (*Looking out of the window*)
  The college building's corner. That's quite near!
SENATOR: (*Going to the window*)
  The doctor's windows!
ONE OF THE SPECTATORS: Why, a woman shrilled!
SOME ONE IN THE STREET: (*Laughing*)
  The devils took him sure!

(*Pelikan runs in, distracted.*)

SENATOR: Our doctor?
PELIKAN: Killed
  By lightning. An occurrence worth research:
  Around his house ten lightning rods were perched,
  Yet the bolt sought him out in the last room.
  A heap of silver rubles brought his doom;
  Close to his pillow, in a desk they lay,
  And surely brought the lightning down today.

137

STAROSTA: I see that Russian rubles may cause fright.
SENATOR: (*To the ladies*)
  You ladies broke the dance – how impolite!

(*Seeing that they are assisting Mrs. Rollison.*)

  Carry her out; come, help the woman there!
  Carry her –
FATHER PETER: To her son?
SENATOR: Yes, anywhere.
FATHER PETER:
  Her son still breathes, though crushed and stuporish.
  May I go?
SENATOR: To the devil if you wish.

(*To himself*)

  The doctor killed. Ah, *c'est inconcevable!*
  The priest foretold it to him. *C'est diable!*

(*To the company*)

  Well, what is dire in this? Clouds come in spring;
  And clouds breed lightning – that's the normal thing.
COUNCILLOR'S WIFE: (*To her husband*)
  Say what you please, but fear is always fear.
  I'll not stay with you 'neath one roof, that's clear.
  I told you: Leave those boys alone, don't pry.
  Though while you flogged poor Jews I raised no cry.
  But children! And the doctor this befell!
COUNCILLOR: You're silly.
COUNCILLOR'S WIFE: I'm for home, I am not well.

(*Thunder is heard again. All run off: first the left side, then the right. There remain only the Senator, Pelikan, and Father Peter.*)

SENATOR: (*Gazing after those who fled*)
  That doctor – while alive, the worst of pests –
  Now that he's croaked, is driving off my guests.

(*To Pelikan*)

See that priest gaze – *voyez, quel oeil hagard;*

A strange chance this, *un singulier hasard.*
Tell me, dear priest, are you a conjurer?
How did you know? Perhaps with God confer?

(*Father Peter is silent.*)

To tell the truth, this doctor was to blame:
He went beyond his duty in this game.
On aurait fort à dire – there may be warnings.
Best keep the straight path and beware of mournings.
What think you, priest? He's silent, hangs his nose.
But he'll go free – *on dirait bien des choses!* . . .

(*Becomes pensive.*)

PELIKAN:
    Ha, ha! If probing cases is a risk,
    The lightning should have given us a frisk.
FATHER PETER:
    I'll tell two stories, old but weighty too.
SENATOR: (*With curiosity*)
    Of thunder? Of the doctor? Speak!
FATHER PETER: I do.
    Once, during summer heat, it did befall
    Some travelers napped beneath a shady wall.
    One was a robber. While the others slept,
    God's angel woke him: "Rise!" And up he leapt,
    By far the worst among them, not the best,
    And down the wall fell, crushing all the rest.
    Then he thanked heaven that he was not dead,
    But the Lord's angel came again, and said:
    "You have sinned most; you shan't escape your fate:
    The worst of all, to die in shame and hate."
        This is the other story. Long ago
    A Roman general did overthrow
    A mighty king, and ordered all slaves slain.
    Centurions and captains died in pain,
    But he slew not the monarch of those regions,
    No, nor the prefects and the heads of legions.
    Then said those foolish prisoners in their ranks:
    "We live and owe the general our thanks."
    Until a Roman soldier, who now served
    The captives, said: "Yes, you have been preserved,

For he will chain you to his chariot
And round the camp will drag you, all the lot,
And thence to Rome; for your sort without pity
They lead about through Rome, that famous city,
So that the folk may shout: 'Our general
Has made these kings and captains hither crawl!'
Then, when he's led you round in golden chains,
He'll hand you over to the hangman's swains;
Then in the deep, dark dungeons, far beneath,
You shall in torment wail and gnash your teeth."
So spoke the soldier. But the king did bellow:
"These are the babblings of a stupid fellow.
Did you at banquet with your general sit,
To know his counsels and his secret wit?"
Having rebuked the man, the monarch quaffed
And with his captive chiefs and captains laughed.

SENATOR: (*Bored.*)
   Il bat la campagne. Priest, go where you will.
   If caught again, I'll scrape your hide until
   You can't be recognized by your own mother;
   Yes, you will look like Rollison's twin brother.

(*The Senator goes off to his own room with Pelikan. Father Peter walks toward the door and meets Konrad, who, conducted to the investigation by two soldiers, stops when he sees the priest and gazes at him for a long time.*)

KONRAD:
   How strange! I swear I've never seen this man,
   Yet I know him as just a brother can.
   Was it in dreams? It was. I now recall
   That face, those eyes – in dreams I saw it all.
   He seemed to snatch me from a gulf of night.

(*To Father Peter*)

   Good priest, though our acquaintance is but slight,
   At least you don't know me. I thank you much
   For favors that my conscience knows as such.
   Dear are the friends seen even in a dream,
   Since, while we wake, so few friends faithful seem.
   Take this ring. Sell it. Give the poor some doles,
   The rest, for mass for purgatorial souls.

If bondage marks their state, I know their pain:
Who knows if ever I'll hear mass again!
FATHER PETER:
    You will. And for this ring, a word I owe:
    A distant, unknown road you soon will go,
    You'll be in throngs of great folk, rich and bright:
    Seek out a man with mind of still more light.*
    You'll know him; he will greet you in God's name.
    Heed well his words.
KONRAD: (*Gazing at him attentively*)
    What! Is it you? The same?
    Wait! In the name of God ...
FATHER PETER: I cannot stay.
KONRAD: One word!
SOLDIER: Forbidden! Each take his own way!

Scene ix

Forefathers' Eve

(*In the background are a cemetery and a chapel. Wizard and Woman in Mourning.*)

WIZARD:
    To church the crowds are passing in;
    Forefathers' Eve will soon begin.
    Come, we must go; the night grows dark.
WOMAN:
    Wizard, I'll not go there; I want
    To stay within this graveyard haunt,
    A certain ghost I wish to mark:
    The one who many years ago
    After my marriage once did show;
    Amid a spirit throng he loomed,
    All bloody, pallid as the doomed.
    And caught me with his frenzied eye,
    And then, without a word, passed by.

---

*Probably an allusion to the Polish painter Oleszkiewicz who introduced Mickiewicz to mystic circles during his stay in Russia. – Ed.

141

WIZARD:
  Perchance he then was still alive;
  If so, no answer could he give.
  For to the spirit festival
  On weird Forefathers' Eve, the shade
  Of one still living we can call.
  The body at a banquet stayed,
  Or at some game or in a fight,
  Will there remain in calm delight:
  The soul that we by name have called,
  A thin, pale shadow, comes enthralled.
  But while it lives, it cannot speak
  But stands there dumb and white and bleak.
WOMAN:
  What meant that wound upon his breast?
WIZARD:
  A wound of soul it would attest.
WOMAN
  All by myself, I'll lose my way.
WIZARD:
  Then here beside you I will stay.
  Their spells without me they'll prepare;
  Another warlock holds forth there.
  Can you make out that distant song?
  Already gathered in a throng,
  The opening revel upon both
  The wreath and distaff takes its oath;
  They have invoked the airy sprites.
  Can you behold those myriad lights
  That swarm like falling meteors there?
  Those fiery chains across the heights?
  Those are the spirits of the air.
  See how above the church they shine
  Under the black expanse of sky:
  Like doves that in the night malign
  Above a burning city fly,
  When, with the down upon each wing
  Reflecting flame's bright scimitars,
  They glitter like a flock of stars.
WOMAN:
  He comes not with this mustering.

WIZARD:
A gleam bursts from the chapel's gloom:
Now have they sworn by fire, and call
From desert places and the tomb
All bodies in the Devil's thrall.
Hither will come the spirit folk;
You'll know him unless memory err.
Hide with me in a stricken oak,
In this old oak, decayed and dried,
Where sorceresses used to hide.
Now the whole graveyard is astir:
The tombs are rent on every side,
'Mid flickerings of bluish flame
The coffined planking bursts its frame,
Whence issuing the damnèd dead
Thrust the long arm and livid head.
Their eyes – like glowing embers, see?
Best shield your eyes! Hide in the tree!
A vampire scorches with his glance,
But I am safe against his trance.
Ah!
WOMAN: What is it?
WIZARD: A corpse arrayed
In recent cerements, undecayed.
About him clings a sulphur smell;
His brow is black as coal from hell.
Placed in the eyeholes of his skull
Two golden plates glow fierce and full;
Within each circlet's central vaults
A devil sits, a pupil bright,
And keeps on turning somersaults;
He twinkles with the speed of light.
The corpse, with gnashing teeth, must trot.
From hand to hand, as sieve to sieve,
He pours out silver, molten hot;
And ghastly groanings does he give.
PHANTOM:
Ah, where is the church, is the church, where men worship?
  Ah, show me, I pray, where it stands!
Ah, see on my brow how this ducat consumes me!
  How hot silver scorches my hands!

5. The Cracow production of *Forefathers' Eve*, Scene ix. The Wizard and the Woman. (Photograph: Wojciech Plewiński)

Ah, pour out, I pray, for the pitiful orphan,
    For prisoners and widows nigh dead;
Ah, pour from my hand this hot torture of silver,
    And pluck out this coin from my head!
You will not? Alas, I must sift this fierce metal
    Till he who eats children depart
And breathe out his greedy and bottomless spirit:
    This metal I'll pour in his heart,
And then I'll pour out through his eyes and his earholes
    And pour in again by that trough;
That corpse is my sieve, and I'll sift it forever,
    Pour ever, pour on, and pour off!
Ah, how to sift him with metal I'm yearning!
Waiting is long, and I'm burning, I'm burning!

(*Flees away.*)

WIZARD: Ha!
WOMAN: Now what see you?
WIZARD: Ha, how near!
    Another crawls out, runs this way:
What a great loathsome corpse is here;
Pale, fat, and freshly marred with clay!
Fresh garments on its body rest,
As for a wedding it is dressed;
The gnawing worm, in brief assize,
Has scarcely eaten half its eyes.
    It rushes from the chapel now:
The devil's wiles will not allow
The corpse to reach the holy door.
The devil like a girl now stands
And beckons with enticing hands,
Winks lewdly, laughs in warm salute.
The cozened carcass, mad for more,
Runs in concupiscent pursuit.
From grave to grave it leaps and swings
Its writhing limbs like windmills' wings.
Just as it falls in her embrace,
From underneath its legs rush out
Ten large black dogs with hellish face
And reeking fang and long black snout;
No act of love this pack permits:

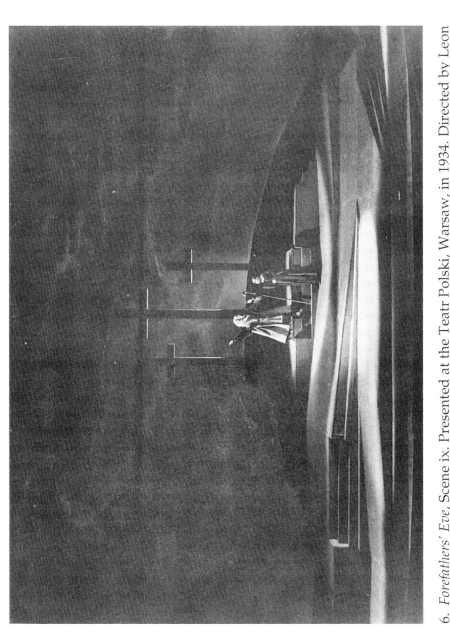

6. *Forefathers' Eve*, Scene ix. Presented at the Teatr Polski, Warsaw, in 1934. Directed by Leon Schiller. Stage design by Andrzej Pronaszko. The Wizard and the Woman at the finale of the play. (Photograph: S. Brzozowski)

They tear the panting corpse to bits,
Worry his parts with bloody jowl,
And scatter them with fiendish howl.
   The dogs are gone. New sights arrive!
Each scattered fragment is alive:
All, all like separate corpses leap
And run together in a heap.
The head hops like a toad, and spouts
Flame from its nose in fiery gouts;
The corpse's chest now crawls to hell
Like an enormous tortoise shell –
Joining its head, the body vile
Then waddles like a crocodile;
The fingers of the torn-off hand
Wriggle like blindworms in the sand;
The palm takes hold, convulses strong,
And pulls a twitching arm along;
The legs crawl up in writhing pain,
And now the corpse stands whole again.
Once more it seeks its sweetheart's charms,
Once more falls prostrate in her arms;
Once more the devil-pack outspreads
And tears it into living shreds –
Ha! Let me see that sight no more!
WOMAN: Are you afraid?
WIZARD: I loathe it sore!
   Toads, turtles, blindworms: Satan wraps
   So many reptiles in one corpse!
WOMAN:
   Not with these spirits is my friend!
WIZARD:
   Forefathers' Eve is soon at end.
   You hear, the third cock now is crowing:
   Our fathers' annals as they leave
   The throngs sing yonder at their going.
WOMAN:
   He came not to Forefathers' Eve!
WIZARD:
   If that spirit in the body
      Lingers yet, now speak his name;
   I with herbs and incantation
      Shall his speedy presence claim:

Let that spirit leave the body!
   Let your eyes behold the same!
WOMAN: The name I've said.
WIZARD: He does not come.
  I've conjured.
WOMAN: And the ghost is dumb!
WIZARD:
  Woman, the lover you hold dear
  Is to his fathers' faith untrue
  Or else has changed the name you knew.
  You see how dawning now draws near;
  Our potent charms have lost their power;
  Your darling comes not at this hour.

(*They come out of the tree.*)

  What's that? What's that? Look, from the west
  Out of Giedymin's city's * breast
  Amid thick clouds of whirling snow
  Full fifty wagons northward go!
  All to the north infuriate fly
  With might of steeds across the sky.
  See one in front, in garments black!
WOMAN: It's he!
WIZARD: And hither lies his track.
WOMAN:
  Behold, he turned in his advance
  And cast on me a single glance:
  Ah, only once – but what an eye!
WIZARD:
  Blood on his bosom was not dry,
  For many wounds are in that breast:
  Torture he knows and fearful dole;
  A thousand swords have pierced his chest,
  And passed into his inmost soul.
  Now, only death can work his cure.
WOMAN:
  Who made him all these wounds endure?

---

* A reference to Wilno, founded by the Lithuanian prince Giedymin. – Ed.

WIZARD:
  Our nation's enemies did this.
WOMAN:
  He had one wound upon his brow,
  A single wound and very small:
  It seemed a drop of black, I vow.[†]
WIZARD:
  That is the sorest wound of all:
  I saw it, I examined it;
  That wound he did himself commit;
  Death cannot heal him of that hurt.
WOMAN:
  Then heal him, God! Your hand assert!

End of Act I

[†] An allusion probably to Konrad's pride which must be expunged before
Father Peter's prophecy can come true. – Ed.

The Un-Divine Comedy

by Zygmunt Krasiński

Translated by
Harold B. Segel

To the errors accumulated by their forebears they added those which their forebears never knew – indecision and timidity. And so it came to pass that they disappeared from the face of the earth and only a great silence remains after them.

Anonymous

To be or not to be, that is the question.

Hamlet

PART I

Stars circle your head. Beneath your feet the waves of the sea. On the waves a rainbow rushes before you and disperses the clouds. Whatever you behold is yours. Shores, towns, and peoples belong to you. The heaven is yours. It seems as though your glory has no equal.

You play inconceivable raptures in the ears of others. You bind and unbind the heart as though it were a garland, a plaything for your fingers. You press out tears and dry them with a smile and then again you strike the smile from the lips of the smiler for a moment, for several moments, perhaps forever and ever. But what do you feel yourself? What do you create? What do you think? Through you flows a stream of beauty, but you are not beauty yourself. Woe unto you, woe! The child that weeps at its nurse's bosom, the field flower that knows not its own fragrance, has more merit before the Lord than you.

Whence do you come, vain shade, who gives witness of the light but does not know the light, has never seen it and never will? Who created you in anger or in irony? Who gave you your vile life, so delusive that you can seem an Angel a moment before you sink into the mud, before, like a reptile, you creep into the slime and are stifled by it. You and woman have the same beginning.

But you, too, suffer, though your pains are creative of nothing and come to naught. The groan of the lowest wretch is numbered among the tones of the celestial harps. Your despair and sighs fall to the depths and Satan gathers them in, adding them joyfully to his falsehoods and delusions. And the Lord one day will deny them as they have denied the Lord.

Not for this do I reproach you, Poetry, mother of Beauty and Salvation. Only he is unhappy who, of a world destined to perish, must remember you or foresee you, for only those do you destroy who have consecrated themselves to you, who have become the living voices of your glory.

Blessed is he in whom you have resided, as God has resided in the world, unseen, unheard, in His every part magnificent, great, the Lord, before whom all created things bow and say: "He is here." Such a one will wear you like a star on his forehead and will not separate himself from your love by the abyss of the word. He will love all men and will walk as a man among his brethren. But he who does not hold to you, who deceives you too soon and betrays you to the vain delights of men, on such a one's head will you strew a few flowers and will turn away, and he will play with the wilted flowers and will weave his funeral wreath all his life. Such a one and woman have the same beginning.

153

GUARDIAN ANGEL: Peace to all men of good will. Blessed be he among created things who has a heart. He may yet be saved. O good and modest wife, come forth for him and may a child be born in your house. (*Flies past.*)

CHORUS OF EVIL SPIRITS: Onward, onward, phantoms, fly toward him! You in front, at the head of the others, shade of his concubine who died yesterday, shade freshened by the mist and decked in flowers, O maiden, mistress of the poet, forward!

Onward and you, too, fame, old eagle, stuffed in hell, taken down from the stake on which the hunter hung you in autumn, fly, spread wide your great wings, white from the sun, o'er the poet's head.

Come forth from our vaults, rotten picture of Eden, the work of Beelzebub. Let us fill your holes and cover them over with varnish, and then, O magic canvas, roll yourself into a cloud and fly to the poet. Swiftly unravel yourself around him, gird him with rocks and waters, night and day by turns. O Mother Nature, encircle the poet!

(*A village. A church, above which the Guardian Angel hovers.*)

GUARDIAN ANGEL: If you keep this oath, forever will you be my brother before the face of the Heavenly Father. (*Disappears.*)

(*The interior of the church. Witnesses. A taper on the altar.*)

PRIEST: (*Conducting the marriage rite*) And remember you this. (*The wedded pair stand up. The Man presses his wife's hand and then gives it to a relative. All go out. He remains alone in the church.*)

THE MAN: I have descended to earthly vows for I have found her of whom I dreamt. May curses rain upon my head if ever I cease to love her.

(*A room full of people. A ball. Music, candles, flowers. The Bride waltzes and after a few turns halts, comes upon her husband in the crowd by chance and leans her head upon his shoulder.*)

BRIDEGROOM: How beautiful you seem to me in your weakness. The flowers and pearls in your hair are in disorder. You are flushed with modesty and weariness. Oh, eternally, eternally, will you be my song.

BRIDE: I will be a faithful wife to you, as my mother told me to be, as my heart tells me now. But there are so many people here. It is so hot and noisy.

BRIDEGROOM: Go dance once more while I stand here and look at you as once in thought I looked at gliding angels.

BRIDE: I shall go, if you want me to, but I have almost no more strength.
BRIDEGROOM: Please go, my darling.

(*Dancing and music.*)

(*A cloudy night. An Evil Spirit in the form of a maiden flying past.*)

EVIL SPIRIT: Not long ago I still ran about the earth just at this time. Now devils are urging me on and ordering me to pretend to be a saint. (*Flies over a garden.*) Flowers, pluck yourselves and fly into my hair. (*Flies above a cemetery.*) O freshness and charm of dead maidens, poured out in the air, floating above the graves, fly to my cheeks!

 Here a black-haired maiden crumbles to dust. O shades of her curls, overhang my forehead! Beneath this stone are two blue eyes from which the light has been extinguished. To me, come to me, O fire that once glowed in them! Behind that grate a hundred tapers burn; today a princess was buried. O satin dress, white as milk, tear yourself from her! Through the grating the dress flies to me, fluttering like a bird. On, on!

(*A bedroom. A nightlamp stands on a table and palely illuminates the Man sleeping beside his wife.*)

THE MAN: (*In his sleep*) Whence do you come, unseen, unheard for so long? As water flows, so flow your feet, two white waves. There is a holy peace on your brow. Everything I ever dreamt and loved has come together in you. (*Awakens.*) Where am I? Ah, beside my wife. This is my wife. (*Looks intently at her.*) I thought that you were my dream, but after a long interval it finally returned to me and it is different from you. You are good and dear, but she... My God, what do I see, wide awake!
MAIDEN: You deceived me. (*Disappears.*)
THE MAN: Cursed be the moment in which I took a woman as wife, in which I abandoned the mistress of my youth, the thought of my thoughts, the soul of my soul.
THE WIFE: (*Awakening*) What is it? Is it day already? Has the carriage come? Today we have various purchases to make.
THE MAN: It is quite late at night. Sleep, sleep soundly.
THE WIFE: Perhaps you have suddenly become ill, dear? I shall get up and give you some ether.
THE MAN: No, just sleep.
THE WIFE: Tell me, dearest, what troubles you, for your voice is different and your cheeks are flushed with fever.

THE MAN: (*Rising abruptly.*) I need some fresh air. Stay here. I beg you, don't come after me. Don't get up, I tell you once more. (*Goes out.*)

(*A moonlit garden. A church can be seen beyond a fence.*)

THE MAN: Since my wedding day I have slept the sleep of the torpid, the sleep of gluttons, the sleep of a German manufacturer alongside his German wife. It was as though the entire world fell asleep around me following my example. I have been going from relative to relative, doctor to doctor, shop to shop, and since a child is to be born to me, I have been thinking of a wetnurse. (*The church clock strikes two.*) Come to me, my former realms, populous, living, gathering together under my thought, harkening to my inspiration. Once upon a time the sound of the night bell was your watchword. (*Walks up and down, wringing his hands.*) O God, did You yourself sanctify the union of two bodies? Was it You that pronounced their inseparability, though their souls repulse each other, go their own ways and leave the bodies like two corpses alongside each other?

Again you are beside me. O my own, my very own, take me with you. If you are but an apparition, if I merely imagined you, and if you emanated from me and now appear unto me, then let me too be a phantom, let me become mist and smoke in order to unite with you.

MAIDEN: Will you follow me whenever I come flying for you?

THE MAN: Oh, every moment I am yours.

MAIDEN: Remember.

THE MAN: Stay. Do not dissolve like a dream. If you are truly the beauty above all beauties, the idea above all thought, why do you not last longer than a single wish, a single thought?

(*A window opens in a nearby house.*)

A WOMAN'S VOICE: My dear, you are certain to catch cold out there. Come back, darling; I am unhappy alone in this large, dark room.

THE MAN: Yes, at once. The spirit has vanished, but it promised to return and when it does, farewell little garden and house and you, who were created for a little garden and house, but not for me.

VOICE: I beg you, the closer to morning the colder it gets.

THE MAN: And my child – oh, God! (*Leaves.*)

(*A drawing room. Two candles on a piano. A cradle with a child asleep in it in a corner. The Man is stretched out in an armchair, his face hidden in his hands. The Wife is at the piano.*)

THE WIFE: I was at Father Benjamin's. He promised me the day after tomorrow.

THE MAN: Thank you.

THE WIFE: I sent to the pastry maker's to have him prepare some cakes since you no doubt have invited many guests to the christening. You know, chocolate cakes with George Stanislas' initials on them.

THE MAN: Thank you.

THE WIFE: Thank God that the real ceremony will be held at last, that our little Georgie will become a full Christian. Although he was baptized right after he was born, it always seemed to me that he was lacking something. (*Goes over to the cradle.*) Sleep, my baby! Did you dream something perhaps, that you threw off your blanket? That's it. Now lie like that. My Georgie is restless today. My little darling, my handsome boy, sleep, sleep!

THE MAN: (*Aside.*) Sultry, stuffy – a storm is on the way. Will lightning soon crackle out there, and my heart burst in here?

THE WIFE: (*Returns, sits down at the piano, plays, stops playing, begins to play again, and again stops.*) Today, yesterday – ah, my God, and all week long and for three weeks now, for a month, you haven't said a word to me and everyone I see tells me that I look bad.

THE MAN: (*Aside*) The hour has come. Nothing can postpone it. (*Aloud*) It seems to me that you look well.

THE WIFE: It's all the same to you, for you no longer look at me, you turn away when I come in and you shut your eyes when I sit near you. Yesterday I was at confession and I recalled all my sins and I couldn't find anything that might have offended you.

THE MAN: You did not offend me.

THE WIFE: My God! My God!

THE MAN: I feel that I ought to love you.

THE WIFE: You finished me off with that one word "ought". Ah, it would be better to get up and say, "I don't love you". At least that way I'd know everything, everything. (*Rises suddenly and takes the baby from the cradle.*) Don't forsake him and I will sacrifice myself on your anger. Love my baby, my child, Henry! (*kneels down.*)

THE MAN: (*Helping her up*) Pay no attention to what I said. I often get bad moments, boredom.

THE WIFE: I ask you for only one word, one promise. Tell me that you will always love him.

THE MAN: Both him and you, believe me. (*He kisses her on the forehead and she embraces him. Then a clap of thunder is heard and immediately afterward the sound of music, one chord after another, all the more wilder.*)

THE WIFE: What does that mean? (*She presses the baby to her breast. The music ceases. The Maiden comes in.*)

MAIDEN: O my beloved, I bring you blessing and delight, come follow me. O my beloved, cast off the earthly chains which fetter you. I come from a new world, a world without end, without night. I am yours.

THE WIFE: Most Holy Virgin, save me! It's a phantom pale as a corpse. Its eyes have no light in them and its voice is like the creaking of a cart on which a corpse lies.

THE MAN: Your brow is bright, your hair intertwined with flowers, O my beloved!

THE WIFE: A shroud in rags falls from her shoulders.

THE MAN: Light flows all about you. Let me hear your voice once more and then I can die.

MAIDEN: She who holds you back is an illusion. Her life is transient, her love like a leaf that perishes amid a thousand faded leaves. But I shall not pass away.

THE WIFE: Henry, Henry, shield me, don't give me up! I smell sulphur and the stench of the grave.

THE MAN: Woman of clay and mud, be not jealous, hold your insults, do not blaspheme. See, that was God's first thought of you, but you followed the counsel of the serpent instead and thus became what you are now.

THE WIFE: I will not let you go.

THE MAN: O my beloved! I leave my home and follow you. (*Goes out.*)

THE WIFE: Henry, Henry ... (*Faints and falls with the child in her arms. A second clap of thunder.*)

(*The christening. Guests. Father Benjamin. The Godfather. The Godmother. The Wetnurse with the child. The Wife sits on a sofa on one side. A servant in the background.*)

FIRST GUEST: (*In a low voice*) Strange where the Count has gone.

SECOND GUEST: Dawdling somewhere or else writing.

FIRST GUEST: And his wife so pale, as though she hadn't slept at all, and she hasn't said a word to anyone.

THIRD GUEST: Today's christening reminds me of a ball, where the host loses everything at cards the night before and then receives the guests he invited with the courtesy of despair.

FOURTH GUEST: I left a beautiful princess and came here. I thought that surely there would be a sumptuous breakfast, but instead what have we except, as the Scriptures say, weeping and the gnashing of teeth.

FATHER BENJAMIN: George Stanislas, do you accept the holy oil?

GODFATHER AND GODMOTHER: I accept it.

ONE OF THE GUESTS: Look, she got up and is walking as though she were asleep.

SECOND GUEST: She has stretched out her hands in front of her and, tottering, is going toward her son.

THIRD GUEST: What are you saying? Let us give her a hand; she's fainting.

FATHER BENJAMIN: George Stanislas, do you renounce Satan and his pride?

GODFATHER AND GODMOTHER: I renounce them.

ONE OF THE GUESTS: Sh! Listen!

THE WIFE: (*Placing her hands on the baby's head*) Where is your father, little Georgie?

FATHER BENJAMIN: Please do not interrupt.

THE WIFE: I bless you, Georgie, I bless you, my child. Be a poet so that your father may love you and not abandon you some time.

GODMOTHER: But come now, Mary dear, please...

THE WIFE: Serve your father and be pleasing to him and then he will forgive your mother.

FATHER BENJAMIN: For God's sake, Countess!

THE WIFE: I curse you if you will not be a poet. (*Faints. Servants carry her out.*)

GUESTS: (*All together*) Something extraordinary has happened in this house. Let us leave it, at once!

(*Meanwhile, the rite comes to an end. The crying baby is returned to its cradle.*)

GODFATHER: (*Before the cradle*) George Stanislas, you have only now become a Christian and entered the society of man. Later you will become a citizen and, through the efforts of your parents and the grace of God, an eminent official. Remember that you must love your country and that it is even beautiful to die for your country. (*All leave.*)

(*A lovely area. Hills and woods. Mountains in the distance.*)

THE MAN: This is what I wanted, what I prayed for for so many long years and at last I am near my goal. I have left the world of men behind. Let every ant there run around and amuse itself with its blade of grass, and when it loses that, let it leap from despair or die of grief.

MAIDEN'S VOICE: This way, this way! (*Goes past.*)

(*Mountains and cliffs above the sea. Thick clouds. A storm.*)

159

THE MAN: Where did she go? The fragrances of the morning have suddenly evaporated and the sky has become darker. I stand upon this height, the abyss beneath me, and the winds roar fearfully.

MAIDEN'S VOICE: (*In the distance*) Come to me, my darling.

THE MAN: How far it still is, and I am unable to cross over the abyss.

VOICE: (*Nearby*) Where are your wings?

THE MAN: Evil spirit mocking me, I despise you.

SECOND VOICE: On the edge of the mountain your great, immortal soul, which was to take flight to heaven in one leap, is expiring. The poor thing begs your feet to go no farther. Great soul! Great heart!

THE MAN: Show yourselves to me; assume a form that I can bend and overthrow. If I fear you, may I be denied her forever.

MAIDEN: (*On the other side of the abyss*) Entwine your hands in mine and fly across.

THE MAN: What is happening to you? The flowers are leaving your temples and falling to the earth, and as soon as they are touched, they slip away like lizards, they slither like serpents.

MAIDEN: My beloved!

THE MAN: My God, the wind has torn the dress from your shoulders and ripped it to shreds.

MAIDEN: Why are you delaying?

THE MAN: The rain drips from your hair. Naked bones protrude from your bosom.

MAIDEN: You promised; you swore.

THE MAN: The lightning has eaten out the pupils of your eyes.

CHORUS OF EVIL SPIRITS: Old woman, return to hell. You have led astray a great and proud heart, admired by men and by itself. Great heart, go after your loved one!

THE MAN: O God, do You damn me because I believed that Your Beauty surpasses the beauty of this earth by a whole heaven? Because I went in pursuit of it and wearied myself for it, only to become an amusement for devils?

EVIL SPIRIT: Listen to him, brothers, listen!

THE MAN: The last hour is about to strike. The storm twists in black whirlwinds. The sea reaches up to the very cliffs and draws near to me. An unseen force thrusts me farther and farther, ever closer. From behind, a crowd of people has sat upon my shoulders and pushes me toward the abyss.

EVIL SPIRIT: Rejoice, brothers, rejoice!

THE MAN: It is vain to struggle. The charm of the abyss tempts me. My soul is giddy. O God, your enemy conquers!

GUARDIAN ANGEL: (*Above the sea*) Peace unto you, waves, be calm. At this moment, the holy water of baptism is being poured upon your baby's head. Return home and sin no more! Return home and love your child!

(*A drawing room with piano. The Man enters, followed by a servant bearing a candle.*)

THE MAN: Where is your mistress?
SERVANT: My lady is ill disposed.
THE MAN: I was in her room; it is empty.
SERVANT: My lord, my lady is no longer here.
THE MAN: And where may she be?
SERVANT: They took her away yesterday...
THE MAN: Where?
SERVANT: To a madhouse. (*Runs from the room.*)
THE MAN: Listen, Mary, perhaps you are pretending, hiding somewhere just to punish me? Speak, please, Mary, Maaary!

No, no one answers. John! Catherine! The whole house has gone deaf and dumb.

Into the ranks of the damned here in this world I myself have cast her to whom I swore fidelity and happiness. Everything I have touched I have destroyed and I shall destroy myself in the end as well. Did hell let me loose just so that I might be its living image on earth a little longer?

On what pillow does she lay her head today? What sounds surround her at night? The whining and singing of the mad. I can see her – that forehead of hers, from which there always emanated a kind, calm, welcoming thought, she holds inclined, and her good thoughts she has sent off to unknown regions, perhaps after me, and the poor soul wanders aimlessly and weeps.
A VOICE FROM SOMEWHERE: You are composing a drama.
THE MAN: Ha! My Satan speaks. (*Rushes to the door and pushes it wide open.*) Saddle Tatar for me! My cloak and pistols!

(*A madhouse with a garden all around it in a mountainous locale.*)

DOCTOR'S WIFE: (*Standing at the door with a bunch of keys in her hand*) Are you a relative of the Countess?
THE MAN: I am a friend of her husband. He sent me here.
DOCTOR'S WIFE: I am afraid that there is not much to hope for in this case. My husband is away right now. He could have explained it all

better. They brought her in yesterday. She was in convulsions. My, how hot it is! (*Wipes her face.*) We have many sick people here. But none of them as dangerously ill as she is. Just imagine, this institution costs us two hundred thousand. Have a look – what a view of the mountains! But I see that you are impatient. Is it true what they say, that Jacobins abducted her husband in the night? Please go in.

(*A room. Barred windows. A few chairs and a bed. The Wife is sitting on a sofa.*)

THE MAN: (*entering*) I should like to be alone with her.

VOICE FROM BEHIND THE DOOR: My husband would be upset if...

THE MAN: Oh, leave me alone, madam! (*Locks the door behind him and approaches his wife.*)

VOICE FROM ABOVE THE CEILING: You have chained up God. One already died on the cross. I am the second God and I, too, am among executioners.

VOICE FROM BENEATH THE FLOOR: To the scaffold with the heads of kings and lords. With me begins the freedom of man.

VOICE FROM BEYOND THE RIGHT WALL: Kneel before the king, your lord!

VOICE FROM BEYOND THE LEFT WALL: A comet already shines in the sky. The day of dreadful judgment is approaching.

THE MAN: Do you recognize me, Mary?

THE WIFE: I swore to be faithful to you until death do us part.

THE MAN: Come, give me your arm. Let us leave here.

THE WIFE: I can't raise myself up. My soul has left my body and has entered my head.

THE MAN: Let me, I'll help you up.

THE WIFE: Allow me a few moments yet, and I shall become worthy of you.

THE MAN: What do you mean?

THE WIFE: I prayed for three nights and God heard me.

THE MAN: I don't understand you.

THE WIFE: From the time I lost you, a change came over me. "Lord God", I said, and beat my breast, and held a taper to my chest, and did penance – "Send down the spirit of poetry unto me" – and on the morning of the third day I became a poet.

THE MAN: Mary...

THE WIFE: Henry, you don't despise me any more? I am filled with inspiration. In the evenings, you won't cast me aside any longer?

THE MAN: Never, never.

THE WlFE: Look at me. Have I not become your equal? I can grasp, understand, express, play, and sing everything. The sea, the stars, a storm, a battle. Yes, the stars, a storm, the sea, ah! Something else escaped me. Ah yes, and a battle. You must take me into a battle some time. I shall look upon it and describe it. A corpse, a shroud, blood, a wave, dew, a coffin.

> Infinity surrounded me,
> And like a bird, with wings I cleave
> The azure of infinity.
> And flying, fade entirely;
> Black nothingness alone I leave.

THE MAN: Damnation! Damnation!

THE WIFE: (*Embracing him and kissing him on the mouth*) Henry, my Henry, how happy I am!

VOICE FROM BENEATH THE FLOOR: I have killed three kings with my own hand. There are still ten left and a hundred priests singing mass.

VOICE ON THE LEFT: The sun has lost a third part of its brilliance. The stars are beginning to stumble in their course, alas, alas!

THE MAN: The Day of Judgment has already come for me.

THE WIFE: Smooth your brow, for you sadden me again. What do you lack? You know, I have something else to tell you.

THE MAN: Speak, and I shall do whatever you ask of me.

THE WIFE: Your son will be a poet.

THE MAN: What?

THE WIFE: At the christening, Poet was the first name the priest gave him. The others you know – George Stanislas. I arranged it that way. I blessed, and then I cursed. He will be a poet. Ah, how I love you, Henry!

VOICE FROM THE CEILING: Forgive them, Father, for they know not what they do.

THE WlFE: That one has a strange madness, hasn't he?

THE MAN: The strangest.

THE WIFE: He doesn't know what he's raving about, but I'll tell you what would happen if God went mad. (*Takes him by the hand.*) All the worlds fly upward and downward, downward and upward. Every man, every worm cries, "I am God!" And every moment, one after the other dies; the comets and the suns go out. Christ can no longer save us. He has taken His cross into both His hands and hurled it into the abyss. Do you hear how that cross, the hope of millions, strikes against the stars, breaks, bursts apart, flies to pieces, falling lower and lower and lower until a great cloud of dust forms from its fragments? The Most Holy Virgin alone prays and the stars, Her handmaidens, have not yet abandoned Her. But She, too, will go whither the entire world is going.

THE MAN: Mary, would you like to see your son?

THE WIFE: I fastened on his wings and dispatched him among the worlds that he might imbibe everything that is lovely and terrible and lofty. One day he will return and will bring you joy. Ah!

THE MAN: Do you feel ill?

THE WIFE: Someone has hung a lamp in my head and the lamp sways back and forth, unbearably.

THE MAN: My dearest Mary, be calm, I beg you, the way you used to be.

THE WIFE: He who is a poet does not live long.

THE MAN: Hello out there! Help, help!

(*Women and the Doctor's Wife rush in.*)

DOCTOR'S WIFE: Pills, powders! No, nothing solid! Of course, some liquid medicine. Maggie, run to the medicine cabinet! You are the cause of this, sir. My husband will give me a good scolding.

THE WIFE: Farewell, Henry.

DOCTOR'S WIFE: Then you are the Count himself!

THE MAN: Mary! Mary! (*Embraces her.*)

THE WIFE: It is well with me, for I die with you near me. (*Lowers her head.*)

DOCTOR'S WIFE: How red she is. The blood has rushed to her brain.

THE MAN: But nothing will happen to her!

(*The Doctor enters and approaches the sofa.*)

DOCTOR: Nothing can any more, she is dead.

[End of Part I]

PART II

Why, O child, do you not ride upon a stick, do you not play with dolls, torment flies, impale butterflies, roll on the grass, steal sweets, or water with your tears all the letters from A to Z? King of flies and butterflies, Punch and Judy's friend, little imp – why are you so much like an angel? What mean your bright blue eyes, downcast yet full of life, of memories, though scarcely have you known a few springs? Why do you rest your brow on your little white hands and seem to dream, and why is your brow burdened with thought, like a flower heavy with dew?

When you blush, you blaze like a rose with a hundred leaves, and with your curls falling back, you measure the heavens with your gaze. Tell me what you hear, what you see, with whom you speak then? For little wrinkles, like fine threads flowing from an invisible ball of yarn, appear on your forehead and in your eyes sparks glitter which no one understands. Your nurse cries and calls to you and thinks that you do not love her. And friends and relatives call to you and think that you do not recognize them. Your father alone remains silent and stares gloomily, till a tear wells up in his eye and, falling, disappears somewhere.

The doctor took your pulse, counted the beats, and declared that you are nervous. Your godfather brought you cakes, patted you on the arm, and prophesied that you would be the citizen of a great nation. A professor came, felt about your head, and declared that you have a talent for the sciences. A poor man, to whom you gave a coin as you passed by, promised you a beautiful wife on earth and a crown in heaven. A military man jumped toward you, seized you, put you down, and shouted, "You will be a colonel". A Gypsy read the palms of both your hands for a long time, but could make out nothing. Groaning, she went away, refusing to take a ducat. A magnetizer waved his long fingers before your eyes, circled your face with them and took fright, for he felt that he was going to sleep himself. A priest prepared you for your first confession, and wanted to kneel before you as before a holy picture. A painter came when you were angry and you stamped your little feet; he sketched you as a little devil and set you in a picture of Judgment Day among the spirits for whom there was no hope.

Meanwhile, you continue to grow and to become beautiful, not with that milk and strawberry freshness of childhood, but with the beauty of strange, inconceivable thoughts which seem to flow to you from another world. Although your eyes are often without light, your face pale, and your chest hollow, everyone who beholds you stops and says, "What a lovely child!" If a flower that fades had a soul of fire and inspiration from heaven, if on every little leaf that bends toward the ground an angel thought lay instead of a drop of dew, the flower would resemble you, O my child. Perhaps children were that way before the fall of Adam.

(*A cemetery. The Man and George beside a tomb with Gothic pillars and turrets.*)

THE MAN: Take off your hat and pray for your mother's soul.

GEORGE: Hail, Mary, full of the grace of God, Queen of Heaven, Lady of everything that blooms on earth, in the fields, by the streams...

THE MAN: Why do you change the words of the prayer? Pray the way you were taught, for your mother who died ten years ago, just at this very hour.

GEORGE: Hail, Virgin Mary, full of the grace of God, the Lord is with Thee, blessed art Thou among Angels, and each of them when Thou approachest plucks one rainbow from his wings and casts it before Thy feet. Thou goest upon them as upon waves...

THE MAN: George!

GEORGE: When those words reel about my head and make it hurt so, I just have to say them, Papa.

THE MAN: Get up. A prayer like that does not reach God. You don't remember your mother. You can't love her.

GEORGE: But I often see Mama.

THE MAN: Where do you see her, dear?

GEORGE: In my sleep. That is, not really in my sleep, but just when I start to fall asleep, like the day before yesterday.

THE MAN: What are you saying, my child?

GEORGE: She was very white and thin.

THE MAN: And did she speak to you?

GEORGE: It seemed to me that she was walking through a great wide darkness, that she herself was all white and that she was saying:

> I wander far and wide,
> My way make everywhere,
> Beyond the moon's dark side,
> Where choirs of angels sing,
> And gather for you there
> A myriad of forms,
> My child, and swarms
> Of thoughts inspiring.
> And from the spirits higher,
> And those of paler fire,

> Colors and shades,
> Sounds and rays
> I gather for you,
> That you, O darling boy,
> May be an angel too,
> And that your father's joy
> May shed his love on you.

You see, father, I remember it word for word. Please believe me, Papa dear, I'm not making it up.

THE MAN: (*Leaning against a pillar of the tomb.*) Mary, do you want to destroy your own child and burden me with two deaths? What am I saying? She is somewhere in heaven, quiet and peaceful, the way she used to be when she was alive on earth. The poor boy is just imagining the whole thing.

GEORGE: Even now I hear her voice, but I can't see her.

THE MAN: Where is it coming from, what side?

GEORGE: As if from those two larch trees on which the light of the setting sun is falling.

> Your lips I fill,
> In you instill
> Sweet melody and might;
> Your brow bestrew
> With bands of light,
> And with a mother's love
> Awake in you
> What people here on earth and angels up above
> Call beautiful and true –
> So that your father's joy,
> O darling boy,
> May shed his love on you.

THE MAN: Do our last thoughts at death accompany the spirit although it ascends to heaven? Can the spirit be happy and holy and yet, at the same time, mad?

GEORGE: Mother's voice is growing weak. It is almost dying out behind the wall of the vault, there, there – oh, it repeats again:

> O darling boy,
> So that your father's joy
> May shed his love on you.

THE MAN: God, have mercy on our child whom, it seems, in Your wrath You have destined for madness and premature death. Lord, deprive not Your own creatures of reason; forsake not the temples that You have built unto Yourself. Look upon my torment and deliver not this angel unto hell. Me, at least, You have endowed with strength to endure crowds of thoughts, passions, and feelings. But him? You have given him a body like a spider web which any great thought can tear apart. O Lord God! O God!

For ten years I have not had a peaceful day. You have sent many people upon me who have congratulated me, who have envied me, who have wished me well. You have let down upon me a hail of pain, of fleeting images, of forebodings, and of dreams. Your grace has fallen upon my mind, not my heart. Let me love my child in peace and let there be peace now between Creator and created. Son, cross yourself and come with me. Eternal rest. (*They go out.*)

(*A promenade. Ladies and gentlemen. A philosopher. The Man.*)

PHILOSOPHER: I repeat that I am of the irrefutable, inescapable conviction that the time is coming when women and blacks will be liberated.
THE MAN: You are right.
PHILOSOPHER: And there will also be a great change both particular and general in human society, from which I deduce the regeneration of the human race through blood and the destruction of old forms.
THE MAN: Do you think so?
PHILOSOPHER: Just as our globe straightens itself or leans on its axis by sudden revolutions.
THE MAN: Do you see that rotten tree?
PHILOSOPHER: The one with young leaves on its lower branches?
THE MAN: Good. What do you think – will it be able to stand for many more years?
PHILOSOPHER: How can I say? A year, two perhaps.
THE MAN: And yet today it let out several fresh leaves, although the roots are rotting more and more.
PHILOSOPHER: And what do you make of that?
THE MAN: Nothing – only that it will collapse and turn into coal and ashes, for even a joiner will have no use for it.
PHILOSOPHER: But that is not what we were talking about.
THE MAN: Yet it is a picture of you and all yours and of your age and of your theory. (*They move on.*)

(*A pass among the mountains.*)

THE MAN: I have labored for many years to discover the final end of all knowledge, pleasure, and thought, and I have discovered a gravelike emptiness in my heart. I know every feeling by name, but there is no desire, no faith, and no love inside me. Only a few forebodings haunt that desert – that my son will go blind, that the society in which I grew up will dissolve – and I suffer, as God is happy, alone within myself, for myself alone.

GUARDIAN ANGEL'S VOICE: Love the sick, the hungry, the despairing, love your neighbors, your poor neighbors, and you will be saved.

THE MAN: Who is that?

MEPHISTO: (*Approaching*) Your humble servant, sir. Sometimes I like to detain travelers by the gift with which nature endowed me. I am a ventriloquist.

THE MAN: (*Raising his hand to his hat*) I remember seeing a face like that in an engraving somewhere.

MEPHISTO: (*Aside*) The Count has a good memory. (*Aloud*) Praise be . . .

THE MAN: For ever and ever. Amen.

MEPHISTO: (*Going in among the rocks*) You and your stupidity!

THE MAN: The poor child, for his father's faults and his mother's madness doomed to eternal blindness – incomplete, ardorless, living only by dreams, the shadow of a fleeting angel cast upon the earth and roaming in aimless transience. What a huge eagle soared above the place where this man disappeared!

EAGLE: Greetings unto you!

THE MAN: It flies toward me, all black – the rush of its wings like the rush of a thousand bullets in battle.

EAGLE: With the sword of your fathers fight for their honor and power.

THE MAN: It has spread itself above me . . . the pupils of my eyes are sucked out by its rattlesnake gaze. Ha! I understand you.

EAGLE: Don't step aside, never step aside – your foul enemies will turn to dust.

THE MAN: I bid you farewell among the rocks amid which you disappear. However it be, false or true, victory or defeat, I believe you, envoy of glory. O past, come to my aid, and if your spirit has already returned to the bosom of the Lord, let it tear itself away from there once again, enter into me, and become thought, strength, and deed! (*He throws off a viper from him.*)

Go, vile reptile – Just as I have cast you away and there is no regret for you in nature, so shall they fall down and there will be no regret for them – no fame will remain after them – no cloud will turn round in its course to look behind it at so many sons of earth perishing together.

They first, I afterward.

O boundless firmament, you enfold the earth – that earth like a babe grinding its teeth and crying. But you tremble not, you do not listen to her, you flow on in your infinity.

Mother Nature, fare thee well! I go to transform myself into a man, to fight together with my brethren.

(*A room. The Man. A doctor. George.*)

THE MAN: Nothing has done him any good. You are our last hope.

DOCTOR: You do me a great honor...

THE MAN: Tell the gentleman what you feel.

GEORGE: I can no longer recognize you, father, nor this gentleman. Sparks and black threads flow before my eyes, and sometimes something in the shape of a very thin snake comes out of them – and then a yellow cloud forms – the cloud flies upward, then falls down, and a rainbow bursts from it. And nothing at all hurts me.

DOCTOR: Stand in the shade, Master George. How old are you? (*Looks into his eyes.*)

THE MAN: He has turned fourteen.

DOCTOR: Now turn around to the window.

THE MAN: What now?

DOCTOR: The eyelids are beautiful, the whites of the eyes as clear as can be, all the veins in perfect order, the muscles strong. (*To George*) Laugh at all of this. You're going to be as well as I am. (*To the Man*) There is no hope. Look at the pupils yourself, Count. They are insensitive to light. There is a complete weakening of the optic nerve.

GEORGE: There is a mist over everything before me, everything...

THE MAN: True, they are wide open, gray, lifeless.

GEORGE: When I close my eyes, I see more than when they are open.

DOCTOR: Thought has utterly destroyed his body – catalepsy is a real danger.

THE MAN: (*Taking the Doctor aside*) Anything you ask for – half my estate.

DOCTOR: Disorganization cannot reorganize itself. (*Takes his hat and cane.*) Your most humble servant, Count; I must now go and operate on a lady with a cataract.

THE MAN: Have mercy – don't leave us yet.

DOCTOR: Perhaps you'd care to know the name of the illness?

THE MAN: You say there is no hope at all, none?

DOCTOR: In Greek, it's called *amaurosis.* (*Goes out.*)

THE MAN: (*Pressing his son to his breast*) But you can still see a little, can't you?

GEORGE: I hear your voice, father.

THE MAN: Look at the window; the sun is shining, the weather is nice.

GEORGE: A mass of shapes float around between my eye and my eyelid – I see faces I've seen before, familiar places, the pages of books read.

THE MAN: You still see then?

GEORGE: Yes, with the eyes of my soul; but the other eyes have gone dark.

THE MAN: (*Falling on his knees. A moment of silence.*) Before whom have I knelt? Where am I to claim the righting of the wrong against my child? (*Getting up*) Better to keep silent. God laughs at prayers, Satan at curses.

VOICE FROM SOMEWHERE: Your son is a poet. What more do you desire?

(*The Doctor. The Godfather.*)

GODFATHER: Certainly, it is a great misfortune to be blind.

DOCTOR: And most unusual at so young an age.

GODFATHER: He was always of a weak constitution, and his mother died somewhat... well...

DOCTOR: What do you mean?

GODFATHER: To some extent, yes... you understand... unbalanced.

(*The Man enters.*)

THE MAN: Please forgive me for calling you at so late an hour but for the last few days my poor son has been waking always around twelve, getting up, and talking in his sleep. Please come with me.

DOCTOR: By all means. I am very curious about this phenomenon.

(*A bedroom. Servants. Relatives. The Godfather. The Doctor. The Man.*)

RELATIVE: Sh!

SECOND RELATIVE: He has awakened, but he doesn't hear us.

DOCTOR: Please say nothing, gentlemen.

GODFATHER: A very strange thing.

GEORGE: (*Getting up*) O God, God!

RELATIVE: How slowly he moves.

SECOND RELATIVE: Look how he has his hands folded across his chest.

THIRD RELATIVE: He doesn't wink. He barely opens his mouth, but a sharp, drawn-out voice comes out of it.

MALE SERVANT: Jesus of Nazareth!

GEORGE: Away, darkness! I was born the son of light and song. What do you want of me? What would you have of me?

I will not surrender to you even though my sight has flown away with the winds and races somewhere through the vast expanses of the universe. But it will return one day, rich in the rays of the stars, and will light my eyes with a flame.

GODFATHER: Just like his late mother, babbling he doesn't know himself about what. This is a sight surely worth thinking about.

DOCTOR: I agree entirely.

WETNURSE: Most Holy Virgin of Częstochowa, take my eyes and give them to him.

GEORGE: Mother dear, please, mother, send me pictures and thoughts now so that I may live inwardly, so that I may create another world within myself, the equal of the one I have lost.

RELATIVE: What do you think, brothers, must we call a family council?

SECOND RELATIVE: Wait a while. Sh!

GEORGE: You don't answer me. O mother! Don't abandon me!

DOCTOR: (*To the Man*) It is my duty to speak the truth.

GODFATHER: Right, the duty – and virtue – of a doctor, Mr. Physician.

DOCTOR: Your son is suffering from mental derangement combined with an extraordinary nervous sensitivity that sometimes brings on, if I may say so, a simultaneous state of sleep and waking, a state similar to what we are obviously observing here.

THE MAN: (*Aside*) O God, he is explaining Your judgments to me!

DOCTOR: I should like to have a pen and ink – two grams of *cerasi laurei*, etc., etc.

THE MAN: You'll find them in the room over there. Now may I ask all of you to please leave.

MINGLED VOICES: Good night – good night – until tomorrow. (*They all go out.*)

GEORGE: (*Awakening*) They wish me good night. Say "long night" or "eternal night", maybe, but not "good" night or a "happy" one.

THE MAN: Lean on me; I'll lead you back to bed.

GEORGE: Father, what does it all mean?

THE MAN: Cover yourself up well and sleep peacefully. The doctor says you are going to get your sight back again.

GEORGE: I feel so unwell – Some voices broke my sleep. (*Falls asleep.*)

THE MAN: May my blessing rest upon you. I can give you nothing more, neither happiness, nor light, nor fame. And the hour is at hand when I must fight, act with a handful of people against hordes. Where will you go, all alone among a hundred abysses, a blind, weak child and poet all in one, a poor singer without an audience living by the spirit beyond the confines of the earth, and chained to the earth by your body. O you unhappy, unhappiest of angels, O my son!

WETNURSE: (*At the door*) The doctor is asking for you, sir.

THE MAN: My good Catherine, stay with the child. (*Goes out.*)

[End of Part II]

PART III

To song – to song!

Who shall begin it, who shall end it? Give me a past armed with steel, resplendent in the fluttering feathers of knightly helmets. I call forth Gothic towers before your eyes, I cast the shadow of holy cathedrals upon your heads. But it is not that – it will never be that!

Whosoever you may be, tell me in what you believe. You would more easily have taken your own life than found a faith or awakened faith within yourself. Shame, shame on all of you, both small and great, but in spite of you, in spite of your mediocrity and misery, your heartlessness and mindlessness, the world advances toward its goal, pulls you after it, rushes ahead, plays with you, throws you about, casts you aside. The world waltzes round and round, couples disappear and appear and soon fall down, for it is slippery – there is much blood – blood everywhere – much blood, I tell you.

Do you see those crowds standing at the gates of the city among the hills and poplar trees – tents pitched, long planks set, covered with meat and drink, propped up by tree stumps and poles? The tankard flies from hand to hand and where it touches a mouth, that mouth emits a threat, an oath, or a curse. It flies, returns, circles, dances, ever full, clinking and shining among the thousands. Long live the cup of drunkenness and comfort!

Do you see how impatiently they wait – murmuring among themselves, prepared to shout – all of them wretched, years of toil inscribed on their brows, their hair disheveled, in rags, their faces flushed, their hands wrinkled from work. Some hold scythes, others shake hammers, planes. Look – this tall one holds an axe by his side and that one waves an iron muzzle rod above his head. Farther on, to a side, beneath a willow tree, a small boy is putting a cherry into his mouth with his left hand, while in his right he grips a long awl. Women have come, too, mothers, wives, as hungry and poor as the men themselves, prematurely faded, without any traces of beauty – on their hair the dust of a beaten track – on their bosoms torn garments – in their eyes something expiring, gloomy, as if an imitation of sight. But soon they grow livelier. The tankard flies every-where, runs all around. Long live the cup of drunkenness and comfort!

Now a great tumult arises in the assembly. Is it joy, is it despair? Who can recognize any feeling in the voices of thousands? This man who has come up, has climbed on a table, has jumped upon a chair and dominates them, is speaking to them. His voice is protracted, sharp, expressive. You can distinguish and understand each and every word. His movements are slow and easy and accompany the words the way music accompanies a song. His forehead is high and broad, his head without a single hair on it, all fallen from thought. The skin has dried to the skull, to the cheeks, yellowishly sinking in between the bones and muscles and, from the temples down, a black beard surrounds the face like a wreath. Never blood, never a change of color in the cheeks – eyes unmoved, fixed intently upon those listening to him – betraying not a single moment of doubt or confusion. And when he raises an arm, stretches it out and extends it above them, they bend their heads and it seems that soon they will kneel before that blessing of great mind – not of heart. Away with heart, away with superstition. Long live the words of comfort and of murder!

This is their fury, their love, the ruler of their souls and of their zeal. He promises them bread and a livelihood. Cries have arisen – they are drawn out, they erupt on all sides: "Long live Pancras!" "Bread for us, bread, bread!" And at the feet of the speaker, his friend, or comrade, or servant leans on the table.

This one has an eastern eye, black, shaded with long lashes. His arms are flabby, his legs bowed, his body bent awkwardly to one side, his mouth voluptuous and malevolent, his fingers adorned with gold rings. And he, too, in a harsh voice cries, "Long live Pancras!" The speaker has turned his glance to him for a moment. "Citizen Convert Jew, give me my handkerchief!"

Meanwhile, the applause and shouting go on. "Bread for us, bread, bread!" "Death to the masters and merchants!" "Bread, bread!"

(A hut. Some lamps. An open book on a table. Converted Jews.)

CONVERT: My vile, vengeful, and beloved brethren, we suck the pages of the Talmud as if it were a breast heavy with milk, a living breast, which pours forth strength and honey for us but bitterness and poison for them.

CHORUS OF CONVERTS: Jehovah is our lord and none other. He has scattered us everywhere, He has entwined the world of those who honor the Cross – our masters, proud, stupid, and illiterate – with us, as with the folds of some measureless reptile. Let us spit three times to their ruin. May they thrice be cursed!

CONVERT: Rejoice, my brethren! The Cross, our enemy, severed and rotting, stands today above a pool of blood. If it falls but once, never will it rise again. Until now, the masters have defended it.

CHORUS: The work of ages is complete, our sullen, painful, relentless work. Death to the masters! Let us spit three times to their ruin. May they thrice be cursed!

CONVERT: Upon freedom without order, upon slaughter without end, upon contention and wrath, upon their stupidity and pride shall we found the power of Israel. Only those few masters more, just those few, must we push down and their corpses strew with the splinters of the Cross.

CHORUS: The Cross is our holy sign. The water of baptism has united us with mankind. The scorners have come to believe in the love of the scorned.

The freedom of men is our law – the good of the people is our goal. The sons of Christians have come to believe in the sons of Caiaphas.

Centuries ago our fathers tortured the Enemy. Today we torture Him again and He shall never again rise from the dead.

CONVERT: A few moments yet, a few drops more of the serpent's venom, and the world will be ours, ours, O my brethren!

CHORUS: Jehovah is the Lord of Israel, and none other. Let us spit three times to their ruin. May they thrice be cursed!

(*A knocking is heard.*)

CONVERT: To your work, and thou, holy book, away, lest the glance of the accursed soil thy pages! (*Puts the Talmud away.*) Who goes there?

VOICE FROM BEHIND THE DOOR: A friend. In the name of liberty, open up.

CONVERT: Brothers, to your hammers and ropes! (*Opens the door.*)

LEONARD: (*Entering*) It is well, citizens, that you are alert and sharpen your daggers for tomorrow. (*Goes up to one of them.*) And what are you making in that corner there?

ONE OF THE CONVERTS: Nooses, citizen.

LEONARD: You are wise, my brother, for he who does not fall in battle by the sword, shall die on a branch.

CONVERT: Good citizen Leonard, is tomorrow's matter certain?

LEONARD: He who thinks and feels the most powerfully of all of us has bade me summon you to parley. He himself will answer your question.

CONVERT: I am going, and the rest of you – slacken not in your work! Yankel, keep a close eye on them! (*Leaves with Leonard.*)

CHORUS: Ropes and daggers, sticks and sabers, the work of our hands, come forth to their destruction! They shall slay the masters in the pasture lands, they shall hang them in the gardens and forests, and afterward we shall slay the slayers and hang them. The scorned will arise in their anger and will clothe themselves in the glory of Jehovah;

7. Zygmunt Krasiński's *The Un-Divine Comedy*, Part III. Presented at the Stary Teatr, Cracow, in 1965. Directed by Konrad Swinarski. Leonard (center) and Converts preparing for battle. (Photograph: Wojciech Plewiński)

the words "His salvation" and "His love for us" are destruction for all. Let us spit three times to their ruin. May they thrice be cursed!

(*A tent. Bottles and goblets thrown all around.*)

PANCRAS: Fifty of them were carousing here a moment ago and at every word of mine shouted, "Vivat!" But did even one of them divine my thoughts or grasp the end of the road at whose beginning he raised such a cry? *O imitatores, servum pecus.* (*Enter Leonard and the Convert.*) Do you know Count Henry?

CONVERT: Great citizen, by sight rather than by conversation. Once, I remember, passing by on Corpus Christi Day, he shouted to me, "Out of my way!" and looked upon me with the gaze of a master. For that, I vowed him a noose in my soul.

PANCRAS: Tomorrow, at the earliest hour, betake yourself to him and inform him that I wish to have a private, secret meeting the day after tomorrow, at night.

CONVERT: Will you give me many men to go along with me, for it would be incautious to set out alone?

PANCRAS: Go alone; my name will be your guard. The gallows on which you hung the baron two days ago will be your support.

CONVERT: Oh dear!

PANCRAS: Say that I will come to him at midnight the day after tomorrow.

CONVERT: And if he orders me imprisoned, or beaten?

PANCRAS: Then you will be a martyr for the Liberty of the People.

CONVERT: Everything, everything for the Liberty of the People. (*Aside*) Oh dear!

PANCRAS: Good night, citizen!

(*The Convert leaves.*)

LEONARD: Why this delay, these halfway measures, negotiations, conversations? When I swore to honor and obey you, it was because to me you were a hero of extremity, an eagle flying straight to its goal, a man staking himself and all his followers on a single card.

PANCRAS: Be silent, child!

LEONARD: All are ready – the converts have forged weapons and spun nooses; the crowds shout and call for an order. Issue the order and it will race like a spark, like lightning, and will turn into flame and pass into a thunderbolt.

PANCRAS: The blood has rushed to your head. That is inevitable at your age, but you cannot fight against it and you call that zeal.

LEONARD: Consider what you are doing. The aristocrats in their weakness have entrenched themselves in Holy Trinity Castle and await our arrival, as if the blade of the guillotine. Forward, master, without delay, forward, and upon them.

PANCRAS: It makes no difference. They have lost the strength of their bodies in sensual pleasures, the strength of their minds in idleness. Tomorrow, or the day after, they must yield.

LEONARD: Whom do you fear? Who restrains you?

PANCRAS: No one. Only my will.

LEONARD: And must I believe in it blindly?

PANCRAS: In truth, I say to you – blindly.

LEONARD: You are betraying us.

PANCRAS: Like a refrain in a song, betrayal appears at the end of every speech of yours. Do not shout, for if we were overheard…

LEONARD: There are no spies here, and what then?

PANCRAS: Nothing – just five bullets in your chest because you dared raise your voice one tone higher in my presence. (*Goes up to him.*) Believe in me, and be at peace with yourself.

LEONARD: I got carried away, I confess, but I am in no fear of punishment. If my death may serve as an example, if it may strengthen the resolve and dignity of our cause, then order it.

PANCRAS: You are quick, full of hope, and believe deeply. Happiest of men, I have no wish to deprive you of life.

LEONARD: What do you say?

PANCRAS: Think more, talk less, and some time you will understand me. Did you send to the magazine for two thousand cartridges?

LEONARD: I sent Deyts with a detachment.

PANCRAS: And has the shoemakers' contribution been turned over to our treasury?

LEONARD: With the sincerest zeal they all paid in, each and every last one of them, and brought a hundred thousand.

PANCRAS: I shall invite them to a dinner tomorrow. Have you heard anything new about Count Henry?

LEONARD: I despise the masters too much to believe what they say about him. Declining races have no energy – they should not, they cannot!

PANCRAS: Yet he is assembling his villagers and, confident of their attachment, he is preparing to come to the relief of Holy Trinity Castle.

LEONARD: Who can oppose us? For we are the embodiment of the Idea of the age.

PANCRAS: I still wish to see him, to gaze into his eyes, to penetrate to the depths of his heart, to win him over to our side.

LEONARD: He is an inveterate aristocrat.

PANCRAS: But at the same time, a poet. Now leave me alone.

LEONARD: Do you forgive me, citizen?

PANCRAS: Sleep peacefully. Had I not pardoned you, you would already be asleep for all eternity.

LEONARD: Then nothing is going to happen tomorrow?

PANCRAS: Good night and sweet dreams! (*Leonard goes out.*) Oh, Leonard, wait!

LEONARD: (*Returning.*) Citizen leader...

PANCRAS: The day after tomorrow, at night, you shall accompany me to Count Henry.

LEONARD: As you command. (*Leaves.*)

PANCRAS: Why should that one man stand in the way of me, the leader of thousands? His forces are small in comparison with mine – a few hundred peasants who blindly believe his word, attached to their master like domestic animals... It is wretchedness, it is nothing. Yet why do I so desire to see him, to lure him to our side? Is it because my spirit has at last met its equal and for a moment stands still? This is the last obstacle before me on this plain. It must be overcome, and then... Oh, thought of mine, can you not delude yourself as you delude others? Shame on you, you know your goal, for you are thought, the mistress of the people, the will and power of all are concentrated in you and what is a crime for others is praise for you. To base and unknown people you have given names; to people without feeling you have given faith, the world made in your own image. You have created a new world about you and yet you yourself go astray and do not know what you are. No, no, no, you are great! (*He falls into a chair, sunk in thought.*)

(*A forest. Linen is hanging in all the trees. In the center there is a meadow in which stands a gallows. Huts. Tents. Campfires. Barrels. Crowds of people.*)

THE MAN: (*Disguised in a black cloak with a red Cap of Liberty on his head,[*] enters holding the Convert by the arm.*) Remember!

CONVERT: (*In a low voice*) Sir, I will conduct you around. On my honor, I will not betray you.

---

[*] The so-called Phrygian Cap (*bonnet phrygien*) of the French Revolution. – Ed.

8. The Cracow production of *The Un-Divine Comedy*, Part III. The Man (Count Henry) in the midst of the dance of the free people. (Photograph: Wojciech Plewiński)

THE MAN: Just wink an eye or raise a finger, and I'll aim straight for your head. You can imagine that I care nothing for your life, since I have dared come this far.

CONVERT: Oh my! You grip my hand with claws of iron. What am I to do?

THE MAN: Talk to me as though I were an acquaintance, a newly arrived friend. What sort of a dance is that there?

CONVERT: The dance of free people.

(*Men and women dance around the gallows and sing.*)

CHORUS: Bread, earnings, wood for fuel in winter, rest in summer! Hurrah! Hurrah!

> God had no mercy on us. Hurrah! Hurrah!
> Kings had no mercy on us. Hurrah! Hurrah!
> Masters had no mercy on us. Hurrah! Hurrah!
> Today we take leave of the service of God, kings, and masters. Hurrah! Hurrah!

THE MAN: (*To a girl*) I am pleased that you are so rosy and merry.

GIRL: We have waited so long for such a day. I washed dishes and rubbed forks with a cloth and never heard a good word. But now it is time for me myself to eat and dance. Hurrah!

THE MAN: Dance, citizeness.

CONVERT: (*Softly*) I beg you, sir. Someone may recognize you. Let us go on.

THE MAN: If someone recognizes me, you die. Let us go farther.

CONVERT: Members of a lackeys' club are sitting beneath this tree.

THE MAN: Let us approach them.

FIRST LACKEY: I have already killed my former master.

SECOND LACKEY: I am still looking for my baron. Your health!

BUTLER: Citizens, bent over boot trees in sweat and humiliation, shining boots, trimming hair, we felt what our rights were. The health of the whole club!

CHORUS: The president's health! He will lead us along the path of honor.

BUTLER: Thank you, citizens.

CHORUS: From the anterooms, our prisons, we rushed out together, in harmony, as though we were one. Hurrah! We know how ridiculous and licentious drawing rooms are. Hurrah! Hurrah!

THE MAN: What voices are those, harder and wilder, coming from that thicket on the left?

CONVERT: That is a chorus of butchers, sir.

CHORUS: The axe and the knife are our arms, the slaughterhouse our life. To us it is all the same, slaughtering cattle or masters.

Children of strength and blood, we look indifferently on others who are weaker and whiter. He who summons us has us in his hire. For the masters we shall slay oxen and for the people masters.

The axe and the knife are our arms, the slaughterhouse our life – the slaughterhouse, the slaughterhouse, the slaughterhouse.

THE MAN: I like these men. At least they make no mention of honor or philosophy. Good evening, madam.

CONVERT: (*Softly*) Sir, say "citizeness" or "free woman."

WOMAN: What does that title mean? Where did it come from? Phew, you stink of old clothes.

THE MAN: My tongue got twisted.

WOMAN: I am as free as you are, a free woman, and I freely distribute my love to the members of my society since they are the ones who acknowledged my rights.

THE MAN: And in return for that your society again gave you those rings and that amethyst chain. O doubly beneficent society!

WOMAN: No, those trifles I tore, before my liberation, from my husband, my enemy, the enemy of freedom, who kept me bound.

THE MAN: I wish the citizeness a pleasant walk. (*He moves on.*) Who is that strange soldier, leaning on his two-edged sword, with a death's-head on his cap, another on his baldric, and a third on his chest? Is it not the famous Bianchetti, today a condottiere of peoples as others were formerly the condottieri of princes and governments?

CONVERT: The same, my lord. He joined us just a week ago.

THE MAN: What were you thinking about, general?

BIANCHETTI: Citizen, do you see that gap among the sycamores? Look carefully. You'll notice a castle on a hill there. I can clearly make out its walls, trenches, and four bastions through my telescope.

THE MAN: It will be hard to take it.

BIANCHETTI: A plague on all kings! It could be surrounded with a ditch, undermined, and . . .

CONVERT: (*Winking*) Citizen general!

THE MAN: (*In a low voice*) Do you feel the pistol cocked underneath my cloak?

CONVERT: (*Aside*) Oh my! (*Aloud*) How have you arranged it then, citizen general?

BIANCHETTI: (*Musing*) Although you are my brothers in liberty, you are not my brothers in genius. After the victory, everyone will learn of my plans. (*Leaves.*)

9. The Cracow production of *The Un-Divine Comedy*, Part III. The Convert, The Man (Count Henry), and the Woman with rings. (Photograph: Wojciech Plewiński)

THE MAN: (*To the Convert*) I advise you to kill him for that is how every aristocracy begins.

ARTISAN: Curses! Curses!

THE MAN: What are you doing beneath that tree, you poor fellow? Why do you have such a wild, dim-eyed look?

ARTISAN: Curses on the merchants, on the factory directors. The best years, when other people are loving girls, fighting in open fields, or sailing the wide seas, there I was, wearing myself out in a narrow room over a silk loom.

THE MAN: Empty the goblet you have in your hand.

ARTISAN: I have no strength. I cannot raise it to my lips. I barely managed to crawl here, but the day of liberty will not dawn for me now. Curses on the merchants, who sell the silk, and on the masters who wear it. Curses! Curses on them all! (*Falls dead.*)

CONVERT: What an ugly corpse!

THE MAN: Coward of liberty, citizen convert, behold that lifeless head floating in the bloody glow of the setting sun. Where now are your phrases, your promises – the equality, perfection, and happiness of the human race?

CONVERT: (*Aside*) May you, too, die before your time and may dogs tear your body to pieces. (*Aloud*) Let me go. I have to make a report on my mission.

THE MAN: Just say that I took you for a spy and detained you. (*He looks all around him.*) The echoes from the feast are dying out behind me. Before us are only pines and spruce trees, bathed in the rays of sunset.

CONVERT: Clouds are gathering above the trees. You had best return to your own people who already have been long awaiting you in Saint Ignatius' ravine.

THE MAN: Thank you for your concern, master Jew. Back! I want to observe the citizens once more in the twilight.

VOICE FROM AMONG THE TREES: The son of boors bids the old sun good night.

VOICE ON THE RIGHT: Your health, old enemy of ours, who drove us to work and toil. Tomorrow, when you rise, you will find your slaves seated before dishes of meat with pots of drink beside them. And now, miserable little glass, go to the devil!

CONVERT: A procession of peasants is coming this way.

THE MAN: You won't get away. Stand behind that tree trunk and keep quiet.

CHORUS OF PEASANTS: Forward, forward, to the tents, to our brethren! Forward, forward, to the shade of the sycamores, to sleep, to

185

10. The Cracow production of *The Un-Divine Comedy*, Part III. The gallows scene. (Photograph: Wojciech Plewiński)

pleasant evening banter. Girls await us there; slaughtered oxen, once harnessed to plows, await us there.

A VOICE: I pull and drag him, but he bridles up and resists me. Come on to the recruiting station, come on!

A MASTER'S VOICE: My children, have pity on me, please have pity on me!

SECOND VOICE: Give me back all the days of my bondage.

THIRD VOICE: Raise my son from the dead, master, from under Cossack whips.

FOURTH VOICE: The boors drink to your health, master; they beg your pardon, master.

CHORUS OF PEASANTS: (*Passing by*) A vampire sucked our blood and sweat. We have the vampire. We will not let the vampire go. By the devil, by the devil, you shall die high up, like a master, like a great master, hoisted up high above all of us. Death to the masters-tyrants. It is for us, the poor, the hungry, the weary, to eat, sleep, and drink. Like sheaves in a field shall their corpses be, like chaff in threshing machines, like the ashes of their castles. By our scythes, hatchets, and sickles, forward, brethren, forward!

THE MAN: I could not discern the face amid the multitude.

CONVERT: Perhaps a friend or relative of yours, sir.

THE MAN: I despise them and I hate you. Poetry will some day gild all of this. Go on, Jew, go on! (*He dashes into bushes.*)

(*Another part of the forest. A hill with fires lit. A gathering of people by torchlight.*)

THE MAN: (*Below, coming out from among trees, with the Convert*) The branches tore my Cap of Liberty to rags. And what hell is this, with its ruddy flames, rising up between these two walls of woods, these two enormities of darkness?

CONVERT: We have gone astray looking for Saint Ignatius' ravine. Back into the bushes, for here Leonard is celebrating the rites of the new faith.

THE MAN: (*Going up the hill*) By God, forward, man! This is just what I wanted. Don't be afraid; no one will recognize us.

CONVERT: Carefully, slowly.

THE MAN: All around lie the ruins of some huge thing which must have stood for centuries before it crumbled – pillars, bases, capitals, quartered statues, scattered ornaments with which ancient vaults were once encircled. Now a broken pane flashed beneath my foot – it seems as though the face of the Blessed Virgin looked out for a moment from the shadows and now it is dark there again. Here, look, lies a whole arcade; here is an iron grating, covered over with rubble. Up above the flash of a torch gleamed. I see half a knight, asleep on half a grave. Where am I, guide?

CONVERT: Our people worked to the point of exhaustion for forty days and nights until at last they had destroyed the last church on these plains. Right now we are passing the cemetery.

THE MAN: Your songs, new people, resound bitterly in my ears. Black forms press in from behind, from in front, from both sides, and the gleams and shadows, driven by the wind, move about through the throng, like living spirits.

A PASSERBY: In the name of Liberty I greet you both!

SECOND PASSERBY: By the death of the masters I greet you both!

THIRD PASSERBY: Why are you not hastening? There the priests of Liberty are singing.

CONVERT: We cannot resist them. They are pressing in on us from all sides.

THE MAN: Who is that young man over there standing on the ruins of the sanctuary? Three campfires are burning beneath him and amid their smoke and glow his face burns, his voice has the sound of madness.

CONVERT: That is Leonard, the inspired prophet of Liberty. All about him stand our priests, philosophers, poets, artists, their daughters, and their mistresses.

THE MAN: Ha! Your aristocracy. Show me him who sent you.

CONVERT: I don't see him here.

LEONARD: Give her to me that I may take her to my lips, to my breast, into my embrace, give me my beautiful one, independent, liberated, stripped of coverings and prejudices, chosen from among the daughters of Liberty, my betrothed.

A GIRL'S VOICE: I rush forth toward you, my beloved.

SECOND VOICE: Look, I stretch out my arms to you – I fall fainting – I roll among the ruins, my beloved.

THIRD VOICE: I have outdistanced them – through ashes and glowing embers, through fire and smoke, I step toward you, my beloved.

THE MAN: With hair loosened, with heaving breast, she climbs the ruins in passionate leaps and bounds.

CONVERT: It happens this way every night.

LEONARD: Come to me, come, oh my delight, daughter of Liberty. You tremble in divine frenzy. Inspiration, possess my soul. Hear me, all of you. Now I will prophesy unto you.

THE MAN: She has bent her head; she is falling into a faint.

LEONARD: We two are an image of the human race, liberated, rising from the dead. Behold, we stand on the ruins of old forms, of the old God. Glory to us, for we have torn asunder His members and now only dust and ashes remain of them. His spirit has been conquered by our spirits; His spirit has descended into nothingness.

CHORUS OF WOMEN: Happy, happy betrothed of the Prophet, we stand here below and envy her glory.

LEONARD: I proclaim a new world. Unto the new God I give the heavens. Lord of freedom and delight, God of the peoples, let each victim of vengeance, the corpse of each oppressor, be Your altar. The old tears and sufferings of the human race shall drown in an ocean of blood. Henceforth its life will be happiness; its law, equality. And he who so dare make other laws will have the noose and cursing for his lot.

CHORUS OF MEN: The edifice of oppression and pride has crumbled. Death and curses to him who raises even a stone of it!

CONVERT: (*Aside*) Blasphemer of Jehovah, three times do I spit to your destruction.

THE MAN: Eagle, keep your promise, and here, upon their necks, I will raise up a new church to Christ.

MINGLED VOICES: Freedom, happiness, hurrah, hey, hallo, hurrah, hurrah!!!

CHOIR OF PRIESTS: Where are the masters, the kings, who lately walked about the earth with scepters and crowns, in pride and wrath?

MURDERER: I killed King Alexander.

SECOND MURDERER: I killed King Henry.

THIRD MURDERER: I killed King Emmanuel.

LEONARD: Go without fear and murder without remorse, for you are the chosen of the chosen, the holy of the holiest, for you are martyrs, heroes of Liberty.

CHORUS OF MURDERERS: Let us go by the dark of night, clenching our daggers in hand, let us go, let us go!

LEONARD: Awaken, my lovely one! (*Thunder is heard.*) Now, answer to the living God. Lift up your songs. Follow me, all of you, all of you! Once more let us go round and trample the temple of the dead God. And you, lift up your head, arise and awaken!

GIRL: I burn with love toward you and toward your God. This love of mine I offer out to the whole world. I flame, I flame.

THE MAN: Someone has run up to him, has fallen on his knees, is wrestling with himself, babbling something, moaning.

CONVERT: I see, I see – that is the son of the famous philosopher.

LEONARD: What is your wish, Herman?

HERMAN: High priest, give me the murderer's consecration!

LEONARD: (*To the priests*) Give me the oil, a dagger, and poison. (*To Herman*) With the oil with which kings were anointed in bygone times, I anoint you today to the ruin of kings. The weapon of former knights and masters I entrust to your hands, to their doom. Upon your breast I hang this medalion full of poison. There, where your iron cannot reach, let it consume and corrode the entrails of tyrants. Go forth and destroy the old generations in all the corners of the earth!

THE MAN: He has left his place and, at the head of a procession, moves over the hill.

CONVERT: Let us get out of the way.

THE MAN: No. I want to see this dream through to the end.

CONVERT: I spit upon you thrice. (*To the Man*) Leonard may recognize me, sir. Look at the knife hanging on his chest.

THE MAN: Cover yourself with my cloak. What women are those dancing before him?

CONVERT: Countesses and princesses who have come over to our faith after abandoning their husbands.

THE MAN: Once my angels. The common people have completely surrounded him; I have lost sight of him in the crowd. Only from the music can I tell that he is moving farther away from us. Follow me. From over there we will be able to see better. (*He climbs on to a fragment of a wall.*)

CONVERT: Oh my heavens, no! Anyone can see us here.

THE MAN: I see him again. Other women are pressing in after him, pale, frenzied, in convulsions. The philosopher's son is foaming at the mouth and shaking his dagger in the air. Now they are coming up to the ruins of the northern tower.

They have stopped. They are dancing on the ruins. They are tearing down the arcades that are still standing. They are scattering sparks on the fallen altars and crosses. The flame takes hold and chases pillars of smoke before it. Woe unto you, woe!

LEONARD: Woe unto those people who still kneel before the dead God.

THE MAN: The black billows are turning round and rushing toward us.

CONVERT: O Abraham!

THE MAN: O eagle, my hour surely is not so near yet.

CONVERT: We are done for.

LEONARD: (*Coming up to them and stopping*) And who may I ask are you, brother, with such a proud face? Why do you not join us?

THE MAN: I have hastened here from afar at the sound of your uprising. I am a murderer from the Spanish club, and have arrived just today.

LEONARD: And the other one who is hiding in the folds of your cloak?

THE MAN: He is my younger brother. He has taken a vow not to show his face to people until he kills at least a baron.

LEONARD: And in whose death do you yourself glory?

THE MAN: Just two days before I set out on the road my elder brothers consecrated me.

LEONARD: Whom do you have in mind?

THE MAN: You, first of all, if you betray us.

LEONARD: Brother, for that purpose take my dagger! (*He draws the dagger from his belt.*)

THE MAN: (*Withdrawing his own dagger*) Brother, for that purpose my own will suffice.

VOICES OF PEOPLE: Long live Leonard! Long live the Spanish murderer!

LEONARD: Tomorrow present yourself at the tent of the citizen commander.

CHORUS OF PRIESTS: We greet you, guest, in the name of the spirit of Liberty. In your hand lies part of our salvation. He who struggles untiringly, murders without giving way to weakness, who day and night believes in the final victory, will triumph at last. (*They move on.*)

CHORUS OF PHILOSOPHERS: We have lifted the human race from its infancy. We have torn truth from the womb of darkness into the light of day. Now it is for you to fight, murder, and perish for it. (*They move on.*)

PHILOSOPHER'S SON: Comrade brother, I drink to your health out of the skull of an old saint. Farewell. (*He throws the skull down.*)

GIRL: (*Dancing.*) Kill Prince John for me!

ANOTHER GIRL: And Count Henry for me!

CHILDREN: Please bring us the head of an aristocrat!

OTHERS: Good fortune to your dagger!

CHORUS OF ARTISTS: On the Gothic ruins of the old temple we are erecting a new one. It has neither pictures nor statues in it. The vaulting is in the form of long poniards. The pillars resemble eight human heads, and the top of each pillar is like hair from which blood drips. The altar alone is white. There is but one symbol on it – the Cap of Liberty. Hurrah!

OTHERS: On, on – the dawn is already breaking!

CONVERT: They will hang us very soon. Where is the gallows?

THE MAN: Quiet, Jew. They are running after Leonard, no longer looking at us. I take in with a glance, for the last time I grasp in thought this chaos emerging from the depths of time, from the womb of darkness, to the ruination of me and all my brethren. Driven by frenzy, borne away by despair, my thoughts whirl madly about in all their might.

God, grant me that power which You did not deny me before and I will encompass this new, immense world in a single word. It does not understand itself. But that one word of mine will be the poetry of the future.

A VOICE IN THE AIR: You are composing a drama.

THE MAN: Thank you for the advice. Revenge for the shamed ashes of my fathers! A curse on the new generation! Their whirlpool encircles me, but I will not be dragged down with it. O eagle, eagle, keep your promise! And now, descend with me into the ravine of Saint Ignatius.

CONVERT: Day is drawing near. I will not go farther.

THE MAN: Find the way for me and then I will let you go.

CONVERT: Where are you dragging me, amid mists and ruins, thorns and ashes? Have mercy on me, I beg you.

THE MAN: Onward, onward, and then down with me! The last songs of the people are fading away behind us; there is scarcely a torch still glowing. Amid these pale vapors, these dewy trees, do you see shadows of the past, do you hear sounds of mourning?

CONVERT: Mist covers everything. We are going farther and farther down.

A CHORUS OF FOREST SPIRITS: Let us weep for the Christ, the exiled, martyred Christ. Where is our God, where is His church?

THE MAN: Faster, faster to arms, to the fight! I will give your God back to you and I will crucify His enemies on a thousand crosses.

CHORUS OF SPIRITS: We have guarded His altars and all the monuments of the saints. We have borne upon our wings the echo of His bells to all the faithful. Our voices were in the music of the organs. Our life was in the gleams of the cathedral panes, in the shadows of its pillars, in the shining of the holy cup, and in the blessing of the Lord's Body. Now whither are we to go?

THE MAN: The morning light is growing brighter. Their forms fade in the rays of the dawning sun.

CONVERT: This is our way. Over there you can see the mouth of the ravine.

THE MAN: Hey! Jesus and my sword! (*Tearing off his cap and folding some money in it*) Take the thing as a keepsake and symbol together.

CONVERT: May I remind you, sir, that you gave me your word for the safety of him who at midnight today...

THE MAN: A member of the old gentry does not give his word twice. Jesus and my sword!

VOICES IN THE BUSHES: Mary and our swords! Long live our master!

THE MAN: All who are true to the faith, come to me! Farewell, citizen! The faithful, to me! Jesus and Mary!

(*Night. Bushes. Trees.*)

PANCRAS: (*To his men*) Lie down with your faces to the grass. Lie quietly. Don't start a single fire, not even to light a pipe, and at the first shot come rushing to my help. If there is no shot, don't move until it's light.

LEONARD: Citizen, once more I conjure you.

PANCRAS: You stand up against that pine tree and meditate.

LEONARD: Take me at least with you. He is a master, an aristocrat, a liar.

PANCRAS: (*Ordering him to remain by a gesture*) The old gentry some-times keeps its word.

(*An oblong room. Pictures of ladies and knights hanging on all the walls. In the background, a column with a coat of arms on it. The Man is sitting at a marble table on which there is a lamp, a pair of pistols, a broadsword, and a watch. Opposite him is another table with silver jugs and goblets.*)

THE MAN: Once long, long ago, at this same time of day, amid threatening dangers and thoughts such as I have now, Caesar's spirit appeared before Brutus as an apparition.

And I, today, await a similar vision. Any moment now there will stand before me a man without a name, without forebears, without a guardian angel, a man who issued forth out of nothingness and who perhaps will begin a new epoch, if I do not repulse him, thrust him back down into the nothingness from which he came.

My fathers, inspire me with that which made you masters of the world. Put all your lionhearts into my breast. Let the glory dignifying your temples flow onto my forehead. Let there enter into me that blind, implacable, seething faith in Christ and His Church which was the inspiration of your deeds on earth – that hope of immortal glory in heaven – and then I shall slay and burn our enemies, I, the son of a hundred generations, the last heir of your thoughts and deeds, of your virtues and failings. (*Midnight strikes.*) Now I am ready. (*He rises.*)

ARMED SERVANT: (*Entering*) My lord, the man who was to come has arrived and awaits you.

THE MAN: Let him come in.

(*The servant goes out.*)

PANCRAS: (*Entering*) My greetings, Count Henry! That word "Count" sounds strange in my throat. (*He sits down, throws off his cloak and Cap of Liberty, and stares intently at the column on which the coat of arms hangs.*)

193

11. The Cracow production of *The Un-Divine Comedy*, Part III.
The confrontation scene – Pancras and Count Henry.
(Photograph: Wojciech Plewiński)

THE MAN: Thank you, that you have seen fit to trust my house. Following the old custom, I drink your health. (*Takes a goblet, drinks from it, and then offers it to Pancras.*) My guest, your turn now!

PANCRAS: If I am not mistaken, those red and blue emblems are called coats of arms in the language of the dead. May there be fewer of such signs on the earth's surface. (*Drinks.*)

THE MAN: With God's help, you shall soon see thousands of them.

PANCRAS: (*Removing the goblet from his lips*) There's the old gentry for you! Always sure of itself, proud, persistent, blossoming with hope – but without a cent to its name, without arms, without soldiers – yet threatening, like the dead man in the fable, the coachman at the cemetery gate – believing or at least pretending to believe in God for it would be hard for it to believe in itself. But show me the thunderbolts sent down in your defense, and the regiments of angels descended from heaven! (*Drinks.*)

THE MAN: Laugh at your own words! Atheism is an old formula. I rather expected something new from you.

PANCRAS: You laugh at your words! My faith is stronger, more immense than yours. The groan torn forth from thousands upon thousands by despair and pain, the hunger of artisans, the misery of peasants, the shame of their wives and daughters, the humiliation of humanity yoked by superstition and indecision and the blind habits of the herd – that is my faith, my God for today, my thought, my power which will distribute bread and glory to them forever and ever. (*Drinks and throws down the goblet.*)

THE MAN: I have placed my strength in the God who gave my fathers rule.

PANCRAS: And your whole life you have been the devil's plaything. Anyway, I leave this discussion to theologians, if any pedant of that profession still lives in these parts. Let's get down to business instead!

THE MAN: What more do you want of me, O savior of nations, O citizen-god?

PANCRAS: I came here because I wanted to meet you, and then, to save you.

THE MAN: I am indeed grateful to you for the first; for the second, trust my sword.

PANCRAS: Your sword is glass; your God, a phantom. You are damned by the voices of thousands; you are encircled by the arms of thousands. All you have left you are a few acres of land which hardly will suffice for your graves. You cannot last a full twenty days. Where are your cannon, your equipment, your supplies – and finally, where is your courage? In your place, I know what I would do.

THE MAN: I am listening. You see how patient I am.

PANCRAS: Then I, Count Henry, would say to Pancras: "All right, I dissolve my troop, my one and only troop. I shall not go to the relief of Holy Trinity Castle, and in return I shall keep my name and my possessions, the integrity of which you guarantee me by your word."

How old are you, Count?

THE MAN: Thirty-six, citizen.

PANCRAS: Another fifteen years, at the most, for such people don't live long. Your son is nearer the grave than youth. One exception will do the masses no harm. Be then the last count on these plains. Reign till your death in the home of your forebears. Have their portraits painted and their heraldic arms carved. But about these wretches think no more. Let the sentence of the people be carried out upon the villains. (*Pours himself another goblet.*) Your health, last count!

THE MAN: You insult me with every word. You seem to be trying to make me your slave on the day of your triumph. Desist, for I am unable to repay you in kind. The providence of my word protects you.

PANCRAS: Holy honor, chivalric honor has come upon the scene. That is a faded rag in the standard of humanity. Oh, I do know you, I see right through you. You are full of life, but you join the dying in order to deceive yourself, in order to go on believing in castes, in your great-grandmother's bones, in the word "fatherland", and so forth. But deep in your soul you know yourself that your brethren deserve to be punished, and, after that, forgotten.

THE MAN: And you and yours deserve otherwise?

PANCRAS: Yes, victory and life. I recognize only one law and before it bow my head. According to this law, the word revolves in ever wider circles. This law is your destruction and it cries now through my lips:

"O you doddering, you worm-eaten, you full of food and drink, make way for the young, the hungry, and the strong!"

But I would save you, just you alone.

THE MAN: May you perish miserably for that pity of yours! I, too, know your world and you. I looked, amid the shadows of night, on the dancing of the rabble, upon whose necks you ascended. I saw all the old crimes of the world, garbed in new robes, whirling in a new dance. But their end will be the same as it was thousands of years ago – depravity, gold, and blood. But you were not there. You did not deign to step down among your children, for in the depths of your soul you despise them. A few moments yet and if your reason doesn't desert you, you will despise yourself as well. Torment me no more! (*Sits down beneath his coat of arms.*)

PANCRAS: My world has not yet deployed itself in the field – I agree; it has not yet grown into a giant. Till now it craves bread and comfort, but the time is coming... (*He gets up, walks toward the Man, and leans against the pillar with the coat of arms.*) But the time is coming when it will understand itself and will say of itself, "I am!", and there will be no other voice on earth which will also be able to respond, "I am".

THE MAN: What else?

PANCRAS: Of this generation, which I nurse with all the strength of my will, there will come a race which will be the last, the highest, and the bravest. The earth has not yet beheld such men. They are free people, her masters from pole to pole. And she herself is one flourishing city, one happy home, one workshop of wealth and industry.

THE MAN: Your words lie, but your pale, immovable face cannot feign inspiration.

PANCRAS: Don't interrupt, for there are people who have begged me for such words on their knees and I stinted them.

There rests the God who will never die, the God from whom the veil has been torn by the labor and torment of ages, the God conquered in heaven by His own children whom He once cast down on earth but who now have penetrated to the truth and grasp it. The God of humanity has appeared to them.

THE MAN: And to us centuries ago. Humanity has already been saved by Him.

PANCRAS: May it enjoy such salvation – two thousand years of misery, proceeding from His death on the cross.

THE MAN: I saw that cross, blasphemer, in old, old Rome. At His feet lay the ruins of powers mightier than yours. A hundred gods like yours were wallowing in the dust and dared not raise their mutilated heads toward Him. And He stood on the heights, extending His holy arms to the east and to the west, bathing His holy brow in the rays of the sun – and it was plain that He was Lord of the world.

PANCRAS: An old tale, empty as the jangle of your coat of arms. (*He strikes the shield.*)

But I read your thoughts long ago. If you can reach infinity, if you love the truth and have sought it sincerely, if you are a man made in the image of man and not in the likeness of nurses' ditties, listen and do not reject this moment of salvation. Of the blood we both will shed today there will not be a trace tomorrow. For the last time I am telling you, if you are what you once seemed to be, arise, forsake your house, and follow me!

THE MAN: You are Satan's younger brother. (*Gets up and walks about.*) Vain dreams – who shall fulfill them? Adam perished in the wilderness; we shall not return to paradise.

PANCRAS: (*Aside*) I have bent my finger beneath his heart. I have touched the nerve of poetry.

THE MAN: Progress, the happiness of the human race – I once believed in them. There you are, take my head just so long as... It's done. A hundred years ago, two centuries ago, we might have reached an amicable accord... but now I know, now there has to be a mutual slaughter for at issue is a very change of race.

PANCRAS: Woe to the vanquished! Do not hesitate! Repeat "woe" only once and conquer with us!

THE MAN: Have you trod all the byways of Destiny? Did Destiny, in visible form, ever stand at the entrance to your tent at night and bless you with a gigantic hand? Or did you ever hear its voice at noontime when all slept in the heat and you alone were deep in thought? That you menace me thus with sure victory, O man of clay, as I am, slave to the first chance shell, the first chance saber slash!

PANCRAS: Don't delude yourself with vain hope for lead will not scratch me nor will iron touch me so long as one of you resists my work. And whatever happens later is no concern of yours.

(*A clock strikes.*)

Time mocks us both. If you are tired of life, at least save your son.

THE MAN: His soul is pure, already saved in heaven, while on earth his father's fate awaits him. (*Bows his head between his hands and stands still.*)

PANCRAS: You refuse then?

(*A moment of silence.*)

You remain silent. You ponder. Good! Let him meditate who stands above a grave.

THE MAN: Stay clear of the mysteries which, beyond the bounds of your thought, are taking place now within the depths of my soul! The world of flesh belongs to you – fatten it with food, pour blood and wine over it, but go no further – and away, away from me!

PANCRAS: O servant of one thought and of its forms, O pedant knight, poet, shame on you! Behold me – thoughts and forms are like wax under my fingers!

THE MAN: It is all in vain. You will never understand me, for each one of your fathers shares a common grave with the rabble, like a dead thing, not like a man with strength and spirit. (*Stretches out his hand toward the pictures.*)

Look at those figures: the thought of their country, of their home, of their family; that thought, your foe, is inscribed in wrinkles on their brows, and what was once in them and has since passed on lives in me today. But you, tell me – where is your land? In the evening you pitch your tent on the ruins of another's home, and at dawn you strike your tent and camp farther on. Till now you have not found your own abode and you will not find it so long as a hundred men say after me, "Glory unto our fathers!"

PANCRAS: Yes, glory to your ancestors on earth and in heaven. In truth, they are something to behold.

That one, a high district official, used to shoot at old women from trees and roast Jews alive.* The one with the seal in his hand, who used to sign himself "chancellor", falsified documents, burned records, bribed judges, and hastened legacies with poison. That's where your estates, income, and power come from. The black-haired one over there, with the fiery gaze, committed adultery in his friends' homes. The one with the Order of the Golden Fleece, in the Italian coat of mail, entered, plainly, the service of foreigners. And the pale lady there, with the dark ringlets, sullied herself with her own pageboy. The one over there reads her lover's letters and smiles, for night is approaching. The other one, with the lapdog on her hoopskirt, was the mistress of kings. There is your lineage, unbroken, unstained. I like the fellow in the green jacket. He drank and hunted with his fellow squires, and sent the peasants to chase the deer with dogs. The stupidity and misfortune of the whole country – that is your sense and your power. But the Day of Judgment is close at hand and when it comes I promise you that I shall forget none of you, none of your forefathers and none of your glory.

THE MAN: You are wrong, you burgher's son you! Neither you nor any one of yours would be alive had not the kindness and the might of my fathers fed you and protected you. In times of famine they distributed wheat among you and in times of plague they built you hospitals. And when you grew from a pack of beasts to babes, they put up churches and schools for you. When war came, they left you at home knowing that you were not for the field of battle.

Your words break against their glory, as did the arrows of the heathen on their holy armor-plates long ago. They do not even stir their ashes. They vanish like the yelping of a mad dog that runs and foams till it dies somewhere by the wayside. And now, it is time for you to leave my house. My guest, I permit you to pass freely!

PANCRAS: Farewell, until the trenches of the Holy Trinity. And when you begin running out of powder and shells...

---

*An allusion to an actual landowner in the Ukraine named Mikołaj Bazyli Potocki, who was notorious for his cruel "amusements". – Ed.

THE MAN: Then we shall approach each other at our sabers' length! Farewell!

PANCRAS: Two eagles are we – but your nest is shattered by a thunderbolt. (*Takes his cloak and Cap of Liberty.*)

Passing over this threshold I cast a curse upon it appropriate to old age. Both you and your son I devote to destruction.

THE MAN: James, here please! (*James comes in.*) Conduct this man as far as my last outposts on the hill.

JAMES: So help me God! (*Goes out.*)

[End of Part III]

PART IV

From the bastions of the Holy Trinity to the peaks of all the rocks, on the right and on the left, in back and in front lies snowy mist, pale, motionless, silent, a phantom ocean which once had its shores, where those black peaks now stand, sharp and ragged, and its depths, where there are an unseen valley and a sun which has not yet broken through the mist.

On a bare, granite island stand the towers of a castle, set deep into the rock by the toil of bygone men and grown together with the rock like the human breast and spine of a centaur. Above the towers, on the highest point, rises a standard, alone amid the gray skies.

Slowly the slumbering distances begin to awake. On the heights, the roaring of the winds is heard. Below, the rays of the sun break their flight, and an ice floe of clouds rushes across that sea of vapors.

Then, other voices, human voices, mingle with the transient storm and borne on its misty billows beat against the base of the castle.

A precipice becomes visible amid the plains from whose cleavage it issued forth. Its depths are black with human heads. The whole valley is covered with men's heads, as the deep of the sea with rocks.

The sun makes its way downward from the hills to the rocks. The clouds rise up in gold and melt, and as they disappear the tumult becomes ever more audible and the crowds moving below more easily seen.

The mists have lifted from the mountains and now they die in the nothingness of the azure. The valley of the Holy Trinity is flooded with the light of gleaming armaments and the people move toward it from all sides, as to the plain of the Last Judgment.

The Cathedral in Holy Trinity Castle

(Lords, senators, and dignitaries are sitting on both sides, each below the statue of some king or knight. Behind the statues there is a crowd of gentry. Before the high altar, in the background, is the Archbishop, in a gilt chair, with a sword resting on his knees. A choir of priests stands behind the altar. The Man stands for a moment on the threshold and then begins to walk slowly in the direction of the Archbishop with a standard in his hand.)

CHOIR OF PRIESTS: Your last servants, in Your Son's last church, implore You for the honor of our fathers – Save us, O Lord, from our enemies!

FIRST COUNT: See how proudly he looks upon all.

SECOND COUNT: He thinks he has conquered the world.

THIRD COUNT: And all he did was force his way through a camp of peasants at night.

FIRST COUNT: He felled a hundred, and lost two hundred of his own men.

SECOND COUNT: We will not allow him to be chosen leader.

THE MAN: (*Kneeling before the Archbishop*) I lay my booty at your feet.

ARCHBISHOP: Gird on this sword, once blessed by the hand of Saint Florian.

VOICES: Long live Count Henry!

ARCHBISHOP: And receive, with the sign of the Holy Cross, leadership in this castle, our last state. By the will of all I name you leader.

VOICES: Long may he live, long may he live!

ONE VOICE: I forbid it.

OTHER VOICES: Out with him, out, show him the door! Long live Count Henry!

THE MAN: If anyone has something to reproach me with, come forward, let him not hide himself amid the crowd.

(*A moment of silence.*)

Father, I accept this sword and may God grant me an early death, before my time, if I fail to save you with it.

CHOIR OF PRIESTS: Give him strength, give him the Holy Spirit, Lord! Save us, O Lord, from the enemy!

THE MAN: Now all of you swear that you will defend the faith and honor of your ancestors, that hunger and thirst may bring you to death but never to shame or surrender or the secession from even one of God's rights or your own.

VOICES: We swear!

(*The Archbishop kneels and raises up the cross. All kneel.*)

CHOIR: May he who breaks the oath be encumbered with Your anger! May the timid be encumbered with Your anger! May the traitor be encumbered with Your anger!

VOICES: We swear!

THE MAN: (*Drawing his sword*) Now I promise you glory. Beseech God for victory! (*Goes out, surrounded by the crowd.*)

(*One of the courtyards of Holy Trinity Castle. The Man. Counts. Barons. Princes. Priests. Gentry.*)

A COUNT: (*Leading the Man aside.*) How goes it? Is all lost?

THE MAN: Not all, unless your hearts fail you before the time.

COUNT: Before what time?

THE MAN: Before death.

A BARON: (*Leading the Man aside in another direction*) Count, it seems you met that awful man. Do you expect that he'll have even a little pity on us when we fall into his hands?

THE MAN: I tell you in all truth that none of your fathers ever heard of such pity – it's called the gallows.

BARON: Then we must defend ourselves as best we can.

THE MAN: What do you say, Prince?

PRINCE: A few words with you in private. (*Moves away with him.*) This is all well and good for the common herd, but between us, it's clear we can't hold out.

THE MAN: What remains then?

PRINCE: You were chosen leader; it's up to you, therefore, to begin negotiations.

THE MAN: Shhh! Quieter!

PRINCE: What for?

THE MAN: Because, Your Grace, you have already earned your death. (*Turns around to the crowd.*) Whosoever speaks of surrender shall be punished with death.

BARON, COUNT, PRINCE: (*Together*) Whosoever speaks of surrender shall be punished with death.

ALL: With death! With death! Hurrah! (*They go out.*)

(*A balcony on the summit of a tower. The Man. James.*)

THE MAN: Where is my son?

JAMES: He is sitting in the northern tower on the threshold of the old prison and is singing prophecies.

THE MAN: Man the Eleanor bastion as strongly as possible! Don't move from there and every few minutes observe the rebels' camp through a telescope.

JAMES: It would be worthwhile, as God be with me, for encouragement, to give the men a glass of brandy each.

THE MAN: If necessary, order even the cellars of all our counts and princes to be opened.

(*James goes out. The Man goes up a few steps, toward the standard itself, on a flat terrace.*)

With all the sight of my eyes, with all the hatred of my heart do I encircle you, my enemies! Now shall I fight you no longer with my poor voice of vapid inspiration, but with iron and with men who have sworn loyalty to me.

How good it is to be a master, a ruler – to look, even from a deathbed if need be, upon the wills of others gathered round me, and upon you, my adversaries, plunged in the abyss, crying out to me from its depths as the damned call out to heaven.

A few days more and perhaps I and all these wretches who have forgotten their great fathers will be no longer. But be that as it may, a few days still remain. I shall enjoy their pleasures to the full, I shall rule, I shall fight, I shall live. That is my final song!

The sun is rising above the cliffs in a long, black coffin of vapor. Blood pours out in rays upon the valley. Prophetic omens of my death, I greet you with a more sincere and open heart than e'er I greeted the promises of gaiety, illusion, and love!

For not by mean labor, nor by stratagem, nor by cunning have I reached the end of my desires. But suddenly, by surprise, in a way I had always dreamed.

And now here I stand on the frontier of eternal sleep, the leader of all those who only yesterday were my equals!

(*A room in the castle illuminated by torches. George is seated on a bed. The Man enters and places his weapons on a table.*)

THE MAN: Leave a hundred men on the redoubts – Let the others rest after such a long battle.
VOICE FROM OUTSIDE THE DOOR: So help me God!
THE MAN: You surely heard the shots and echoes of our sally, but don't be upset, my child, we shall not fall – either today or tomorrow.
GEORGE: I heard, but that did not touch my heart. The rumble passed and is no more. But there is something else that makes me tremble, father.
THE MAN: You feared for me.
GEORGE: No, for I know that your hour has not yet come.
THE MAN: We are alone. A heavy weight has fallen from my soul today, for there in the valley lie the bodies of conquered enemies. Tell me all your thoughts. I shall listen to them as once at home.
GEORGE: Come with me, father, come with me... (*Goes toward a door hidden in the wall and opens it.*) Behind this door a dreadful judgment is repeated every night.

THE MAN: Where are you going? Who showed you that passageway? There are eternally dark dungeons there and the rotting bones of former victims.

GEORGE: Where your eye, used to the sun, sees not – there my spirit can go. The darkness, descend to the darkness! (*Goes down.*)

(*Underground dungeons. Iron bars, chains, and instruments of torture, lying on the ground, broken. The Man with a torch in his hand at the base of the rock on which George is standing.*)

THE MAN: Come down, I beg you, come down to me.

GEORGE: Don't you hear their voices, don't you see their forms?

THE MAN: The silence of the graves – and the torch lights up only a few steps in front of us.

GEORGE: Nearer and nearer, clearer and clearer – they come from under the low vaulting, one after the other, and seat themselves there in the depths.

THE MAN: In your madness is my damnation. You are mad, my child, and you destroy my strength when I need it so much.

GEORGE: I see with my spirit their pale, stern forms, gathering together for that terrible judgment. The accused is approaching now, floating like mist.

CHORUS OF VOICES: With the strength given us in return for our torments, we, who once were chained, flogged, tortured, torn with iron, given poison for drink, stoned with bricks and gravel, let us torment and judge, judge and condemn, and Satan will undertake the punishment.

THE MAN: What do you see?

GEORGE: The accused – the accused – there, he has wrung his hands.

THE MAN: Who is he?

GEORGE: Father! Father!

ONE VOICE: With you ends the accursed race. In you, the last, it has gathered all its strength and all its passions and all its pride – in order to perish.

CHOIR OF VOICES: Because you have loved nothing, honored nothing save yourself, save yourself and your own thoughts, you are damned, damned for all eternity.

THE MAN: I cannot see a thing, but I hear from under the ground, from above the ground, and on both sides, sighs and lamentations, judgments and threats.

GEORGE: Now he has raised his head, like you, father, when you are angry, and he has answered with a proud word, like you, father, when you scorn.

205

CHOIR OF VOICES: In vain! In vain! There is no hope for him either on earth or in heaven.

ONE VOICE: A few more days of earthly, transient fame, of which your forefathers deprived me and my brethren, and then you and your brethren shall perish and your grave shall be without the tolling of mourning bells, without the sobbing of friend and kin, as ours was once on this same rock of pain.

THE MAN: I know you, miserable spirits, vain will-o'-the-wisps, flitting amid angelic majesties. (*He takes a few steps forward.*)

GEORGE: Father, don't go in any deeper – by Christ's holy name I entreat you, father!

THE MAN: (*Returning*) Tell me, tell me, whom do you see?

GEORGE: There is a figure.

THE MAN: Whose?

GEORGE: That second one is you – you are all pale – fettered – now they torment you – I hear your groans. (*He falls on his knees.*) Forgive me, father. Mother came during the night and ordered me ... (*He faints.*)

THE MAN: (*Taking him up in his arms*) Only this was lacking! Ha! My own child has led me to the threshold of hell! Mary! Inexorable spirit! O God, and you, the other Mary, to whom I have prayed so much!

There begins an infinity of torment and darkness. Back! I must still fight with men. Afterward – the eternal struggle! (*Runs out with his son.*)

CHOIR OF VOICES: (*In the distance*) Because you have loved nothing, honored nothing save yourself, save yourself and your own thoughts, you are damned, damned for all eternity!

(*A hall in Holy Trinity Castle. The Man. Women, children, several old men, and counts, all lying at the Man's feet. The Godfather stands in the center of the hall. There is a crowd in the background. Walls hung with weapons, Gothic pillars, ornaments, and windows.*)

THE MAN: No, by my son, by my dead wife, no, once more I say, no!

WOMEN'S VOICES: Have pity! Hunger burns our insides and our children's. Fear devours us day and night.

MEN'S VOICES: There is still time. Hear the envoy. Don't send the envoy away!

THE GODFATHER: My whole life has been that of an exemplary citizen and I do not deserve your reproaches, Henry. If I assumed the office of envoy, which I hold presently, that is because I know the age in which we live and can estimate its true significance. Pancras is a representative citizen, if I may say so ...

THE MAN: Out of my sight, old man! (*Aside, to James.*) Lead in a troop of our men.

(*James goes out. The women stand up and weep. The men move back a few steps.*)

A BARON: You have doomed us, Count.

ANOTHER BARON: We refuse you obedience.

A PRINCE: We ourselves will arrange with this worthy citizen the conditions for the surrender of the castle.

THE GODFATHER: The great man, who sent me here, promises you life just as long as you agree to join him and recognize the trend of the age.

A FEW VOICES: We recognize it – we recognize it.

THE MAN: When you called upon me, I swore to perish within these walls. I shall keep my word and all of you shall perish along with me.

Ha! You still want to live!

Ha! Ask your fathers why they oppressed and reigned!

(*To a count*) And you – why did you oppress those under you?

(*To another*) And you – why did you fritter away your youth on cards and travels far from your own country?

(*To another*) And you corrupted those of higher station and despised those of lower.

(*To one of the women*) Why did you not raise your children to be your defenders, to be knights? Now they would have served you well. But you loved Jews, lawyers – ask them now for your life.

(*He stands with outstretched arms.*) Why do you so hasten to shame? What entices you so to debase your last moments? Rather forward with me, forward, gentlemen, where there are bullets and bayonets – not there where wait the gallows and the silent executioner, with rope for your necks in his hands.

A FEW VOICES: He speaks well. Fix bayonets!

OTHER VOICES: Not even a crumb of bread remains.

WOMEN'S VOICES: Our children, your children!

MANY VOICES: We must surrender. Let us seek terms, terms!

THE GODFATHER: I promise you the wholeness, if I may say so, the inviolability of your persons and of your bodies.

THE MAN: (*Approaching the Godfather and seizing him by the chest*) O sacred personage of an envoy, go hide your gray head beneath the tents of baptized Jews and shoemakers, lest I stain it with your own blood.

(*A troop of armed men enters with James.*)

Aim at that brow, furrowed with the wrinkles of vain learning – aim at that Cap of Liberty, trembling at the breath of my words, on that brainless head!

(*The Godfather slips away.*)

ALL: (*Together*) Bind him! Turn him over to Pancras!
THE MAN: One moment, gentlemen! (*He walks from one soldier to another.*)

With you, as I recall, I climbed the mountains in pursuit of wild game – you remember – I saved you from falling into a precipice.

(*To others*) With you I was shipwrecked on the rocks of the Danube – Jeremy – Christopher – you were with me on the Black Sea.

(*To others*) Remember, how I rebuilt your cottages after they burnt down?

(*To others*) And you escaped to me from a bad master. Now tell me – will you follow me or will you leave me alone, with a smile on my lips, because among so many people I have not found a single man?
ALL: Long live Count Henry! Long may he live!
THE MAN: Distribute among them whatever meat and drink remain, and then – to the ramparts!
ALL THE SOLDIERS: Brandy – meat – and then to the ramparts!
THE MAN: (*To James*) Go with them, and in an hour be ready to fight.
JAMES: So help me God!
WOMEN'S VOICES: We curse you for our innocent children's sake!
OTHER VOICES: And we, for our fathers'.
OTHER VOICES: And we, for our wives'.
THE MAN: And I, for your miserableness! (*He goes out.*)

(*The trenches of Holy Trinity Castle. Corpses all around. Smashed, upturned cannon. Weapons lying on the ground. Soldiers here and there. The Man, leaning on an entrenchment. James by his side.*)

THE MAN: (*Returning his saber to its sheath*) No delight compares to playing with danger and always winning – and when it comes time to lose, it's only once.
JAMES: Sprinkled by our last rounds they have retreated, but down below there they are regrouping and will soon renew the siege. We have no chance – since the world began no one has escaped the fate destined for him.
THE MAN: Are we already out of ammunition?

JAMES: There are neither bullets, shells, nor buckshot. Eventually you reach the bottom of everything.

THE MAN: Bring me my son, then, that I may embrace him once again.

(*James leaves.*)

The smoke of battle has dimmed my eyes. It seems to me as though the valley had become swollen and then shrank back. In a hundred corners the rocks break and intersect one another. My thoughts, too, follow a strange path. (*Sits down on the wall.*)

It's not worth it to be a man. Or an angel. After a few ages, the first archangel, as we did after a few years, felt weariness in his heart, and longed for greater strength. One must be God or nothing.

(*James comes in with George.*)

Take a few of our men, go around the castle halls, and drive all you meet to the ramparts.

JAMES: Bankers and counts and princes! (*Goes out.*)

THE MAN: Come, son, put your hand in mine. Touch your brow to my lips. Your mother's brow was once as white and soft as yours.

GEORGE: I heard her voice today before your men leaped to their arms. Her words flowed as lightly as a fragrance, and she said: "This evening you will sit beside me."

THE MAN: Did she at least mention my name?

GEORGE: She said: "This evening I await my son."

THE MAN: (*Aside*) Will my strength fail at the end of the road? God, keep me from that! For one moment's courage I am your prisoner for all eternity. (*Aloud*) O son, forgive me for giving you life. We are parting. Do you know for how long?

GEORGE: Take me and don't let me go. Don't let me go. I'll draw you after me.

THE MAN: Our paths are different. You will forget me among angelic choirs. You will never cast a single drop of dew on me from above. O George, George, my son!

GEORGE: What are those shouts? I'm trembling all over! More and more menacing – and nearer – the roar of cannon and musket resounds – the final, foretold hour approaches us.

THE MAN: Hurry, James, hurry!

(*A procession of counts and princes passes through the lower courtyard. James and some soldiers follow them.*)

A VOICE: You gave us broken bits of weapons and now you order us to fight!

SECOND VOICE: Henry, have mercy!

THIRD VOICE: Do not drive us, weak and famished, to the walls!

OTHER VOICES: Where are they driving us, where?

THE MAN: (*To them*) To death! (*To his son*) With this embrace I would unite with you for all eternity, but I must go in another direction.

(*George falls, struck by a bullet.*)

A VOICE ON HIGH: To me, to me, pure spirit! To me, my son!

THE MAN: Hey, to me, my men! (*Withdraws his saber and places it on the lips of the fallen boy.*)

   The blade is as clear as before. Breath and life have fled together.

   Hey! Here – forward! They've now penetrated within my saber's length. Back, to the precipice, sons of freedom!

(*Confusion and fighting.*)

(*Another part of the trenches. The echoes of the battle can be heard. James lies stretched out along the wall. The Man runs in, blood all over him.*)

THE MAN: What troubles you, my faithful old servant?

JAMES: May the devil pay you back in hell for your stubborness and my torments. So help me God! (*Dies.*)

THE MAN: (*Casting away his cloak*) I need you no longer. My best men have persished and those kneeling over there are stretching out their arms to the victors and bellowing for mercy! (*He looks all around him.*)

   They are not coming up this side yet. There is still time. Let us rest a while. Ha, now they have battered their way up the northern tower. New troops have plunged into the tower and they are looking to see if Count Henry is hidden somewhere there. I am here, here – but you shall not judge me! I have already started on my way. I am going toward the judgment of God. (*He mounts a fragment of a bastion overhanging the very precipice.*)

   I see it, all black, with dark expanses, flowing toward me, my eternity, without shores, without islands, without end, and in its midst is God, like an eternally burning sun – ever shining – and illuminating nothing. (*Advances a step farther.*)

   They run, they've seen me! Jesus, Mary! O poetry, be you as cursed as I am for all the ages! Arms of mine, go before and cut me a path through those ramparts! (*He leaps into the precipice.*)

(The castle courtyard. Pancras, Leonard, Bianchetti at the head of a throng. Before them pass the counts and princes with their wives and children, all in chains.)

PANCRAS: Your name?

A COUNT: Christopher of Volsagun.

PANCRAS: You have pronounced it for the last time. And yours?

A PRINCE: Ladislas, master of Blackwood.

PANCRAS: You have pronounced it for the last time. And yours?

A BARON: Alexander of Godalberg.

PANCRAS: Struck out from among the living! On your way!

BIANCHETTI: *(To Leonard)* Two months they stood us off, with one miserable line of guns and worthless parapets.

LEONARD: Are there many of them still?

PANCRAS: I am handing them all over to you. Let their blood flow as an example for the whole world. But whoever tells me where Henry is will be spared.

VARIOUS VOICES: He disappeared at the very end.

THE GODFATHER: I stand now as a mediator between you and your captives – those citizens of noble race who have placed the keys of Holy Trinity Castle in your hands, O great man.

PANCRAS: I recognize no mediators where I have conquered with my own strength. You yourself shall see to their execution.

THE GODFATHER: My whole life has been that of an exemplary citizen, of which there are many proofs, and if I joined you it was not to do away with my own kith and kin...

PANCRAS: Take the old doctrinaire away! Put him on the same road with the rest of them!

(Soldiers surround the Godfather and the other prisoners.)

Where is Henry! Didn't any one of you see him, alive or dead? A sack full of gold for Henry! Even for his corpse!

(A troop of armed men descendsfrom the ramparts.)

And did you see Henry!

THE LEADER OF THE TROOP: Citizen commander, in accordance with General Bianchetti's order, I proceeded to the western side of the ramparts, at the very beginning of our entry into the fortress. On the third corner of the bastion I saw a man wounded and unarmed standing beside a body. I ordered my men to double their steps in order to seize him, but before we caught up with him he stepped down a bit lower, stood on a swaying stone, and looked around him with a mad gaze. Then he stretched out his arms like a swimmer about to dive and thrust himself forward with all his might. We all heard the echo of his body falling along the rocks. Here is the saber which was found a few steps beyond.

PANCRAS: (*Taking the saber*) Traces of blood on the hilt. Below them the coat of arms of his house. This is Count Henry's sword. He alone of you has kept his word. For that, praise to him, and to you – the guillotine! General Bianchetti, look after the razing of the stronghold and the carrying out of my sentence.

Leonard! (*He mounts the bastion accompanied by Leonard.*)

LEONARD: After so many sleepless nights you should rest, master. The fatigue is written on your face.

PANCRAS: It is not yet time for me to sleep, my child, for only half the work is done when they breathe their last. Behold those vast expanses, those immensities that lie crosswise between me and my thought. This wasteland must be peopled – these rocks must be leveled – these lakes united – the land dealt out to each so that twice as much life should be born on these plains as the death that lies on them now. Otherwise, the work of destruction will not be redeemed.

LEONARD: The God of Liberty will give us strength.

PANCRAS: What are you saying about God? It is slippery here from the blood of men. Whose blood is this? Behind us are the castle courtyards – we are alone, yet it seems to me as though some third person were here.

LEONARD: Perhaps that body pierced through.

PANCRAS: The body of his loyal friend – a dead body – but here some spirit rules. And that cap, the same arms on it! Farther on, look, the stone projecting above the precipice. On that spot his heart burst.

LEONARD: You grow pale, master.

PANCRAS: Do you see there, high up, high up?

LEONARD: Above the sharp summit I see an oblique cloud on which the rays of the setting sun expire.

PANCRAS: A terrible sign is burning on it.

LEONARD: Your eyes must deceive you.

PANCRAS: A million of the people obeyed me but a moment ago. Where are my people now?

LEONARD: You hear their shouts. They are calling you, they are waiting for you.

PANCRAS: Women and children babbled that this is how He must appear, but only on the Last Day.

12. The Cracow production of *The Un-Divine Comedy*, Part IV. Final
scene: the death of Pancras. (Photograph: Wojciech Plewiński)

LEONARD: Who?

PANCRAS: Like a column of snowy brightness He stands above the precipices, both hands on the cross, like an avenger on his sword. His crown of thorns is woven of thunderbolts.

LEONARD: What is the matter with you? What is it?

PANCRAS: Surely every man alive must die from the lightning of His gaze.

LEONARD: Your face is becoming paler and paler. Let us go away from here. Come! Do you hear me?

PANCRAS: Put your hands over my eyes. Crush my eyeballs with your fists. Separate me from His look, which turns me into dust.

LEONARD: (*Covering Pancras' eyes with his hands*) Is this all right?

PANCRAS: How wretched your hands – like the hands of a ghost without bones or flesh – transparent like water – transparent like glass – transparent like the air. I still see!

LEONARD: Lean on me.

PANCRAS: Give me at least a particle of darkness!

LEONARD: O my master!

PANCRAS: Darkness, darkness!

LEONARD: Citizens! Brethren! Democrats! Help! To the rescue! Help! Help!

PANCRAS: *Galilaee, vicisti!** (*He staggers into Leonard's arms and dies.*)

[THE END]

---

*Words attributed to the dying Roman emperor Julian the Apostate (ruled 361–363 A.D.), an enemy of Christianity. – Ed.

Fantazy

by Juliusz Słowacki

Translated by
Harold B. Segel

DRAMATIS PERSONAE

COUNT RESPEKT, a former district marshal
COUNTESS RESPEKT, his wife
DIANA ⎫
STELLA ⎭ their daughters
COUNT FANTAZY DAFNICKI
RZECZNICKI, a district marshal, his companion
COUNTESS IDALIA
VLADIMIR GAVRILOVICH, a Russian major
JAN, a former insurrectionist, exiled to Siberia and the Caucasus
FATHER LOGA
KAYETAN, a servant of the Respekts
HELENKA, Idalia's chambermaid
Idalia's lackey
A Kalmyk,* the Major's servant

The action takes place in Podolia, a region in the western Ukraine, around the year 1841; the first three acts are set in the home of Count and Countess Respekt, the last two on the estate of Countess Idalia.

---

*A member of a Buddhist Mongol tribe, found mostly around the Caspian Sea, absorbed by the Russian empire in the eighteenth century. – Ed.

ACT I

Scene i

(The drawing room of Count Respekt. Fantazy and Rzecznicki. Later, Count Respekt.)

FANTAZY: Did you see, my dear fellow, the Apollos, Hamadryads, and
  Laocoons standing in the anteroom in the holiest garb of Adam
  the father...in perfect harmony with the servants? And the servants
  themselves more like statues...all of them so much larger than nature
  intended. Why, they almost reach the ceiling...their gigantic forms
  remind me of the limbs of Hercules. I imagine that the young
  ladies here we'll find to be veritable Dryads or Amazons, superhuman. I
  shall be blind, therefore, or dumb. But you're sensible... You do the
  looking for me and let me know what you find human beneath the
  divinity of form. Get to the bottom of it. Make the father bare his political
  conscience and establish the closest relations with her ladyship, until she
  confesses under what yoke she intends driving her son-in-law. To put it
  simply, conduct yourself just as if you were handling some financial
  matter; talk, act, and keep your eyes open, while I pretend to be a
  child...and let everyone lead me around by the nose.
RZECZNICKI: But they know you.
FANTAZY: How? Because of a few letters which could have been
  composed in a fever, transcribed even by hired copyists, on behalf of
  someone who doesn't know how to write himself; because of a few
  letters which some educated young ladies in Podolia read, swooning
  and shouting: oh, this letter was written on the Capitoline Hill in
  Rome, or this one flew from Mount Vesuvius like a pigeon after a
  swallow of water. Because they exclaimed ecstatically: oh, what a soul!
  Oh, what long, splendid sentences! They shouted things like that
  hundreds of times here. Don't I, Count Fantazius, have a right to be
  stupid then? And besides, what does a woman's opinion matter
  anyway? Is it anything worthy of respect? Is it any nourishment on
  which the heart can grow fat? A pillow on which the head can repose?
  My dear Rzecznicki, you're my bridesman, my...more like my brides-
  maid, because I'm blushing like a country damsel at a lord's banquet.
  Praise me for all you're worth, raise me to the azure heavens above the
  Vesuviuses, above the Alps, above the clouds. Say that I wrote a long
  poetic work, a melancholic one about the four seasons; gild me like the
  horns of a ram about to be sacrificed to the gods, and let me gape a
  little and cast off from myself the Byronic veneer of a satan.

RZECZNICKI: Fantazy! You're liable to make a mess of things here and come out badly.

FANTAZY: What do you mean?

RZECZNICKI: It's hard to erase the bad first impression.

FANTAZY: Don't worry. Don't give it a thought. If I fall in love, I'll change. If not, Count Respekt...

Scene ii

(*Count Respekt enters.*)

RESPEKT: What's this? Alone? Nobody here to greet you? Alone? I apologize for my womenfolk. At least...

RZECZNICKI: (*Aside to Fantazy*) Stop stepping on my heels!

RESPEKT: At least my chief anteroom staff could have...

FANTAZY: (*To Rzecznicki*) Introduce me.

RZECZNICKI: Allow me to present my friend, Count Fantazy.

RESPEKT: A most pleasant guest in my home. Our estates are like plots of land alongside each other...and God grant that our relations will be like...heart against heart. But where is my wife and those rascally daughters of mine? Probably at prayer now...or maybe exciting their spleens devouring some dark romances in a corner somewhere. (*To a lackey*) Kayetan, announce the guests to the ladies. Ah, there they are now, on their way here.

Scene iii

(*Enter Countess Respekt, Diana, and Stella.*)

RESPEKT: Count Dafnicki.

COUNTESS: We owe the Count's descriptions of Rome some very pleasant moments. We know him well. So much fire in his pen, and so much heart, so much enthusiasm! Ah! The Count's letters – why it's as though they were inscribed in marble by lava. Isn't it so, Diana? Those two fountains in front of the Vatican like spirits girdled by a morning rainbow; that wooden cross in the Circus, oh! We've known the Count for a long time, a long time indeed.

FANTAZY: Perhaps we knew each other in another existence...

COUNTESS: I heard that you are a mystic. Now I'll swear to it that you're one. Ah! How much I feared that I'd find you mystical.

RESPEKT: Marianna, don't start right in arguing with our guest! Please come with me, gentlemen. Diana, you'll play a little something for us. And I warn you all that I suspect melancholic people of a lack of sincerity.

(*All exit except the Countess.*)

Scene iv

(*The Countess, then Kayetan.*)

COUNTESS: Kayetan! (*Kayetan comes in.*)
KAYETAN: Yes, madam, what is it you wish?
COUNTESS: Have the flocks driven into the small meadow and tell old Anton to lower his fishing net into the water and sit himself down beneath the willow tree alongside a pair of peasant youths weaving baskets, just the way it is in Tasso. Place a group of harvesters in the back and have them sing. Let Anna pasture some goats along the slopes. And, oh yes, be sure to have a cascade of water flowing! Remember, start the cascade in the evening, before we get up from the dinner table. Oh, and one more thing: tell Dubyna to stand behind the fence and sing Padura's * Ukrainian folk songs!
KAYETAN: But the rains spoiled the pipe in the cascade...
COUNTESS: What luck! Well, no matter then.
KAYETAN: But madam...
COUNTESS: What is it now?
KAYETAN: But Dubyna went to Berdichev today, to buy sugar and arrack.
COUNTESS: Well then, we'll have to get along somehow without the folk songs. But don't forget what I told you about the fisherman, the flocks, and...
KAYETAN: Just as you ordered, ma'am; fisherman and flocks...
COUNTESS: And the little peasants weaving baskets.
KAYETAN: And the baskets.
COUNTESS: And the harvesters.
KAYETAN: But the harvest has already been gathered!
COUNTESS: My dear Kayetan, do as you wish. This wild English garden – it's nothing but a nuisance! There's always something going wrong. Either the bower breaks or the cross on the hilltop intentionally

---

*Tymko Padura (1801–1871), a Polish-Ukrainian poet of sentimentally stylized folk songs. – Ed.

goes crooked. Why, it almost fell on top of my husband and killed him. The trouble we've had because of that garden! (*She motions to Kayetan to leave. He goes out.*) Stella!

Scene v

(*The Countess, Stella, and later Kayetan*)

STELLA: (*Offstage*) What is it?
COUNTESS: Stella, come here!
STELLA: (*Entering*) What is it, Mama?
COUNTESS: Is Count Fantazy chatting already with Diana?
STELLA: No...
COUNTESS: Leave her by herself in the drawing room, Stella, and go bring grandfather here. Then get all dressed up in white and go stand by the pond, you know, underneath our weeping willow there, below the crag, and call the swans. In a little while we'll be going outside with our guests to have some coffee by the oak tree.
STELLA: All right, Mama, but afterwards will you let me go to vespers with Hanka?
COUNTESS: As you like...but what's that I see – oh, some kind of a wagon near the fence and mounted Bashkirs! * (*To Kayetan as he enters*) What's going on there?
KAYETAN: A Russian officer of the Guards.
COUNTESS: Heavens! I'm trembling all over! Do you think he's come here looking to be quartered?
KAYETAN: I don't know what to think.
COUNTESS: Mother of mercy! If it's a special courier, a *Feldjäger*... Oh, I just can't stop trembling. Stella, go and warn your father! (*Stella runs out.*)

Scene vi

(*The Countess, the Major.*)

COUNTESS: (*To the Major as he enters*) Welcome. Whom do I have the honor to...

---

* A Turkic people inhabiting the southwestern slopes of the Urals who came under Russian domination in the time of Ivan the Terrible. – Ed.

MAJOR: You don't recognize me?

COUNTESS: Oh, why yes! Master Vladimir! What an absolutely delightful surprise! I'll call my husband and daughters. Darling! Stella! Diana! (*They rush in followed by Fantazy and Rzecznicki.*)

Scene vii

(*The Respekts and their daughters, Fantazy, Rzecznicki, the Major.*)

RESPEKT: What's going on?

COUNTESS: Look – our old acquaintance!

RESPEKT: Ah, the Major! Receive him with full tankard! Let my humble cottage be illuminated! My courtyard strewn with silver sugar and transformed into Siberia! My dear fellow! (*Embraces him.*) You see now here I am, a Pole from the Ukraine, no longer your prisoner. No longer do I look anxiously at your uniform expecting to see the white horn of a tsarist ukase protruding from it. ... Ladies and gentlemen, my fate rested in the hands of this officer but never, not even once, did he make me feel that I had lost my freedom. On the contrary, when I and my wife and children were in the vicinity of Tobolsk after I was sent there for the "healthier climate" lest the Polish plague contaminate me – you know, of course, that as the leading official in this district the government showed the greatest concern for the state of my health – the Major here, full of pity, seeing me and my family in a miserable little village, in a hole of a barn, was our one help and defense. Thanks to him none of the Siberian Aeoluses blew us away.

MAJOR: I'm happy that you're well...

COUNTESS: And how is Father Osip?

MAJOR: Drunk as usual.

STELLA: And my red bullfinches?

MAJOR: Chirping for all they're worth in the trees...and puffing themselves up like roses. They're sad you're no longer in Siberia.

STELLA: And the tame goldfinches?

MAJOR: As in paradise, at the bookkeeper's...

DIANA: And the three Polish crosses?

MAJOR: Still standing.

COUNTESS: And Mrs. Potopov?

MAJOR: Drinking tea as usual in her green dress...

COUNTESS: Always in her green dress?

MAJOR: And in her cap.

STELLA: Out of which I wanted to make a little house for a puppy. My, how cold it must be there now! I get shivers thinking how cold Mrs. Potopov must be. Diana, remember our...

DIANA: Our who?

STELLA: Who? Our dear poor Jan, who was taken prisoner while leading a band of peasants armed with scythes. Arrested...someone like him, so poor and yet so good and as beautiful as the archangel Michael in the painting.

MAJOR: That friend of yours gave us quite a lot of trouble. He stirred up the peasants against us. But today he's serving in the Caucasus as a simple Russian conscript.

STELLA: Can you imagine, Diana?

COUNTESS: Enough, Stella! Take the Major and serve him some good Polish tea which you promised you'd treat him to after all the Siberian *kvas* he gave us.

(*All go out except Fantazy and Rzecznicki.*)

Scene viii

(*Fantazy, Rzecznicki.*)

FANTAZY: They've forgotten all about us...

RZECZNICKI: Are you angry?

FANTAZY: Oh no!

RZECZNICKI: But you are a little envious.

FANTAZY: Of what?

RZECZNICKl: Diana's gazes, and Stella's tears.

FANTAZY: I'm not yet in love.

RZECZNICKI: But you're already irritated, confess it.

FANTAZY: Not at all. But tell me, Rzecznicki, who is he, that Jan, the one who was captured with a scythe?

RZECZNICKI: Some scytheman or other.

FANTAZY: You're like a Delphic statue. Those oracular utterances of yours. They go straight to the target and to the very heart of the truth. But I'd be very happy to find out what kind of a sad phantom it is who bares his breast somewhere above the silver waves of Siberia and rattles the terrible chains that bind him...and remains in the crowded memory of our young ladies with his wounded breast and with the diamond of that tear which, though shed in vain, wells up in his misty eyes. Against a captive like that, Adonis himself wouldn't stand a chance in the contest for the love of a noble Polish maiden.

RZECZNICKI: A splendid tirade. Long periods.

FANTAZY: That bygone Siberian intimacy...that pale-azure cloud of golden hoarfrost...that surround him, those ravines beneath him full of the bones of wolves, the black pines above him...frightful trees, and that dark misfortune...

RZECZNICKI: And the chimneys in blackness...the name of Diana written in white chalk...

FANTAZY: Damned man whom the temples of Cnidus even today still supply Castalian waters. O nail from Byron's cross... O ram whom Sancho Panza once dreamed of in a mystic vision... beast unexpectedly beheld in heaven! O you who are a salamander in the eternal flame of stupidity and grow fat while in the fire... O Rzecznicki!

RZECZNICKI: O hapless seer!

FANTAZY: O prenuptial Cassandra!

RZECZNICKI: O you needer of good sense!

FANTAZY: You bore you! Look, they've all gone into the garden and nobody's given us even the slightest thought.

RZECZNICKI: For you are a pen that writes sonnets... *et andronas scribit*...and you amuse people when they are bored and you yourself are bored when they amuse themselves.

FANTAZY: Perhaps.

RZECZNICKI: To see yourself as you really are, take someone else's head and put it on your shoulders.

FANTAZY: And shall I put mine on yours?

RZECZNICKI: Lose your head at cards, if the gamblers let you put up air for a bet instead of hard cash. But sooner grab hold of it just the way they salt a sparrow's tail, otherwise it will fly right out of your hands.

FANTAZY: What you say is true. There seem to be lights moving about my head, like a child's, light green, red – like the figures of saints cast by Veneziano against golden backgrounds; various sorts of tones each of which recalls something melancholic and possesses an inexplicable charm for my soul. I seem to hear the memories of different places resounding in the air, passing all about me each with its own countenance, its own fragrance, each transformed into a nymph, into the shape of... Oh! How the emotions are injured by thoughts explained to excess! I imagine that apparitions are the more beautiful because they are hazy, that flowers are sadder when cut, that deities not thirsting for blood but glowing with the sunniness of their countenances, in wreaths of laurel, in camellias of stars whose indistinct colors, like the half rainbows of the moon, take on a silvery hue... My thoughts are already demiapparitions, but still thoughts...

RZECZNICKI: Farewell, you coachman trading in the steeds of Apollo!

FANTAZY: Wait!

RZECZNICKI: Now what is it?

FANTAZY: My heart felt something.

RZECZNICKI: Phenomenal!

FANTAZY: Listen. That girl in black, that Diana blanched by the wind of Siberia who with those black eyes of hers sees graves and crosses there, hears chains rattling, and clasps her hands to her bosom like a statue of obedience and pain... just listen, don't interrupt... that proud Diana who holds her head high like the last remaining column from beneath the ruins of a temple, who, beholding her mother's histrionics and her father's face, pale but affecting a gay manner for people, senses the whole gladiatorial character of domestic misery struggling with the world, who must look upon me as a fiancé but feels in her burning soul that she will be purchased with an inheritance which she is obliged to repay with patience, that girl... oh, I know how low it is of me, but some devil inside me tempts me to fulfill that lowness by buying her after all... for half a million Polish *zlotys*!

RZECZNICKI: The matter's already arranged then?

FANTAZY: Yes, but what tone should I assume in talking to her?

RZECZNICKI: The tone of a plain ordinary merchant.

Scene ix

(*Stella comes in.*)

STELLA: Mama sent me to ask you to join us underneath the oak tree... on the little island of Matilda.

FANTAZY: From Marie Cottin's novel... *

STELLA: And afterwards we're going for a walk to Three Hills.

FANTAZY: Splendid!

---

*A reference to the novel *Mathilde* (1805), by the French Sentimentalist Marie Cottin (1770–1807). – Ed.

Scene x

STELLA: (*Alone*) Everyone seems so melancholic today. Diana is pale, like a wafer. And the way she recoils so violently and trembles as though she were in fever, so unsteady on her feet. Papa isn't telling his anecdotes the way he usually does and Mama, when I looked at her, how frightened I got! That sapphire shading around her eyes and the big tears that burst in them; how care-burdened her face seems. Oh! A Bashkir, a Bashkir coming toward the door. A Bashkir!

(*Jan runs into the room.*)

Scene xi

(*Stella, Jan.*)

STELLA: What do you want? I'm all alone here...
JAN: Aren't you glad to see me?
STELLA: Oh, it's Jan!
JAN: Sh, sh!
STELLA: Master Jan – disguised!
JAN: Stella dear, I beg you, shhh! My, how you've grown. What a lovely white and rose flower you've become.
STELLA: Let me go tell Diana that you're here.
JAN: My dear little angel – not a word about it! Remember that you invited me in for milk and honey from your apiary, like a queen of undines, the sovereign of all the flowers of Podolia. Be loyal to me now and as bewitched as a spell, for this entire region must exist for me like a dream, a holy vision upon which I must look as though in dream – with a smile on my lips, but in silence. Woe to those who have lost their country!
STELLA: You speak painfully and I hear how the mute Siberian wind which blew so terribly, beating against windowpanes with a roar, speaks through you.
JAN: Please, dear, behave prudently now that I'm here. One short moment of joy could plunge me and your entire home into misfortune.
STELLA: Are you still not free?
JAN: Still.
STELLA: And are you returning again to white Siberia?
JAN: I am.

STELLA: And you don't permit me to tell anyone that you've come here?

JAN: If you did, you'd destroy both me and the Major.

STELLA: What am I to do?

JAN: Listen, Stella. I'm looking for some way this evening to return to Diana this golden ring which was lost in the snow...a long time ago. We're leaving again at sunrise.

STELLA: But how to do it? Wait. There's a big pond in back of the house and a boat that we sail, sometimes just we girls alone, to the other shore, to a nice apiary there. The little forest belongs entirely to Diana. But there's one problem. After the Insurrection, Russian Orthodox monks took over our church and parish. Our priest, Father Loga, is living now in the apiary house. We call it our little monastery. I've often gone there with Diana to pray to God to watch over you...our poor Master Jan...in the evening...when the corn crakes are shouting in the meadows and the pond is covered by a dense silver fog full of rosy-colored streaks...and the nightingale's voice falls from the oak trees throughout the black forest...like garlands...till it seems to groan right at the pond itself...and beyond the pond. Diana often talks to Father Loga about you, about the snowy gold rainbow that shone when the two of you asked the Gypsy woman about your destiny. I don't know if you remembered both of us the way we remembered you... How you sighed! What more? What was I saying? Oh yes, if you want, I'll take my sister to that cottage, Father Loga's place, on the other side of the pond.

JAN: But say nothing!

STELLA: Nothing.

JAN: Winged little bird! As always, I see, you have the power of an undine over your sister.

STELLA: Oh, she always obeys me.

JAN: All right, then, in that case I will be in the apiary this eveniñg. (*Goes out.*)

STELLA: I'll tell Diana that she's going to see a spirit. A spirit! I'll hurry now and tell Diana that this evening she's going to lay eyes on a real spirit.

(*Countess Idalia comes in.*)

Scene xii

(*Stella and Countess Idalia.*)

IDALIA: Stella!

STELLA: Oh! Countess...
IDALIA: Where's Mama?
STELLA: Please wait here a little while. I'll run and tell her...
IDALIA: Hold on! I'll go myself. Tell me...
STELLA: You're trembling all over.
IDALIA: It's nothing, just my heart beating. I'm not feeling very well, I got feverish from my trip, traveling so fast...despite my doctor's advice, despite the admonitions I've given myself a hundred times over. (*Aside*) How miserable I am! How insane! (*Aloud*) Do you have guests here?
STELLA: Count Fantazy and Mr. Rzecznicki are here with us now.
IDALIA: Tell me, do you think it would be all right if I went – unobtrusively – where all the others are?
STELLA: They're all down by the pond now.
IDALIA: Is there a glade there that can veil me, you know, some trees leading right up to them...close...so that I could make a sign to your Mama without the others seeing me? Stella! Just see how my knees are quivering, how my eyes... (*Aside*) Oh, how they're casting thunderbolts at the forehead of that fickle man – how they pierce his heart like a stiletto.
STELLA: Let's go. We'll stand behind the trees along the paths in the dahlia beds.
IDALIA: (*To herself*) Ah, I'll emerge from the abyss of flowers... like a vision, all garlanded with dahlias like a rainbow of different stars.
STELLA: Mama will be surprised at your unexpected visit. So many travelers today! (*They leave.*)

Scene xiii

(*Beneath the oak tree in the garden. Count and Countess Respekt, Diana, the Major, Fantazy, and Rzecznicki.*)

DIANA: Would the Major like some tea?
MAJOR: It's been a long time since I've seen bright flowers and trees like these.
COUNTESS: They grow without any cultivation...
MAJOR: To someone garrisoned in snow your country seems like spring itself. No wonder that you longed for your own land, that you sighed for it so deeply. I understood it well.
DIANA: (*To Fantazy, who appears sunk in thought*) That cup with golden handles is a grotesque. It belongs to Count Respekt. Count Fantazy, aren't you listening?

227

RZECZNICKI: Fantazy!

FANTAZY: Strike me down if I'm wrong! Even though I'm wearing a coral amulet to protect me against the evil eye, I could swear I heard something rustling behind me, and the familiar step...of a purgatorial spirit.

COUNTESS: The spirit must be someone dear to you if it deafens everything in your heart and leads your thoughts so far from us...and plunges you into such unconsciousness.

FANTAZY: Please forgive me. It doesn't prevent me from being here... just as the light of a pale moon does not obstruct lamps.

COUNTESS: Then you are with us?

FANTAZY: Body and soul, heart and eyes.

COUNTESS: And nothing of the spirits has remained?

FANTAZY: Not a single hair.

DIANA: Your cup! Hold onto your cup! Oh! You're dropping it! (*The cup falls and shatters.*)

COUNTESS: It's nothing. Diana, pour Count Fantazy another cup!

FANTAZY: I swear by everything that's holy that it was unintentional! I am your most humble servant who begs your forgiveness. But at just that moment...even if you had poured hot tea into my eyes, I wouldn't have felt a thing... (*Aside*) The devil himself is playing a comedy with me... and the saddest at that.

COUNTESS: Diana, pour the Count a cup, but see to it that you give him the weakest tea possible, no more than the tea's shadow.

FANTAZY: The weakest? But why?

COUNTESS: Out of respect for your nerves. (*Suddenly catching sight behind Fantazy's shoulders of Idalia standing in the bushes*) What do I see? (*Nods.*)

FANTAZY: What's this? Whom are you nodding to?

COUNTESS: Oh, it's nothing, nothing at all. Stella saw a rare flower on a single stem together with a dahlia and made a gesture asking if it was all right to pluck it; I was just nodding back to her... Did you come to Podolia from Rome a long time ago?

FANTAZY: Six months ago.

COUNTESS: Whom of our own people did you come across in Rome?

FANTAZY: To tell the truth, apart from several dreadful nuisances who trail after each other all dried out like the old Roman aqueducts and seem guardians over the ruins like moss and overgrown weeds, there's nobody I really care to recall.

COUNTESS: But to country people like ourselves everything is interesting.

FANTAZY: Well, if you insist... There's one Catholic gentleman who likes to doze alongside the ruins – a Pole and chamberlain of his Imperial Majesty; a great devotee of music, crowned with the golden lyre of Apollo, he also loves to sing, but like a murmuring spring of the goddess Egeria that never turns windmills but constantly trickles along like an Italian operatic roulade, only a livid barbule of voice flows from his lips. The angel of silence sits in him and hums; so does Pythagoras and his wordless retinue of neophytes, and you can imagine that none of them breaks the rule of the order against speaking.

COUNTESS: Who else did you know there?

FANTAZY: A pious countess with tresses falling to her shoulders and a canon or monsignore hidden in each ring of hair.

COUNTESS: A fanatic... And what about the other women?

FANTAZY: For the most part pale and very ill... The wrecks of women, the dregs of Karlsbad; stalactites, extinguished Vesuviuses.

COUNTESS: Can you give me an example of what you mean, you know, someone in particular?

FANTAZY: Can I? There's one who's practically on her last legs; I'm positive you know her – Countess Idalia. Something on the order of a Madame de Staël, a letter-writing steam engine.

COUNTESS: Is she attractive?

FANTAZY: Half her body is like a siren's, without any bones, and she seems to move as though propelled by the release of coiled springs. And her eyes...

COUNTESS: Are they pretty?

FANTAZY: Two black ink spots on a white sheet.

COUNTESS: Is she so white?

FANTAZY: Like a sheet!

COUNTESS: And she has eyes like that?

FANTAZY: Like ink.

COUNTESS: I can just picture her.

FANTAZY: If anyone bloodied the sheet with a stiletto, he'd be committing great poetry with a person who today would gladly give ten years of her life for such a splendid and tragic scene. She's the kind of person who needs wounds. Her lips are made for the drinking of poison. If her heart were torn to shreds or if she could go on endlessly praying disconsolately to the moonlight, she'd be a beautiful person. Unfortunately, it's the poor thing's destiny to sit and wait, like a shipwrecked vessel on sand, but the tempests she needs to carry her away from earth never come.

When I arrived in Rome, she wanted to make my acquaintance. I'm happy to be of whatever service I can to women, but one thing I will not do is agree to be a bottomless Danaid's cask into which they pour all the oxides of their rusty hearts. Anyway, when I met her she was obsessed with the idea that love, everywhere and always, is something holy because faith is at the heart of it and faith is the only thing you can rely on in life. When I heard that, I said, "Hold on!" And I told the dear lady quite sincerely that love is nothing so narcotic or shortsighted and that what she needed was to perceive through the alabaster countenance of some Phoebus that lovely star shining in the gleam of the eyes or on the coral of feverish lips... When I said that, a sigh tore loose from the burnous-like shawl she had on, and the shawl – of amianthus – enveloped the flames, and afire, turned silver before my eyes, like true amianthus... I told her then that I saw the star of misfortune in her bluish raven locks. She thought at first that I was mocking. But when she saw that I remained firm, like a ship at anchor, she said, "Oh! You shall be my soul brother! You alone, in a single flash of feeling, understood what I am suffering, what I feel, to what loneliness I have been sentenced". I replied that I pitied her with all my heart, that I needed a sister spirit in the same way that an odd glove needs another of the identical style and size to make a pair.

COUNTESS: Excuse me, but Stella is signaling me. (*She goes over to Idalia and exits with her. Count Respekt and the Major leave in the direction of the other side of the garden.*)

RZECZNICKI: (*To Fantazy, aside*) Now, Fantazy, strew Diana's eyes from the other crater!

FANTAZY: Oh, go to the devil!

RZECZNICKI: (*To Diana*) Something surely must have happened to your mother. Perhaps Stella got sick. I'll go have a look. (*To Fantazy*) Now's the time to attack – be bold! (*Goes out.*)

Scene xiv

(*Fantazy and Diana alone.*)

DIANA: Would you care for some tea?

FANTAZY: No.

DIANA: Would you like to visit my aviary?

FANTAZY: No... But while I am near this samovar that has begun filtering the boiling water, please allow me to extract from the abyss of Pluto a word which in the cemetery of the living is like a death's-head among flowers.

DIANA: Meaning?

FANTAZY: In a word – marriage.

DIANA: Aha!

FANTAZY: Must I kneel now?

DIANA: In the passionate worlds you inhabit, kneeling isn't in fashion
   any more.

FANTAZY: True enough; it is a bit out of date.

DIANA: Then...

FANTAZY: Then?

DIANA: At the bottom of your words there's a declaration...

FANTAZY: There's sugar...

DIANA: Too bold, Count! You come for your...goods...just like a
   merchant. Where are your weights and measures? To a child of noble
   origin God gave... Look, Count, even this nail on my finger, it's like a
   ruby washed somewhere with the blood of my ancestors or much
   admired somewhere on a vizier! My tears...see, they're like the pearls
   of Amphitrite, for I have been offended in tears... In this sapphire of
   my eye you'll find a spring of familial thoughts muddied by tears.
   Everything that a sad child could inherit from deceased forbears...a
   whole hearth of hearts, all their nobilities and all the beauty of their
   thoughts... I possess, inherited from them, and my dowry – is my
   body. If I've left for last my soul – and I've said nothing about it since
   you and I are dealing about myself in *pounds* – then the bright coral of
   my lips and my eyes, which rise in fiery revolt but now hold back the
   tears, would still command me to be proud and difficult in this
   transaction. Well? Not kneeling as before a lonely Raphael's Madonna
   of the steppes, didn't you want, Count, to cause her face to blush and
   with coarse behavior bring off the holy miracle of her eyes filling with
   tears or of blood streaming from the canvas? Because you're admired
   and well known in these parts, because love pursues you, because
   you're all crimped like a strange Calcutta pearl which is all the more
   costly for its unfathomable shape and doesn't even resemble a pearl but
   rather some strange, precious monstrosity, you thought that I'd go into
   ecstasy over the marvel... just like a poor child who sees the brilliant
   diamond on your shirt for the first time. Confess, Count, that you had
   no need of the myrtles and moons of Endymion here where they rake
   hay full of such lowly little flowers as I. That being the case, I'll tell you
   sincerely, the more so since we don't have any witnesses, that my father
   is giving me to you and taking your money in return. Please forgive
   me for expressing myself so frankly. My father is heavily in debt and
   tomorrow they're going to come and take the plows away from all the
   peasants and station soldiers in each cottage. Now if tomorrow I hear
   these cottages crying "God!" and God doesn't send down bolts of
   lightning, if the spirit that breathes with prayer within me doesn't
   protect this village, if the peasants surround me and fall at my feet – as
   though I appeared in the heavens with stars about my temples – and I

couldn't save the people no matter what sacrifice I make, if God wants only from my misfortune the strength which will protect this people like a miracle, then, and only then, will I consent to marry you. (*Goes out.*)

Scene xv

(*Fantazy, Rzecznicki.*)

FANTAZY: What spirit! Jesus!

RZECZNICKI: (*Emerging from the trees*) What? I was behind a tree.

FANTAZY: Gales! Tempests! I'm absolutely beside myself!

RZECZNICKI: Have a little sherry, you'll feel better.

FANTAZY: Rzecznicki! A great, a gigantic change has taken place in my spiritual nature.

RZECZNICKI: Congratulations! What happened? The matter worked out the way you wanted? The girl is madly in love with you?

FANTAZY: She slapped my spirit in the face and left!

RZECZNICKI: Congratulations!

FANTAZY: But the game isn't over yet... (*Runs out.*)

RZECZNICKI: Off he goes. This Fantazius certainly lives strangely: fights with the ladies as though he were in a duel!

[End of Act I]

ACT II

Scene i

(The garden.)

IDALIA: *(Alone)* No! No! I'll not remain under the same roof with them. I'll just rest a while from my journey, right here where the pine trees are overgrown with ivy... and afterwards I'll lodge in Father Loga's little house... Let the springs in which the goddess Diana saw her face behold my countenance; let them see that though I've been wounded in the heart, I am without venom. No! I don't wish her any torture. I am exalted, they shall say, *because* I have forgiven... And dressed in my thorny thistles which I made sparkle with my tears I am like... some woman of Rome or Florence who listens to poets and wears prickly wreaths in her tresses as if the tempest emerging from within her soul expressed itself through the disheveling of her garland and the thorns of tousled leaves on her head... My poet is the past and the singing of my poet makes me half-sad and yet half-happy because his song raises me above all others. I see that I'll have to take up a weaver's loom as in old Poland, that I'll have to intoxicate with the beauty of simplicity that spirit that begs for beauty and yet once wanted to make the golden moon a common lodger. Instead of the moon above my table, I'll have to have my great-grandmother's fearful white face... a lamp of holiness... a dead face. Yes... my spindle will rumble and rumble and as it dances along will unravel my golden carpets. Looking at this I shall think, this is the way the world goes round... the way every young dandy dances, spinning after himself a similar thread of silken memory, coiling himself into the silk of fashion. And... but the spindle flies from my hands... has already begun to move away from me... no longer knows me! Truly, that's how I'll jeer at the world, spinning silk...

Scene ii

(Stella and Jan come in.)

JAN: Stella *lubiezna!* * But what's the matter?

---

*A Russian word meaning "dear". – Ed.

IDALIA: Someone's coming! I'd best hide in the grotto. (*She enters the grotto.*)

STELLA: Please don't talk to me in Russian.

JAN: Listen... that's the language of my longing, the language that rushes from my breast and howls like a dog beside a coffin. And sometimes it barks in the ears like a rifle.

STELLA: Fine. But you're here as my guest, in my apiary. It's not at all nice for you to speak Russian in my kingdom and in the presence of my little dog, who happens to be my superintendent of police.

JAN: How witty we are.

STELLA: As soon as he sniffs you for a Muscovite, he'll grab you by the heel. That's the way he's been taught; after all, he's had some education.

JAN: Where is Diana:

STELLA: She's very sorry she couldn't come here.

JAN: Aha!

STELLA: She's playing a Hummel variation on the piano.

JAN: And she won't come?

STELLA: I don't know. When she finishes, perhaps she'll take a walk this way. You know, don't you, that she's getting married tomorrow.

JAN: Tomorrow...

STELLA: What is it to you?

JAN: True, just a zero in my account. Tomorrow, though... I'm trembling. Diana's getting married, but to whom, may I ask?

STELLA: Oh! How strangely your arrows rattled in their quiver! Listen. I'm looking at you with considerable anxiety. Right now you're a real Bashkir... a real black Bashkir you've become! Why are you looking at the full moon that way?

JAN: It's nothing, Stella. I was searching the heavens for those stars, the seven stars bound together that you showed me once, my golden astronomer... above the terrible image of frozen misery – of an extinguished life, of a snowy hell. It ought to be right here, in this part of the sky, that violin of stars across which you led the bow like an innocent angel. The honey of your apiary isn't as sweet as the music that remained after you in the stars. And when I sat down by gravestones in a cemetery it played to me, played to me there in Siberia, it played... like your voice. (*To himself*) Should I blow my brains out... or go get myself good and drunk soldier's style?

STELLA: The violin of stars?

JAN: Take it from the sky for your sister's wedding!

STELLA: Must you hide then? Aren't you coming to church tomorrow?

JAN: Oh, woe to him that loses his country!

STELLA: Don't hide your face! Diana and I used to end our daily prayers with your name. You were with us every Sunday, and every Friday.

Diana used to talk with your words and at peasant baptisms she'd give the name Jan to every baby boy. But how she's sobbing today, how pale she is, how sick. Oh, you know, you know – it's *you* Diana loves!

JAN: Ha!

STELLA: But Mama and Papa came here yesterday, sat down on the bed, ordered me out, locked the door after me and began having a talk with Diana. In a while, I heard her shouting: "That's a sword! Give me poison! I'll sharpen a knife and slit my own throat after the wedding!" Mama and Papa were arguing with her: "You're being stupid! You're talking as if you were living in a dark cellar somewhere or in romantic novels! Think of the miserable straits we're in and how we have to do what we can to save the honor of our family! You silly little thing, what are you thinking of? Going around begging for a piece of bread and the two of us old people and your sister Stella following after you playing on old harps in all the coffeehouses of Kiev?" At this point, Mama began to swoon and Papa to throw his hands up in despair, and I don't know what else... But I started crying and carrying on myself on the other side of the door till poor Diana rushed out to me, took me in her arms and began shouting: "I'll enter a convent! I'll become a nun!" Dragging the bed linen after her, she pulled me out into the garden like a madwoman and kept on shouting: I'll become a nun because I see that that's what I was raised to be in this house!

JAN: Is that so? Then tell that martyr to keep her distance from me! Stella, give me your hand...please...now... I beg you by everything that's holy, take this golden ring here! Wait, I'm forgetting something. Take, too, this withered flower plucked in a far-off land of tears to which I'll return to finish out my misery...in chains. What good is anything if here... I'll bring my heart greater pain and open wounds instead of... Oh, Stella! You know what I want to say! Keep these things I've given you that are precious to me and some day, later on, when your old friend, a simple soldier, intrudes suddenly on your conversation some nostalgic evening when pictures of the past become vivid again, when that black evil-looking house all garbed in the purple of a Siberian dawn looms before you, and when everything that grieved our hearts long ago returns like an apparition, take them, these traces of the past, and throw them into the fireplace in front of your sister. And when they've been consumed in the flames, show her how black they are, sated of tears, and turned to ashes. And as you do these things, let your face be as sweet as that of an angel who recalls in heaven the pain we endured far in the past.

STELLA: Does that mean that with you...no longer...

JAN: ...is anything at all possible.

STELLA: But I'll see you?

JAN: In this house I'm not a person, but a uniform. I count for less than a person and I want more than God Himself! I'd rather have nothing than have to accept compromises I couldn't live with. Even those pearllike tears you dry when you turn away from me, Stella, are offensive to me because they come from pity. Well, on your way... I'll lie down by the stream and sharpen the tips of my arrows. In my poverty, I got accustomed to work. Work is my beloved. Besides, I have songs we soldiers sing, songs full of laughter... and pain! Good-bye!

(*Stella leaves.*)

Scene iii

(*Jan, Idalia.*)

IDALIA: She's gone! Oh, what a marvelous scene!

JAN: (*Lies down and begins to sing*)

> Hey! Hey! Caucasus,
> With your mines of tin!
> The cudgel is my sweetheart,
> And my mother – gin!
> I'm my country's loyal son,
> Of none else will I be one! Hey!

How well the frightful song howls with an echo here. Let some water sprite inspire me... and at the same time grasp me by the throat so that I'll grunt and scream like a hyena.

> Hey! Hey! Stay alert!
> Shells are in the air!
> Vodka is my sister,
> Death, my commander!
> I'm my country's loyal son,
> Of none else will I be one!
> Mount your horses! Let's ride out!

IDALIA: What a wonderful song! The crags roar as though a hundred wolves opened their jaws and belched out black blood together with

their cries. The air groans and applauds after the song like a sorceress...
And he, lying by the stream like a splendid knight out of Ariosto, rests
his head on his silvery quiver and, it seems, lashes the warm air with
the energy of his voice. The last syllables are still resounding. Oh! He
must be one of those wounded spirits which I've so long felt a kinship
with... I know him, I know I do! And I must touch that red facing on
his uniform, not like the others here would, but as if they were holy
relics. (*Approaches him.*)

JAN: (*Pretending a Russian accent*) Who's there?

IDALIA: A Polish woman.

JAN: So? I'm a Russian.

IDALIA: Are there many forced conscripts like you in Siberia? Forgive
me for speaking to you so informally before we've even been introduced
and not addressing you as "sir" or "mister". But the informal "you" of
mine means a great, great deal, for I grant you more superiority over
other men than the world will ever give its "sirs" and "excellencies"
and the rest of them.

JAN: (*Still affecting a Russian accent*) As you like, madam. I'm here with
my Khan, with the Major. We arrived by post, on our way to pick up
fresh horses.

IDALIA: You poor man you, having to guard your speech that way,
pretending to be a Russian, and constantly hung by the heart on the
nail of your cross! I overheard the last part of your story, while I was
hidden in the grotto. I can easily imagine the rest.

JAN: (*Dropping his Russian speech*) Since that's the case, then I'll tell you
that I was really singing from pain... from torture.

IDALIA: And do you know that as I listened to you I swore on Christ's
thorns that I would take unto myself half of that pain and that I would
serve you faithfully with a heart likewise burning with pain in me,
likewise wounded. Don't ask me anything more. But know that our goals
here are the same. You yield, because you love more ardently, since you
are a man and since you have much strength and your masculine dignity
prevents you from rebelling against the laws of earth for the law of the
heart. But I... as I was being borne along by golden sails a wave of blood
tossed me against these shores and now I am rotting here, I who once
was beloved of rose-hued stars and flowers, I who was more renowned
for love than... any Neapolitan who ever ended a romance with a
stiletto... and yet am abandoned now like some ordinary provincial
damsel whom all the gentry in the district are enamored of and who
declare in verse that her little mouth is full of sugar! Horrible, I tell you!
And because this country of ours is dying, it seems that all the flowers

13. Juliusz Słowacki's *Fantazy*, Act II, Scene iii. Presented at the Stary Teatr, Cracow, in 1967. Directed by Konrad Swinarski. A chance meeting of Jan and Idalia. (Photograph: Wojciech Plewiński)

are withering on the grave and all nobility is perishing. With the masters gone, the lackeys are dressing themselves in their clothes and conducting romances in their places. The conquered hearts they hang alongside their watches and afterwards they write poetry – and account sheets. These people have such fine heads for management that there's a time – and place – for everything. And that's why everything is so bland, so color-less; each of them holds himself a lord, a young master and upstart, and each of them takes counsel of a scullion. Whenever they do anything they're always asking themselves whether or not the valet isn't laughing his head off at them somewhere on the side. Listen. I am a woman. What I feel in my heart you can see in my eyes – contempt, profound contempt, lightning! But because of this contempt, this terrible scorn, God, I fell into a storm of misfortune. I am hurling something against the mist, I am creating something, something, I don't know myself what, but I am certain that something will happen yet, some event that will bring me a piece of driftwood to save myself with before I completely drown. And if not? Ha! I have a shelter not among people ...

JAN: Forgive me, but if there's a woman's vengeance here ...

IDALIA: Then she will not don a suit of armor! Come now, good knight, will you not descend from the moon on Ariosto's steed and, like a falcon, swoop down and take yourself a mistress from a courtyard? Will you not enter the lists and fight for my honor? Ha! Ha! Ha! People think that except for bruises there's nothing a woman can be offered. If you don't extend me your hand, at least give me a prayer, give me your heart; help me with your heart secretly! Suspend your thought above me like a sea swallow, its heart pounding, screeching. Let it protect me, let me know that there's someone above me, who's mine, with a true pair of wings, with a scale of weights not falsified by a mean hand. Oh, and more, more do I want from you, but it will take at least several thousand years before a person will be able to give of himself immedia-tely at the first angelic and sincere request.

JAN: And what kind of a request is it you're talking about?

IDALIA: A request for humbleness.

JAN: Ah! For me, dear lady, that is a big zero! I, who receive half a ruble in pay from the quartermaster's each year and have to go begging for everything else from the peasants, have humbleness enough!

IDALIA: No, you still don't have enough.

JAN: Take a look at the hole in my boot.

IDALIA: Listen ... I'll bend down and kiss that crying wound in your boot if you give me your word ...

JAN: That ...

IDALIA: Just listen. These villages here are ruined beyond repair. Half still belong to the gentry, but the other half are completely mortgaged. Diana's marriage is just like the patch on your boot.

JAN: Then it's holy!

IDALIA: She's been made an expensive commodity, involving a lot of bargaining. The girl is up for sale at half a million, and comes out of a home a half a million in debt. Understand?

JAN: Cheap!

IDALIA: What I want you to do now is head straight for the marketplace and say that a sister of yours died and left you care of a foreign bank just the amount that these people are asking for their daughter. I am your sister, as of now.

JAN: My dear lady! This reminds me of a Russian song called "From Hill to Hill".

IDALIA: From below, your brow seems made of copper, your face somehow not human . . .

JAN: No, no! Something Polish sits in my heart and prohibits such a deed on my part, some kind of fearful veto which nothing, not even the whole world, can countermand. Even if you weren't a woman, I feel that I'd immediately have to answer your golden bullet with a heavy beggar's bullet of lead. What fate! You can sit by a stream and breathe the rosy fragrance of flowers and find relief in pain from nature which knows, it seems, all the aching parts and where to touch the bones and where the flesh. But a man, even though higher than thousands of other men, even though he comes forward with the best of intentions, even though like you, my lady . . . he takes the fragrance of roses in words, something immediately either abases him or lets fall over him such a tear that it burns right through his forehead and blackens it with shame.

IDALIA: Ha! You see how difficult it is to enter the magic circle of those angels for whom such a deed would already be the wondrous humbleness of a brother.

JAN: For God's sake, enough! Let me alone! It's the gift of a madwoman you're making me.

IDALIA: Because I *am* mad! Because an ominous star shone early to a woman born among people who are still growing and do not dare to take a step off the main road. Yes – your noblemindedness is the marvelous spring of your mature years. Believe me, today every poor wretch – I'm not speaking of a lackey or some little clerk – would throw gold back in my face as you do! But don't think that your rejection will earn you any godliness. It rolls along the same beaten track of human custom as the old carriage of the Rzecznickis.

JAN: I don't understand that, my lady, and yet I can't help laughing.

IDALIA: Why? Because a woman like me tosses her fortune away as though it were mud?

JAN: Who are you really?

IDALIA: Just an angel passing by in flight. I hurled a bolt of lightning at your eyes and I am now as evanescent to them as a flash of light in the sky.

JAN: Wait!

IDALIA: Don't follow me. (*Leaves.*)

Scene iv

JAN: (*Alone*) A madwoman! But I see that if the need arose she'd willingly give her soul even to the devil. As for me, she can take her gold and throw it right into the pond here for God's hands provide for me as a prisoner and I'm like a second Ariosto in my misery. Still – I don't know – she instilled in my heart a kind of anger at this man who, like the power of money, like a commander, awaits a victory from his coin soldiers and then takes it for himself calmly and quietly, without exerting any strength of heart. But I'd best be off, for there's a devil dogging me, smudged like me with a little soot, fierce as a Bashkir I saw in a picture somewhere with his gnashing teeth bared. Oh! What I wouldn't give, though, for a plot of land measured off in so many paces and a pair of burning pistols in my hands! Oh, if it weren't for the promise I gave the Major that I'd be as docile as a lamb and take nothing on my own head. I'll follow orders, though, like an automaton and do everything he commands. But how I'd like nothing better than to knock those dolls over and look these worldly people right in their faces calmly, but as cold as marble, sanguine, the way I looked at cannon aimed at my throat once near Warsaw.

Scene v

(*Father Loga comes in.*)

FATHER LOGA: She ran off. Some terrible torment pursuing that woman through the woods. I wanted to come with sound counsel, but in a flash she was beyond the house flying off in the direction of the pond like a wild duck. And I'd have given her some very good advice, and shown her death and her lover in the proper light. What does this Russian soldier here want from me?

JAN: To speak with you.

FATHER LOGA: Are you a Pole?

JAN: Yes, a Pole.

FATHER LOGA: But basely in the service of Moscow, of your own free will, even though speaking a perfect Polish and a member of the gentry, not a conscripted peasant? What is it you want?

JAN: One can sense from your ardor, my dear old fellow, that treachery doesn't grow in your soil. I'll confide in you then, as if under the secrecy of confession, that I do belong to the gentry but was sent off as an ordinary recruit for my part in the revolution, that I have Poland within me and that I came here secretly to rid myself of a burden that's bothered me now for a good ten years' time, and in the form of a terrible spell constantly kept thrusting my thoughts from the flames and wasted my heart in another fire... I beg you, Father, take this ring. (*Removes a ring from his finger and hands it to Father Loga*)...

FATHER LOGA: (*Looking it over*) A gold ring.

JAN: Which has always gleamed like the star that used to shine on the Christmas Eve supper in my own home.

FATHER LOGA: And what am I to do with the ring?

JAN: Make restitution with it, for I stole it.

FATHER LOGA: No...

JAN: I swear it on God's name! I stole it.

FATHER LOGA: You're speaking in dreadful torment now, and I tell you, as the old priest that I am: Don't swear falsely to me because I know this ring; I blessed it some time ago in the parsonage.

JAN: Then you know it's been stolen, don't you? That I have no right to it, Father?

FATHER LOGA: All right, you're fulfilling a holy obligation. May faith and glory and fatherland be auspicious to you and grant you their three laurel wreaths, those ordinary wreaths that these three beloved ones place on the graves of great men. I'm sure it's no secret to you that people first lead you to the grave then love you. Suffer then according to your station but bear your sufferings in the manner of a great soul and I shall remember you in my prayers.

JAN: (*To himself*) And sprinkle pearls from your eyes as a certain king did from his coffers. (*Aloud*) Farewell, old man! There are good people in Poland yet. (*Goes out.*)

Scene vi

FATHER LOGA: (*Alone*) Well, now the conscience of this young girl who got married in a Siberian cabin is clean. I'll go and give back the ring.

[End of Act II]

ACT III

Scene i

(The same drawing room as in Act I. Fantazy and Rzecznicki.)

FANTAZY: Rzecznicki! Idalia is here or was here.

RZECZNICKI: Nonsense!

FANTAZY: I can tell from the scent.

RZECZNICKI: Stuff and nonsense!

FANTAZY: I tell you, she's already avenged herself on me through that devil of a Goliath, the tall fellow, that Bashkir. I've already felt her Venetian stiletto, and a wind from her mouth full of needles has already enveloped me. I've already had a pasty from her kitchen. The butterfly of vengeance has already cast off its pupa and is flying about here. It's already made a treaty with people for my destruction!

RZECZNICKI: She's out to avenge herself on you?

FANTAZY: Like a fieldpiece loaded with a charge of nails.

RZECZNICKI: Give me a better idea of what you mean; I still can't believe...

FANTAZY: That hired Bashkir, for example; he wants to devour me as the whale did Jonah. This very morning, when morning diamonds were on the flowers...

RZECZNICKI: Listen, can't we get along without that porridge of stars and diamonds and flowers...

FANTAZY: Oh, you're an idiot. I'll tell you as simply as I can. We were standing on the veranda today. The Bashkir, with a huge whip in hand and dressed in firs like a kind of Siberian winter deity, was exercising some horses. The girls were looking on from the veranda, the old man was telling his little jokes...

RZECZNICKI: You ought to see yourself now; your face is paler than the moon, like Byron's Manfred.

FANTAZY: And you, my matchmaker, look like a local bumpkin in his Sunday best.

RZECZNICKI: All right, enough now!

FANTAZY: Anyway, the damned Bashkir practically backed a horse up against my chest, then forced it to bolt, driving it into the mud like a sparrow. His saber caught on the gold spectacles I have hanging down on my chest and started to pull...

RZECZNICKI: Oh, it's just an accident; why fuss about it? Even Themistocles had such accidents at the Olympic games. Next time get off the

244

footbridge when horses are riding through mud at a trot. It's not the Bashkir's fault at all.

FANTAZY: But afterwards the beast slew my Spartacus!

RZECZNICKI: What on earth are you talking about?

FANTAZY: When he had already splattered me with mud, a devil must have whispered in Stella's ear. She ran over to the Major and asked him to have the Bashkir fire an arrow from his bow. Her father immediately seconded her request, launching an imposing learned discourse on the Bashkirs' famous skill with bow and arrow. He wanted to prove that he could tell how a shot was going to land from its trajectory. Everyone came down to look, conducting the arrow to the sapphire heavens with their eyes. I myself followed it to the very stars and saw how it hung in the sky, silvery and small, a gnat beneath the globe of heaven. Then it inclined, turned, aimed at the earth with its silvery little head, whirled and finally fell, like a drill. Where did it strike? Have a look. There's my Spartacus, my spaniel, lying in the middle of the courtyard quivering all over. Would you have believed or expected that anything like that could happen? He fired at the sky but really aimed at my Spartacus!

RZECZNICKI: Not hard to understand at all, because Spartacus was strolling around the courtyard at the time. That's fate...

FANTAZY: But there were other dogs there, too...

RZECZNICKI: (*Interrupting him*) Then the Bashkir was right for choosing the prettiest target. You know, Fantazy, that when you fire an arrow up high like that you have to have beauty for your target.

FANTAZY: I'm telling you for the hundredth time that I can sense Idalia's hand in this.

RZECZNICKI: She fired the arrow?

FANTAZY: Well, I felt as though it had struck me. Anyway, right after the firing, Stella, who fawns on everyone and has something of the devil in her, asked the Bashkir how he wears the quiver over his shoulder, and if it's heavy, and if it's made of tinplate...

RZECZNICKI: And what did he do?

FANTAZY: The son of a Tatar removed the quiver and suddenly threw it over my head like a harness. I come up only to his shoulders and when he threw the quiver at me I had just crawled out of a corner and was standing next to him together with a little girl. The straps of the quiver were painted with a yellowish potter's clay and when the thing hit me I suddenly disappeared from the women's sight, like Apollo, saddled, enveloped in a cloud of white dust. There was a terrible uproar on the veranda. When the dust settled, I appeared alongside the Bashkir looking like Cupid in my black frock coat and the quiver crossed with a cartridge belt.

RZECZNICKI: You think Idalia and the Bashkir planned it all that way? Just to make you look foolish in front of all the others?

FANTAZY: I swear she must have been standing somewhere in the vicinity in a tower or an oak tree with a telescope.

RZECZNICKI: Oh, come now!

FANTAZY: You and your "Oh, come now!"

Scene ii

(*Fantazy, Rzecznicki, Count Respekt.*)

RESPEKT: (*Entering*) What is going on, gentlemen? The Major is most unhappy about what has happened and promises to be most severe with the Bashkir. Perhaps you loved that dog, and secretly shed a few tears over him? If it's any comfort to you, my wife, whose head you turned long ago with those letters of yours, is already concerned with finding a pretty place in the garden for a grave for your dog, and for a monument to him. If you and my daughter were on better terms with one another, perhaps she'd be able to find some appropriate sentiments in an English book of hers. But you and my daughter somehow... Count, I'd like to be able to see into you like the clearest blue lapis lazuli; I'd like to see if you have a heart. Of course, you do have a heart, but what I mean is that I'd like to see if you really... Well, I am a father, after all...and the wedding arrangements have already been made...

FANTAZY: And it's precisely to test *your* hearts that we are here now.

RESPEKT: Please go on, but if possible without any florid phrases for the moment.

FANTAZY: (*Indicating Rzecznicki*) This gentleman has my signature.

RESPEKT: Ha! Ha! I see you have no liking for commerce. Fine. Go pluck just the roses, but we'll snare you in our net and take all those beautiful thoughts of yours into a lovely imprisonment. You have a father and mother. In me you have a father, and in my wife, a mother. (*To Rzecznicki*) And you and I, like cold people, shall go tend to our writing. (*Leaves with Rzecznicki.*)

Scene iii

FANTAZY: (*Alone*) My face is still burning with shame on account of the old man. How he must have rolled with laughter, throwing his daughter at me, half-joking and half-serious. Red blood doesn't stick any closer to a murderer's hands or snakes entwine the shoulders of the Laocoons any more tightly than he clings to a son-in-law! Amazing, how much he resembled a beggar, how he was trembling when he embraced me, how he began with my dog and ended up with himself, as if really trying to say, "I'm crying for the dog, so you cry for me!" When I understand the meaning of those two tears I saw glistening in his eyes, then I'll forgive him that false smile which he hid from me as if from behind a mask.

Scene iv

(*Fantazy, Countess Respekt.*)

COUNTESS: (*Entering*) Count!

FANTAZY: Your servant!

COUNTESS: My husband . . . What a happy day! I think that God in all His mercy is helping us. Count! I'm all in tears. You see how I'm trembling from head to foot. Don't be surprised. I am a mother.

FANTAZY: You've greatly obligated me by making me the first witness of those tears. I know how to value them.

COUNTESS: Be assured, Count, that my Diana will understand your heart and will go anywhere you go, or almost anywhere – she can't fly about the stars, after all – and never abandon you in misfortune. She will be a lovely blossom in your home. Before your lightning, she will lower her eyes and will cry without knowing where the tears are coming from or why they are rolling down her cheeks. She will never insult you for any of your activities nor will she quarrel with your prophetic thought of the future nor contend with the past of your golden memories. For all of us she was always like an enchanted corner of the house where it's best of all when you're sad. But, sir, I am a mother and I must look out for her, and I must entrust this mother's foresight to you.

FANTAZY: From this moment on you and I must not keep any secrets from one another.

COUNTESS: Oh, yes! Isn't that so? Both open, we shall plunge our eyes into the most hidden recesses of our feelings. Count, I'm afraid that here, beneath this lava, there's a Vestal Virgin with a fire not yet extinguished.

FANTAZY: (*To himself*) As I can see, my Idalia has already been here. (*Aloud*) Madam, various – what shall I say – various salamanders have grazed on this fire and lived in the fire . . .

COUNTESS: And are they still alive?

FANTAZY: I don't know. In the past, such nymphs were transformed into oleanders, or the unhappy ones into weeping springs. But in the hands of a poet, Daphne usually became a laurel tree. This is something Polish women should carefully consider today...

COUNTESS: You are all giaours, giaours! You always return to your first dreams...on your deathbed...

FANTAZY: Did *she* come here?

COUNTESS: She's here.

FANTAZY: Where?

COUNTESS: In Father Loga's little cottage.

FANTAZY: Is she ill?

COUNTESS: As if at sea!

FANTAZY: What's that? She's seasick?

COUNTESS: Constantly swooning.

FANTAZY: I'll go to her. That's my *fatum*, that woman!

(*Runs out.*)

COUNTESS: Husband! Diana! Stella!

Scene v

(*The Respekts, Diana, Stella, the Major, and Rzecznicki.*)

RESPEKT: What's going on?

COUNTESS: He ran to her!

RESPEKT: It's war then? How will it all end?

COUNTESS: Oh! How will it end? In some misfortune...

MAJOR: Ladies and gentlemen! The devil joined them, a Russian will separate them. I could see what's been going on here from where I've been standing. My Bashkir and I had a little talk about it today and we could understand that here there's a marriage and there some woman is spinning around like a whirlpool. Since I was more grieved than you that my Bashkir was in collusion with that woman and made fun of your son-in-law, I knocked it into his head that he was causing your child unhappiness. I was upset myself on your account and swore to do whatever I could to help against that madwoman. So if you have no objections, let's make a plan of action ourselves. I've kept my Kalmyk on duty with me, but ordered a Bashkir to ride out. He'll look for that Idalia woman and when he gets hold of her, he'll shove her in a carriage and pack her on her way home across the whole of Podolia, if necessary.

RESPEKT: Blazes!

MAJOR: I told him to be polite, of course...but if she refuses, then he'll handle her Cossack style...

COUNTESS: Oh my! In our home...

MAJOR: There's nothing for you to worry about, please!

RESPEKT: But, Major...

MAJOR: Well? I do have grounds, after all – I've got a decree against her for concealing an Italian Freemason* in her house.

RESPEKT: But an abduction, on my estate!

MAJOR: What's the matter? Did I do something wrong?

RESPEKT: It never entered anyone's head that you'd dare act that way.

MAJOR: I've behaved badly then?

COUNTESS: Major, it would have been better if you had arrested the two of us...

RESPEKT: And brought me to court...

COUNTESS: Ordered all of us taken to Kiev...

RESPEKT: Ordered me flung into a kibitka...

MAJOR: What have I done...

COUNTESS: Nothing at all! Not a word more! My husband, order the horses harnessed! Diana, put on your black topcoat, the one with the swans sewn on it! Stella, go fetch my boa! You yourself put on a gown! Since we're such a mighty assemblage here, let us be on our way! (*Count Respekt goes toward the door. The servants begin bustling about. The girls leave and return after having changed clothes.*)

MAJOR: I've gone and done it now!

RZECZNICKI: You'd best pack some smelling salts with you.

COUNTESS: Indeed yes! Kayetan! Put these two bottles in the carriage. Let's be off everyone!

MAJOR: My Kalmyk and I will catch up to you at once.

KAYETAN: The carriage is harnessed...

COUNTESS: Let us all ride forth now to a reconciliation! Would the Major be so kind as to take the lead on horseback?

MAJOR: Why, of course! I'll lead the way...

RESPEKT: Through the small birchwood forest...

(*All leave except Rzecznicki.*)

RZECZNICKI: I'm waiting for my Fantazy.

---

*In the first half of the nineteenth century, political agents sent into Poland by émigré organizations were frequently called Freemasons.

Scene vi

(*Fantazy, Rzecznicki.*)

FANTAZY: (*Rushing in*) Rzecznicki!

RZECZNICKI: What is it?

FANTAZY: A horse!

RZECZNICKI: Too late; the marriage agreement has already been signed.

FANTAZY: Listen to me! Before my very eyes he snatched her, plucked her by the waist like a narcissus! He shook out the roses in her black tresses and carried her away like a whirlwind! A steed and pistols!

RZECZNICKI: Wait!

FANTAZY: As long as one small ossicle of Pole can stay in the saddle, he'll keep on fighting!

RZECZNICKI: Oh, come now!

FANTAZY: If I abandon her like a cad, then you can spit in my face! Goodbye!

RZECZNICKI: Wait a while! What on earth happened?

FANTAZY: I came up and saw her from the distance sadly walking along the bank of the stream. I was already half in line with the old Pleiad of my thoughts, when all of a sudden I caught sight of some Bashkir standing before her. At first, he seemed to be cap in hand, you know, humble, like a servant, with some counsel or request, I presumed. I tried to hear better. Just then a clap resounded through the groves. She slapped him in the face, then went for his eyes. He grabbed her around the waist and began carrying her off like a wild animal. It's terrible! Let me go! I'll saddle my horse and fly there straightaway. If the Major answers for his man in court, mark my word, as soon as that fellow is struck from his regiment he'll find himself in hell! (*Races out.*)

Scene vii

RZECZNICKI: (*Alone*) I see that he's approached the matter from the poetic side. Well, I think I'd better shuffle along too, if only for the bringing around of all the people sure to be fainting there. For protection against the devil, with whom I can no longer fight, I'd best take Father Loga along in my carriage. (*Just as he is about to leave, Idalia comes in.*)

Scene viii

(*Rzecznicki, Idalia.*)

IDALIA: Aha! Mr. Rzecznicki!

RZECZNICKI: What's this?

IDALIA: Why are you so surprised? No doubt I seem to you to be a shade, an apparition! Both of you have such plaintive hearts; you even cry for corpses before they're dead, while you take living people for phantoms when they appear right before your eyes. What's the matter? Am I such a nuisance to the fortunate?

RZECZNICKI: Am I dreaming?

IDALIA: Are you making fun of me?

RZECZNICKI: The roses in her tresses, Fantazy said, flew in all directions. The Bashkir grabbed her around the waist as if she were a narcissus ...

IDALIA: Where is everyone here, where have they all gone? I heard that Fantazy's and Diana's marriage agreement has already been signed. I gathered all the strength of my heart and came here to be a witness of their happiness ...

RZECZNICKI: Then the Bashkir ...

IDALIA: What Bashkir?

RZECZNICKI: Nights of Scheherezade!

IDALIA: Am I getting in the way of any intrigues of yours?

RZECZNICKI: Not in the least. I don't see that you've gotten in my way now at all. The only thing is I myself am in the midst of a great intrigue. A short while ago you were supposed to have been abducted ...

IDALIA: What? I? By whom? Please tell me.

RZECZNICKI: By ... by ... by ... (*To himself*) She must be in league with the Bashkir. (*Aloud*) My dear, as I see, you still have your great charms. The bow of love you wield as skillfully as ever, transforming everything into a picture full of roses and Cupids as though with the brush of Albani.*

IDALIA: What new inscrutable Sphinx is this? Please speak prose, if you don't mind.

RZECZNICKI: Standing amid roses and jasmine, like the sun that causes the eyes to squint ... Disappearing from the blinded eyes of your lover, disappearing ... with a Centaur, like Deianira.

---

*Francesco Albani (1578–1660), Italian Baroque artist known for his pastoral mythological paintings.

IDALIA: Like Deianira? You've either become accustomed to poetry or spirits. In either case, you have my sympathy.

RZECZNICKI: One can see that you needed only a little time for that trip that was so beneficial to the health and so fantastic.

IDALIA: Are you speaking to me?

RZECZNICKI: I am asking you if the horse rides well.

IDALIA: What horse?

RZECZNICKI: The Centaur.

IDALIA: I'm truly delighted that you're so expert a mythologist – in the field of your own stupidity.

RZECZNICKI: No more so than I am at your safe return.

IDALIA: Thank you for being so concerned about me.

RZECZNICKI: And where, may I ask, is Nessus?

IDALIA: You won't give up, I see. My dear man, when Fantazy was in Rome you always fulfilled the duties of a lackey. It was you who used to receive for him from my maidservant a bouquet of roses which withered on a burning breast during a ball. Like a spy, you stood waiting by a gate to find out and later report where I was going. I used to say, "That man bears the sign of a dog, he's so faithful, and because of his faithfulness towers above other men. His heart must be good and his thoughts fine". I thought these things even though a disagreeable spark darted out from beneath your gray, serpentine eyelids and you seemed to emit ignoble vapors which instinctively repelled me ... yet I tried to think only of your good qualities so that the sight of you became pleasant to me and my ears were pleased at the sound of your voice. But today suffer the one torture that can gnaw deeply: the thought that you were raised up high, that in the opinion of one person you stood tall, that in one person's mind you were a being higher than other people, that I was ready to go on my knees before you – yet you were mud, not worth a single glance or word, walking proof that my judgment of the world was merely the judgment of a young woman, a mistake. Now you're a district marshal. His money has elevated you. I shan't send you on errands any longer. No more going after my boot or after a withered flower, you're a gentleman now! But what opens people's hearts here – happiness – is burrowing you into intrigues like a mole, into underground dungeons, into the adulation you find so useful with him. Well? Why aren't you making fun of me any longer? What kind of a journey across the steppes is it that you're persecuting me with? Speak! I'll crown your comic talent with a laurel. Well? I'm curious what Centaur you have me riding away with. You aren't saying anything?

RZECZNICKI: So that's the bloody garment the Centaur offered Deianira after being wounded by Heracles...

IDALIA: Is there no end to your joking?

RZECZNICKI: Forgive me! Ha, ha, ha! I can't help it. Forgive me for being candid and asking if you had a good trip. Was the road paved and smooth, dry? Was the Capitol visible in the distance? Ah! What are those fireflies called? Oh yes – did the *lucciole* fly after the horse's mane like a mane of stars? No doubt that is the way it is in Italy. In other words, did the Centaur who seized the maiden by the waist from his horse offend you?

IDALIA: Then you think I was abducted, is that it?

RZECZNICKI: That's what the rumor is. As you can see for yourself, everyone here, masters and servants alike, has run off in all directions through the forest looking for you.

IDALIA: Where?

RZECZNICKI: The entire assemblage that was here has gone off in pursuit of you. Besides, the morning hour favors it. Fantazy even took a horn with him as though he were off on a hunt.

IDALIA: He went too?

RZECZNICKI: And Miss Diana took her field glass along.

IDALIA: Ha!

RZECZNICKI: And our dear *Mistress* Fantazy also went armed with pistols.

IDALIA: I can't understand it.

RZECZNICKI: Even I, faithful servant that I am, wanted to race after *her* like the wind, taking Father Loga along with me. I had no idea, you see, whether a wedding or a funeral would result from the enterprise.

IDALIA: Are you alone here now?

RZECZNICKI: All by my lonesome self.

IDALIA: The whole estate left en masse?

RZECZNICKI: Everyone. Even the Major and his Kalmyk went galloping off.

IDALIA: And your wife?

RZECZNICKI: My *wife*?

IDALIA: And did your wife go along with the others?

RZECZNICKI: My dear lady, I'm like the shepherd in the idyll pining after her distant image. Fortunate for her, for with that Catholic soul of hers hearing about your adventure, she'd...

IDALIA: What do you mean? Why, no more than an hour ago I was chatting with Mrs. Omfalia Rzecznicki in the garden.

RZECZNICKI: You must be joking.

IDALIA: Not in the least! On the contrary. She told me that she wanted to surprise you and so she put on a blue shawl and my big blonde ruff.

RZECZNICKI: Your big blonde ruff?

IDALIA: I must confess, too, that she wanted to approach you dressed like me and changed hats with me.

RZECZNICKI: She was going on foot?

IDALIA: As though for the conquest of a gentleman's heart.

RZECZNICKI: She was going on foot, you say... Through the garden?

IDALIA: She jumped to me across the boarding from the carriage.

RZECZNICKI: Oh, my God!! Brrr!

IDALIA: Imitating my walk, you know...

RZECZNICKI: (*To himself*) I feel a chill going up and down my spine. Brrr! My blood is running cold.

IDALIA: Is there anything wrong with you?

RZECZNICKI: It's nothing. (*To himself*) Ants are crawling out of my belly...something's got me by the throat! (*Aloud*) Are you certain that it was my wife?

IDALIA: What do you mean?

RZECZNICKI: Maybe it was someone else, you know, someone coming to pay a visit? Someone the same height. Her waist is rather small...

IDALIA: I'm telling you quite clearly that it was Mrs. Omfalia Rzecznicki with whom I was...

RZECZNICKI: Then...then...Your servant, madam! (*Starts to leave.*)

IDALIA: Where are you going?

RZECZNICKI: I beg your forgiveness. Every second is dear to me now. (*To himself*) That Bashkir... My wife... Damn it all!

IDALIA: Aha! Some intrigue spoiled here, eh?

RZECZNICKI: Yes, yes, some intrigue. (*Shouts through the window*) Unharness the carriage and saddle the horse!

IDALIA: You're all upset.

RZECZNICKI: But are you really certain it was she?

IDALIA: She was going through the little lanes of jasmine...

RZECZNICKI: And the Bashkir is armed, on top of it...

IDALIA: What did you say?

RZECZNICKI: The Bashkir was armed when he left?

IDALIA: Ha, ha, ha! Now I understand!

RZECZNICKI: Yes, you understand that such an affront...

IDALIA: What a ride! Flying somewhere with the Bashkir like the wind...

RZECZNICKI: (*Looking out the window*) That idiot doesn't know how to strap on a saddle! Let the stirrups down! But I beseech you again, on bended knee, are you sure that it's my wife whom...

IDALIA: Whom...
RZECZNICKI: He's carrying off over the hills... No, no, no! That would be going beyond all bounds. It just couldn't have been! But...
IDALIA: It could have...
RZECZNICKI: (*Shouting through the window*) Put on the saddle! For God's sake! Don't you have a heart, Havrylo? What are you thinking of?
IDALIA: So you also trot like the Cupid in Albani's pictures?
RZECZNICKI: Did you see her?
IDALIA: Before she was abducted by Nessus...
RZECZNICKI: You saw her today, since morning?
IDALIA: Today...
RZECZNICKI: May I ask then, how long ago?
IDALIA: Not too long ago.
RZECZNICKI: There are two inns along the way. That means that if they were riding slowly they ought to be somewhere near them. It's clear enough that they're not yet in the forest. Right! They must be around the inns. Now if an acquaintance there would just be so kind...
IDALIA: Before they reach the woods...
RZECZNICKI: Are you mocking me? May lightning strike me and my shame! (*Runs out.*)
IDALIA: Well, he's human after all! Pain was wrenching his teeth out, he was suffering in his heart and his blood...the spark of a man spurted out of his eyes. But how long he's been floundering in mud... And he let me look from above upon his ridiculous convulsive agonies. Amid each torment I extend hope from my heart but poison from my hand. I'm always ready to greet every accident with a smile or a deathlike pallor. But this sensible but decrepit grandfather flew out after his abducted spouse like an absolute madman...on an emaciated jade, his trousers way up over the tops of his boots. And that's what's called the cold world, capable only of snoring! Speak to it of the heart, of love, of faith, and it dismisses everything as just romance. But when it falls into romance itself, then it's off and away! If they stopped along the road, he'll overturn the statues of Apollo and return with his wife in hand like one of the Hesperides with a golden apple. Oh, this world. No wonder it saddens even the angels. I am overcome with contempt and disgust when I see such serpents hissing at exaltation with common sense. And indeed, what are the great accomplishments of the people of this house who are so proud of their hearts and minds? They sold their daughter and wanted to drive me away like some repugnant phantom so affronted that I might just as well have taken up the gray habit of a nun and lived out the rest of my days behind the walls of a convent. Away, you venal hearts! I blush because of you like the rose

of shame. Fortunate for me that I have relay horses nearby – I'll return, alone, to my forlorn house, with my old grief and suffering but a hundred percent wiser in experience.

[End of Act III]

ACT IV

Scene i

(Idalia's quarters. Rzecznicki and Helenka.)

RZECZNICKI: Helenka, you see – I had to come to your house with my wife. She was ill. Please, dear, don't tell anyone that I came here with her by horse. I had an accident this evening. My carriage broke down. I had to take her on horseback; she got weak. Has the doctor been here already?

HELENKA: (*To herself*) There's a liar for you! His wife keeps saying in a coma that she was abducted by the devil.

RZECZNICKI: What did you say?

HELENKA: Just that your wife is ill.

RZECZNICKI: Yes, a bit out of sorts. That morning ride... Her nerves are weak. On horse till evening. Bad weather. It's understandable she's somewhat weak. After all, she's a woman delicate, holy...

HELENKA: (*Aside*) Delicate my foot! Though it's true right now she looks as though they just took her down from the Cross and so disheveled...

RZECZNICKI: Look, my dear, isn't that a carriage?

HELENKA: My lady is coming back!

RZECZNICKI: Go and see if my wife's bath is ready. And be sure that this episode isn't proclaimed among the servants. Off with you! I'll greet the mistress here.

(Helenka goes out.)

Scene ii

(Idalia, Rzecznicki.)

IDALIA: (*Entering without noticing Rzecznicki*) Oh, how pleasant it is here! The windows all shaded over by dark trees. I grasp the air full of flowers with my breast... (*Seeing Rzecznicki*) What? You here?

RZECZNICKI: Under your very roof. I had to come here.

IDALIA: And your wife?

RZECZNICKI: As though in a coffin, like some frightful funereal apparition.

IDALIA: Here?

RZECZNICKI: Yes, my dear lady, carried here in my arms.

IDALIA: Where did you find her? But no, I'm not so barbaric that I'd seek revenge in your awful torments. Could you conceal everything from the servants' curiosity?

RZECZNICKI: I think...

IDALIA: That...

RZECZNICKI: They do not know.

IDALIA: I'd like to protect you; therefore I must... and Nessus?

RZECZNICKI: He took money for his silence.

IDALIA: Then listen to me. For people like you, who are so prim and proper and worried about appearances, such an escapade could be a death blow. The ludicrousness of the whole affair could destroy you forever and fall on your children and grandchildren. Imagine what would happen if it all fell into the mouth of every local wag who's also half an actor and as well known in his district as the different jars on an apothecary's shelves are by their labels. This one's an aggressive little politician, that one a sensation monger, another a clever jokester, and so on. How you could be ridiculed, but they'd make fun of you the way they do of cripples... without ever actually touching the twisted part of your body. In a sense, you are a hunchback. Your weakness has always been your passion for displaying wit, and now you've been wounded in the hump of that intelligence of yours which is so renowned in these parts. Horned by the moon of the goddess Diana, you're a lost man if I don't take your hump upon myself and bear the burden in such a way that it will grace my proud shoulders with the wingedness and brilliance of the moon... and beautify me instead of killing you. So I ask you, then, change that forlorn expression on your face. I promise at least to weaken the first impression once I've arranged the sapphires of my eyes and the rest of me in keeping with the sad role of a new Deianira.

RZECZNICKI: No, it can't be that way. I'll prove that I am... a man!

IDALIA: But my dear sir... you came here with your wife, in your coach. The Bashkir got money and will get a command of silence. I am ready to offer the loan of my honor. You're a nobleman, take my offer, without any questions, take it without any interest.

RZECZNICKI: I also have my pride and am no less concerned about the principle of the thing.

IDALIA: But look, Count and Countess Respekt are coming. You'll tell them that your wife...

RZECZNICKI: That I won't say.

IDALIA: In that case, take the advice I gave you. The matter is settled. I was rescued by you in the steppe today and am sick abed now. Say what you will, make fun of me, entertain them, be a woman, amuse them with silly gossip.

RZECZNICKI: But this evening I'm going to take care of things my way.

IDALIA: All right, I permit you. But until evening I'll do as *I* wish. Either I break up those marriages of yours or I'll leave you all and you'll be left to play a comedy in the graveyard. (*Goes out.*)

Scene iii

RZECZNICKI: (*Alone*) Good advice, it seems. For the time being let her be the target of jokes here; later on, I'll do exactly as I like. A citizen, after all, must be unblemished.

Scene iv

(*Rzecznicki, Count and Countess Respekt, Diana, Stella.*)

RESPEKT: Greetings! What's this I hear about Idalia being ill?

RZECZNICKI: Yes, the ride and all that.

RESPEKT: Now, now! So this is her house…a Delphic temple! You see, I've brought my whole nest along with me. Even the Major is with us. But I've concealed him for the time being in the wings. When the time is ripe I'll bring him on stage. I've known him for a long time. He's a simple, good person.

COUNTESS: Is she in full control of all her members?

RZECZNICKI: What?

COUNTESS: Did he spare her?

RZECZNICKI: Yes, enough…

RESPEKT: He didn't go astray in the woods?

RZECZNICKI: No…

STELLA: Then he didn't drive the steed too hard?

RESPEKT: Well, you see he got within sight of his goal, didn't he? Anyway, enough about the matter…But I must say, he caused us trouble; we're all wearing a crown of thorns! You see, Rzecznicki, nobody would wish his own wife such an adventure. When you think about it, it's nothing to take lightly, is it? Why it's enough to rouse anyone's anger.

RZECZNICKI: Where is Fantazy?

RESPEKT: He didn't have courage. He's walking about the garden, the Muse at his service. Composing something or other no doubt. (*To his wife*) Send Diana out to the garden; let her and Stella go together.

COUNTESS: Did they put some ice on Idalia's head?

259

RZECZNICKI: Yes, they did.

RESPEKT: We've brought you a hat.

RZECZNICKI: A hat?

RESPEKT: Shot through with an arrow. Horned by an arrow, yes sir! You see, the Kalmyk was ordered to fly like winged Eros and to see to it that Idalia was not to be stopped. The Major himself gave him the order quite explicitly. But when he saw your knightly behavior when you caught up with him, he took aim and fired, as though replying to a summons to duel, straight from his bow. Lucky he hit just your hat! Stella, dear, tell Kayetan to go and fetch it and bring it here. (*Stella goes out*.) We want to show you that your chivalric deeds did not escape notice and so we're going to attire you ... in arrows.

RZECZNICKI: The matter is too serious for levity.

RESPEKT: Well, you certainly are modest. I know, you are modest. Your head always in the clouds, perhaps you weren't even conscious when the Kalmyk ...

RZECZNICKI: (*Interrupting him*) Really, Count!

RESPEKT: When the Kalmyk decked you out in arrows, like some ancient Numidian ...

RZECZNICKI: Then you know?

RESPEKT: Like some ancient Numidian, I tell you. My, but you are a splendid rider! You see, such talent must out! My dear Rzecznicki.

RZECZNICKI: What is it, Count?

RESPEKT: Come, let me embrace you with all my heart! You restless spirit, you! If the years don't weaken your blood, you're bound to break your neck somewhere. Orlando Furioso ... raced all over as though after – God knows what! Orlando ...

RZECZNICKI: You're repeating ...

RESPEKT: The route!

RZECZNICKI: (*Aside*) I'll get even yet! (*Aloud*) Following my tracks, did you happen to come across some paper ... What bad luck! The marriage contract fell out of my pocket along the way.

RESPEKT: No matter. You yourself are a witness to the arrangements. If the contract is lost, it's of little consequence. A new one can be drawn up. We'll have the official seal stamped on it; it's as good as money nowadays. But you're angry, I see. It's customary with people; they're embarrassed by heroism. They get all red like beet salad when they suddenly see themselves high above ordinary mortals, in brilliant laurels. It's as though they were contemptuous of them. (*To his wife*) Come dear, let's go to the garden together with the girls before Countess Idalia agrees to behold our saddened figures. (*They go out*.)

RZECZNICKI: Hell and damnation! The old fellow is driving splinters under my fingernails! I'm in torture!

Scene v

(*Rzecznicki, Fantazy.*)

FANTAZY: (*Rushing in*) Rzecznicki, I'm as good as dead.
RZECZNICKI: What on earth are you talking about?
FANTAZY: I had a frightful duel, I tell you.
RZECZNICKI: With whom?
FANTAZY: With that Russian.
RZECZNICKI: You don't mean it! Without seconds?
FANTAZY: You might as well start saying the last rites over me; I'm a corpse already.
RZECZNICKI: For God's sake! Where are you wounded? But you're alive, and all in one piece!
FANTAZY: I'm telling you that I've already got one foot in the grave. And my golden ideals are taking on the face...of a skull... My thoughts are all confused. Do you have any paper? Sit down, please, and take a pen. I'd like to write down, in just a few words, my last will and testament.
RZECZNICKI: Listen...
FANTAZY: Write! (*Rzecznicki sits down and takes a pen in hand.*) Take a million advance on my estate. After you've got the cash, change it into gold. Have it all made into a single ring in the shape of Saturn's serpent and then have this dedication inscribed on it: From The Husband's Corpse To His Betrothed. Offer it to Diana, and if she doesn't accept it, throw it into the pond.
RZECZNICKI: Have you gone completely out of your mind?
FANTAZY: I owe that young woman a lot. If I could return from the grave, I'd start life all over again in a different way. More simply. And, young again, I'd go after her. Tomorrow, when she sees me in the coffin, I'm certain that she'll touch me with a sister's hand. But my last hour alive, I should be thinking of other things.
RZECZNICKI: My dear Fantazy! In the name of the Father, the Son... If only I didn't know you so well.
FANTAZY: Enough! Time is running out. I'm in a rush to the grave. Don't come after me! If you try to, you won't succeed anyway. Death

has a Theban capital of a hundred gates. Some are red, like blood-colored coral; others are as white as pearls, and white spirits, without wounds, enter through the latter. Farewell! The kingdom of my soul is not at all agitated, but worms are already breeding in my body and these cold words on my lips are worms.

RZECZNICKI: Oh, rot and tommyrot!

FANTAZY: Ha! Now I'll doze beneath the laurels and in dream mount the racers of Pluto. I am a Roman... (*Goes out.*)

Scene vi

RZECZNICKI: (*Alone*) What was that all about? God in heaven! I have to get together with the Major as soon as possible. He'll explain everything to me, and considering the nature of the matter, he'll have to see me...and treat me decently, like a human being...

(*Idalia comes in.*)

Scene vii

(*Rzecznicki, Idalia.*)

IDALIA: What, may I ask, is going on?

RZECZNICKI: Please hurry. Fantazy has started to go mad. Everyone in this house acts as though he's crazy. I'll probably end up insane myself. Your servant... (*Leaves.*)

Scene viii

IDALIA: (*Alone*) What did he say? Fantazy going mad? How easy it is to link love and insanity. They're two inseparable ideas. Love, insanity. He's going mad. That means that he's returning to those rosy feelings wreathed in a garland of flowers and stars...that the realm of spirits will again be enriched by the power of inspired songs tossed carefree to the four winds. Oh, what I'd give for just an hour of that life...when he nourished me constantly from his heart as though from a bottomless vessel...when he would steal up to me armed with a stiletto, like a dark Othello, and hold the blade to my chest waiting to see whether fear or a smile came to my eyes! But a smile never left them. Instead, like a spider who spins golden webs out of bright luminosity in the sapphire of some flower, happiness made my eyes radiant at the thought that death at his hands would bring me closer to heaven. Oh, how far from that whiteness, which he used to call alabaster, was the paleness of death! How good it was to lie on a bed of Roman granite, my head inclined over him, inhale the roses of the Caesars and see being born in this man a new ideal of the ages, full of the spell of magic, that will bring delight to the whole future – that is, if he doesn't inflict harm on himself with the mud of ordinary mortals and can resist the desire to drink himself drunk on the wine of earthly temptations.

Scene ix

(*Idalia, Helenka.*)

HELENKA: (*Entering*) You won't receive the Countess then?
IDALIA: Later.
HELENKA: The Countess is most anxious to see you, begs to with tears in her eyes...
IDALIA: Then let her in, Helenka. But if Mr. Fantazy wants to come in, too, then warn me ahead of time by some song or other. Or cough a few times outside the door. And now admit that Walter-Scottian.

(*Helenka goes out.*)

Scene x

(*Idalia, Countess Respekt.*)

COUNTESS: My dear! The tears I've shed! I'd have given my blood! May I never set foot here again, never, if I am 'n any way guilty for what happened... Oh, my dear! Like a knife in the chest... I can feel it myself. All my veins feel just like bursting. I'm a woman, too... This world is just as poisonous to me; it's against us – constantly, every-where, always acting in a contrary way... If it weren't for my husband, I would have packed that Major off to his command in chains yester-day, out of this house, for good. Oh, this unfortunate country of ours! Where a drunken Muscovite can raise havoc while we have to bear it. As God is my witness, in the old days the Poles were certainly rowdies, but now – they're less than...

IDALIA: Don't weep, Countess, and don't lament. My reputation is so tarnished today...

COUNTESS: I know that the approval of people doesn't mean anything to you, because you are gold yourself, enclosed in yourself like a priceless gem... You despise every handful of mud the world throws... But that Major from some God-forsaken corner of Siberia is a real barbarian. I'm ashamed, so ashamed, that in my home... But I'm resigned, I'll go out to the highway and sit down in a tavern, since my house has become one anyway...

IDALIA: Please let's change the subject. Tell me, where was your Diana's trousseau sewn?

COUNTESS: Oh, I'm losing my mind! That marriage! For me to be so blind! But I simply didn't realize that Mr. Fantazy isn't free.

IDALIA: But he is free.

COUNTESS: How can you, of all people, say that, Idalia? Free...a man who should have, but was incapable of sensing that, as your rival, my Diana would expire like a candle in the sun's brilliance? Mind you, I am intending no flattery. Oh, no. I'll call him a liar to his face now. But please don't think that we are keeping him here under lock and key like some rare bird we captured. He can do as he wishes...

IDALIA: As he wishes? But the marriage contract you already have between you?

COUNTESS: Oh, no! You've exceeded reality. Could some official documents make right...a deed...when love itself... You understand. Marriage is founded on the heart.

IDALIA: Yes, on the heart...

Scene xi

(*Stella rushes in. Countess Respekt, Idalia.*)

STELLA: Mama, come fast!
COUNTESS: What is it?
STELLA: Diana...
COUNTESS: But what? (*Runs out after Stella.*)

Scene xii

IDALIA: (*Alone*) A marriage spoiled by the heart. Diana and Jan met. She looked through my album with Fantazy's soul inscribed in it and then came face to face in the entrance hall with this handsome bronzed uhlan who now wears a hair shirt and a felt coat – a fearful actor on the stage of love.

(*Helenka runs in.*)

Scene xiii

(*Idalia, Helenka.*)

IDALIA: Helenka, what is it?
HELENKA: The young lady fainted and struck her head on the stones when she fell. When she was lifted up, blood was pouring from her forehead, she was as white as chalk and was crying like a baby.
IDALIA: But she wasn't badly hurt?
HELENKA: No; she's conscious.
IDALIA: (*Aside*) I have the feeling that the entire scene was staged. The album, then he. Such great urgency…and such a transition. (*Aloud*) Give me my burnous. (*Aside*) But no; I won't put in an appearance there now. I'll remain here like that bronze Saturn who sits motionless on the clock and has the hours revolving beneath his legs.

Scene xiv

(*Idalia, Helenka. A lackey comes in carrying a calling card and a stiletto.*)

LACKEY: Madam, this card…
IDALIA: What's this I see? My God in heaven! (*Reads.*) Fetch me my burnous. Ha! Ha! That Venetian stiletto here! Jesus! Mary! (*Runs out with the stiletto, leaving the card behind.*)

Scene xv

(*Helenka, the Lackey.*)

HELENKA: What's this?
LACKEY: Mr. Fantazy gave it to me and ordered me to deliver it to the Countess.

(*Helenka takes the card and reads it.*)

HELENKA: I don't understand what it means. And if I hold it longer, I still won't make any more sense of it. I must go after her.

LACKEY: Give it here, let me read it. *The last meeting of our souls on earth today ... at midnight ...*

HELENKA: In God's name, what does it mean?

LACKEY: *Our last toast with golden goblets ... today ... Either I drink to the angels together with you ... or alone ...* Jesus! There's an exclamation mark after every word and the letter was so damp, you can clearly see the imprint of my fingers on it. Must be devils doing the writing for those gentlemen. All zigzag and shaky. (*Continues reading.*) *There, where all people in the world come together and remain eternally, where Juliet awoke and then fell asleep again, I shall be waiting ...*

HELENKA: I have to take Countess Idalia her silk swan jacket, since there's dew out and she's apt to catch cold, and then I'll get the dogs stirred up and yelping so that they'll frighten her out of these awful nightly strolls through the woods. After all, she's kinder to the people who serve her than any queen usually is. At the Rzecznickis it's impossible to work because you're always so cold and hungry there. And if you happen to be in a house that's already in the hands of the Jesuit fathers, you have to weep for no reason at all every Friday, or rub your eyes with onion, when you accompany some ladyship to mass ... But here, it's almost as though you were being fondled, and ...

(*Count Respekt rushes in, the Major after him.*)

Scene xvi

(*The same, Count Respekt, and the Major.*)

RESPEKT: Where is your mistress?

HELENKA: I don't know.

RESPEKT: Death hangs above my daughter's head! Please, call a doctor! (*Helenka and the Lackey go out.*) Major! I see that you and our region are not in harmony. One evening here and you've spoiled so much for me! Why on earth did you have to bring that person with you? Don't you realize that children who got to know each other there and were stirred by the power of feeling amid the snow and the terrible white

Siberian horrors dreamed up a rainbow for themselves out of fondness for each other? Was it necessary to bring here to our very home a page torn out of that anthology? To put it briefly, perhaps you meant no harm but nevertheless you strewed a terrible bed of nails beneath my feet!

MAJOR: Well, but you're wealthy...why not let your daughter follow her heart?

RESPEKT: What are you saying, man? Maybe you're good when it comes to weapons, but not where hearts are concerned. I'll tell you sincerely that... oh, curse you, Major! My son-in-law is all ready to break our contract!

MAJOR: What son-in-law?

RESPEKT: But you know, after all, that I do have a son-in-law.

MAJOR: Perhaps.

RESPEKT: What do you mean "perhaps?" Since you were present at the signing of the marriage agreement, how can you doubt that I'll soon be rocking grandchildren? Eh? You doubt it, do you?

MAJOR: Doubt it I do.

RESPEKT: Ha, ha, ha! Lose a son-in-law, you think? May I ask, how?

MAJOR: Well now! How? When a card is bent in a corner it loses, and the money is lost with it. Maybe that's how, playing with me, your son-in-law got lost to you.

RESPEKT: What? How could it be? Why? My son-in-law gambled with you? Is that what you're trying to say?

MAJOR: Why yes, that's it more or less.

RESPEKT: My son-in-law lost at cards with you? You're just nodding your head at me. Tell me, please, please, be frank with me! You don't know how much I have at stake here.

MAJOR: Well, Count, here's the marriage contract in this billfold; take it. Your son-in-law's slap cost me face, but he lost his whole head at cards. Anyway, I'm giving you his head back as a present, and the honor torn from my mug by his hand maybe I'll find with God... (*Hands him a slip of paper.*) I want you to understand that I'm not a bad man. Out of stupidity I caused you harm, but I paid for it with my own honor.

RESPEKT: (*After reading the paper given him*) Oh, my heavens! The lightning of insanity has struck the brains of such people. My son-in-law has gone stark raving mad! Marianna! Our son-in-law is poisoning himself! Marianna! Our son-in-law is killing himself... (*Runs out.*)

MAJOR: And theatre, too!

(*Jan comes in.*)

Scene xvii

(Jan, the Major.)

JAN: Major!

MAJOR: What is it now? Did you see the young lady?

JAN: Let's leave. Back to our Siberian mists and winds. You'll be a father to me again, as you used to be, and a friend. This world's a puzzle. If only you knew how funny it all was. The mother was the angriest of all. "You've killed my child! Away with you! Don't stand near me! Foul person! You smell like an ordinary foot soldier, a hireling. There's the stench about you of the lowest lackey. You stink of cheap vodka and moldy tobacco. Out of my sight!" When she heard these shouts the daughter who had fainted raised her eyelids and threw the mother such a wild look, and me such an angelic one, that I'll remember it for ages. What balsam there is in a girl's loving eyes!

MAJOR: Well, we'll give you the prettiest girls in Siberia.

JAN: Let's leave this land which was always a paradise of happiness in my dreams, a mother to me. But now . . . what a stepmother it's become! Listen, she called an exile a lackey and frivolously threw a seed of anger into this painful heart of mine.

MAJOR: Oh, the hell with her! And I'll help. You see, there you are – your Polish counts! By the way, did you order that Kalmyk rascal to saddle up the horses?

JAN: Already.

MAJOR: Well, let's light our pipes and leave the smoke as farewell to the fine gentry here.

JAN: Let's be on our way, Major. The person who falls once into the sea of misfortune has to go to the bottom and give his head to the waves. Lovely little eyes livid in tears–farewell!

[End of Act IV]

268

14. The Cracow production of *Fantazy*, Act V, Scene i. Fantazy and Idalia in the graveyard. (Photograph: Wojciech Plewiński)

ACT V

Scene i

(*A graveyard in back of which can be seen a closed chapel. A moonlit night. Enter Fantazy and Idalia.*)

FANTAZY: Caesar's mortal Ides of March are upon me, for you are my Ida. Well, have I not kept my word! My last few hours – with you! Our stars are coming, our golden moon is already here, and I have kept my word to be the first at the banquet of death. The world had fettered me with such chains that now when I am surrendering my soul, my eternal sleep can only be a liberation. My mocking tones were the last pain of my soul. Sit down here. In your eyes I see two azure moons. You shall be my eternal harmony, and your eyes – an eternal source of light. I shall drink from them all the golden rays...

IDALIA: This graveyard has always been the nicest part of my estate. See the dark shadows there beneath the thicket of linden trees, and the faces of snakes, and the death's-heads on the blackness of invisible crosses...

FANTAZY: I shall show you the rainbow spirits, the visages of fatal deities which have always been close to me at night and are the cause of my throwing my life away so stupidly, so vainly.

IDALIA: What vision is it I seem to see there?

FANTAZY: No, it's nothing. Just people walking with lanterns in the mist, probably out looking for us.

IDALIA: Forgive me, dear, but I'm asking you again, again... Can you just give your life away so cheaply? After all, God has us all inscribed and it is because of Him that we have been put on earth. Listen... some anxiety is taking hold of me, and you, too, are trembling... Both of us have been touched by the wings of death. That shapeless future does have its dreadful aspect. Listen to me, please... I experienced no violence and the cause of my death – that abduction – was so arranged by fate that the shame of the whole thing fell on another person entirely. Therefore, I am the one who is guilty, guilty for having lied, for having wanted to be an actress for a whole day... and according to the world, it is wrong to help oneself by deceit. Indeed. This death that flies about now like a nocturnal butterfly beating the air with wings of bone is mean and insults us as though we were stupid children... Because you did not avenge yourself on account of me, but for some fury, some monster, for Rzecznicki. And he, like the miserable man he

270

is, hid himself behind his own shame, behind that common wife of his, behind those aired-out rags I found in the house this morning in a bath of camomile, behind the red cockade on his cap, behind the crowing and face of a cock, shouting "Help" from one end of the house to the other!

FANTAZY: Ha, ha, ha! Mrs. Rzecznicki ruined! Ha, ha, ha! If Rzecznicki himself stood here and asked me for poison, I wouldn't give him even the smallest drop. Ha! Live on, Brutus! Ha, ha, ha! I should dearly love to encounter Rzecznicki once more on earth and in this famulus of mine mock the unridiculed side of my Faustism, so that he'd stand as a monument of mockery over my grave. Ha, ha, ha! I'll drown in tears of laughter! Ha! The Bashkir archangel snatching Mrs. Rzecznicki from the hands of the Jesuits! And at a gallop, mind you! Ha, ha, ha! My laughter will reach the very stars in the sky! Long may she live! The model of all religious bigots and domestic slatterns... Mrs. Rzecznicki, who was a spirit, on a pilgrimage! Oh my! Ha, ha, ha!

IDALIA: That laugh...

FANTAZY: Struck the head of the statue of beauty like the back of an axe and changed into gray fear the death that stood before us like a wondrous figure of alabaster, all in stars, butterflies, and moons, with a carpet of poppies, mulleins, and asters beneath a silent step. Just see what jesters Poland produces; they can amuse you to the death! Come now, concert of laughter and nightingales, play! Surrounded by a crowd of monsters, terrible to behold, the new Deianira, in a cap, marches at the head of the retinue – our retinue... our two coffins. And she shouts, "It is for me that the son of Zephyr and the daughter of Aurora perish!"

IDALIA: Oh! What incoherent madness!

FANTAZY: What? Am I rousing you from sleep? Here! In this phial, this golden globe, there's enough sleep for you for a thousand years.

IDALIA: Then it is poison you offer me?

FANTAZY: Yes. Anger concealed in a mask of sugar. You have to admit, it's an honorable way...

IDALIA: And there's no remedy?

FANTAZY: There is.

IDALIA: Then use it, live for your country!

FANTAZY: For that, ha, something truly great would have to happen.

IDALIA: Such as?

FANTAZY: Such as a bolt of lightning or a meteorite falling within a quarter of an hour on the Major's gray head that groaned beneath my slap like the harp of Aeolus.

15. The Cracow production of *Fantazy*, Act V, Scene i. The "suicide" scene – Fantazy and Idalia before the chapel. (Photograph: Wojciech Plewiński)

IDALIA: What?

FANTAZY: Or if the harp on which I snapped the string of honor burst. A contract, you see, is explicit. Midnight tonight will see one coffin filled. The paper is duly stamped. Half a ruble fee, for a paper that someday will be an important document. Give me that phial!

IDALIA: Seer! Lift your spirits! Death is a terrible sacrament. Don't take poison with such an expression on your face!

FANTAZY: What?

IDALIA: Your face is twisted satanically.

FANTAZY: What you said about death isn't so. Death is a golden column of air. And in this air there is strength! Oh! this warm, fragrant air, embraced by my arms, has lovely, immortal spirits within it, spirits, like me, torn from bodies conceived long ago, full of love, like me, invisible, distending the world by their form. Wait, I'll stand alongside you for a moment like the very air...

IDALIA: Do you see my bosom heaving? Oh, find some word, of greater power, to make me love dark death!

FANTAZY: Look there, the chapel with the golden cross standing in the night like some spirit...it will begin to rule with the power of our souls...and from its stones will pour forth the love of the world... sacramentally! Tomorrow this church...will be infused, like a melancholy light, with our radiance...and will act upon sad spirits and young hearts like a song that resounds within us when we are children. Come! I shall lead you to the dark chapel. Astarte... O Thou, without laurel wreath on thy temple, Beatrice of an unknown spirit whom I abducted and bear now like an angel, come, come, and gaze upon the countenance of the Madonna and in holy ecstasy place thy head beneath the moon's scythe of still death. What am I saying? Stand upon it as though on the moon itself and the winged spirit will fly away with us to new worlds and in the heat of fiery suns will place our foreheads on the final border...whither flees the human soul. Come, come! Come to the chapel, my sister! Come with me! You will not depart there without a brother nor I without a sister, though both of us will leave without bodies...

IDALIA: My soul is in your hands, upon your lips!

FANTAZY: Your mouth gives forth words like lightning, my soul!

IDALIA: Come to the chapel, let the world race after us!

(*The sound of a shot nearby is heard.*)

FANTAZY: Wait! What's that? A shot...

IDALIA: Listen! A groan...
MAJOR'S VOICE: God, forgive me!
FANTAZY: What is it? Who dares break the silence of the moon?
RZECZNICKI'S VOICE: Help!
IDALIA: Don't go!
RZECZNICKI'S VOICE: Help, anyone!
FANTAZY: On the mound, near the graveyard.
RZECZNICKI'S VOICE: If there's anyone there, please help!
FANTAZY: It's Rzecznicki shouting.
RESPEKT'S VOICE: (*Offstage*) Someone's shot! Whoever can, run to the graveyard! The shot came from there.
FANTAZY: The Count! I have five minutes of life left on my watch. Must I waste these moments on a garrulous old fool?

Scene ii

(*The same, Count Respekt, Rzecznicki, and the Major, servants with lanterns.*)

RESPEKT: The shot came from here. Here they are! Here! Here! I see something white on a grave there. Over here! Here! Lanterns! It's Fantazy and Countess Idalia! Both alive, thank God! What are you doing? My child, wait a moment! Young people die going against ramparts, redoubts, and cannons, not the way you are! (*He hands Fantazy the promissory note the Major had returned.*) Poison yourself instead with this paper and swallow the secret, and live with us! (*He espies the Major lying in a pool of blood.*) What now?
RZECZNICKI: Someone go fill his cap with water!
MAJOR: I'm done for. Under the banners of the Holy Mother, I gave satisfaction...as a man of honor...and I am dying for honor... (*To Fantazy*) Well, I guess now we won't have to argue about a coffin, Count... At twelve o'clock I'll be reporting to God. You say a prayer for me. Shake hands; be well! A pity I can't express myself clearer. I don't feel your rap in the face any longer. If I felt it, I forgot it; or if I didn't forget, I forgave – from my soul.
IDALIA: How this simple man has grown so marvelously immense in the hour of his death!
MAJOR: (*To Idalia*) Dry your tears, my darling. Give me your hand! Don't cry. I'm an old man and should have gone to my grave a long time ago.
FANTAZY: Have a carriage brought!

MAJOR: Why, are you thinking of taking me to Christ on wheels? Splendid! There's a joke for you. They'll put a corpse in a coach! (*To Count Respekt*) I want to whisper something in your ear...

RESPEKT: (*After a moment's conversation*) Rzecznicki, bring my women here. The Major...as a Catholic...

MAJOR: Greek Catholic!

RESPEKT: Wishes to see my family...and reveal some testaments of his thought...

MAJOR: That's it. Let mother and daughter come. And let them remember that I, a simple man, on death's doorstep, asked for their grace...

(*Rzecznicki goes out.*)

Scene iii

(*Jan and the Kalmyk rush in.*)

JAN: Where's the Major?

RESPEKT: Here, on this grave.

MAJOR: By God's side.

JAN: What's happened? I found an empty coach at the inn. The Major sent me on ahead with a parcel. I'd have raced all the way to Tobolsk if it hadn't been for a premonition and fear. What's happened? His head is lowered as if...as if...

MAJOR: Give me your hand!

FANTAZY: (*To Idalia*) Our poisoning was foolishness! Look! Look how they're talking to each other just with their hands! Ten Siberian years compressed in those hands, like wax...

Scene iv

(*Countess Respekt runs in with her daughters. Rzecznicki some distance behind them.*)

COUNTESS: Oh, my God! What is it?

RESPEKT: Quiet! A frightful accident. Our Major was shot in a duel.

COUNTESS: Look here, this letter...

RESPEKT: What is it?

COUNTESS: Grandfather died.

RESPEKT: What did you say?

COUNTESS: This very night...

RESPEKT: Oh!

COUNTESS: (*Quietly*) You're as red as a beet!

RESPEKT: The blood rushed to my head.

COUNTESS: Take that expression off your face!

RESPEKT: This has brought a great change... and our domestic affairs...

COUNTESS: Put this letter away in your pocket for the time being and don't show your face. His death is written all over it and people will reach conclusions.

RESPEKT: Do the children know?

COUNTESS: No... (*Aloud*) Perhaps it's possible to put him in a coach.

FANTAZY: Sh! Don't disturb the sleep that brings a smile to his face as the angel of death touches his gray hair. He's dreaming about something, that his soul must surely be like the sun. Sh! He's opening his eyes. Major! The Countess is here with the children.

MAJOR: Let me have some water! (*Drinks.*) So, the world is still here. In the name of the Father, the Son, and the Holy Ghost! Please come closer Countess with your children, here, next to the grave. I couldn't love anybody more sincerely and openly than you people. The son of Gavrila, Major Vladimir, your old friend, sincerely loved you. And visited your good home as a friend... and stayed with you till Judgment Day... Kalmyk! A casket! (*The Kalmyk leaves.*) Listen, Countess. I was a Circassian prisoner, abducted once upon a time when I was still a child. This Russified Greek, thief, and swindler (forgive me, God!) would have been a general if not for those Muravevs, the Decembrists, with whom I was always honorable and liberal as long as they were alive. Now, lying mortally wounded under these trees, I remembered them warmly, looking at my own blood. Oh, if I'd have had the bullets in my heart beneath the Senate then that I do now underneath these trees here, it'd have been much better. Piff, piff – and it's all over with me and the world. Ahhh, the Muravevs, Alexander, Sergey... why did I recall you now, after so long?

COUNTESS: Major!

FANTAZY: Quiet, madam!

MAJOR: This ring here, see, is from Sergey... I had an old mother who brought me a little piece of wood from his gallows... Ahhh, fff! The old woman... Anyway, later on, thanks to Minister Arakcheev, I managed to get myself packed off to a command in Siberia, stripped of rank, degraded, humiliated... The way I was when you met me. I used to sit all day in my little house or in the garden, smoking my pipe, while you stood looking at my sadness... And I kept silent and didn't tell you where my heart ached. That liberalism burning like a hot flame, the black gloom... There's what caused my grief! You know, miss, whenever you used to sing sad songs, I often thought, standing in a corner and listening to them, of Bestuzhev* and how he recalled afterwards that I stood alongside the fuse and didn't fire. When you knew me, Vladimir Gavrila, the pain in my heart was like a snake eating away at me on the inside and a heavy rock weighing me down. I stood before you then in humiliation and anxiety thinking that you were despising me as a poor old, gray-haired, foolish liberal who had a weapon and the tsar's life in his hand, and held his fire... Seeing the tsar in what looked like a row of stars, and the chief staff in banners the colors of the rainbow, he took the hissing fuse and shoved it in the snow. He felt fear in his heart, his head, his toes, and he made a fool of himself...

IDALIA: For God's sake, Major! Blood is pouring out of the wound... try to talk more calmly!

MAJOR: Well, it's done and gone now and for God to judge. Once I saw action in the Turkish war, I fought the Persians... I served in areas under quarantine and touched death with my fingers...and never paled! But that one time before the tsar I became a coward and then as meekly as a child handed over my sword to them when they came after it...

(*The Kalmyk returns bearing a casket.*)

RESPEKT: What's this? The Major's talking, wounded? Forbid him! Forbid him!

MAJOR: Please, Count, sit down here and listen seriously for I've already got a foot in the grave. I'm speaking with my last breath... In Siberia, I had only one true friend. The two of us often used to walk among crosses bearing the names of Ryumin, Pestel,† and others... In back of one church we placed a silent keepsake... That's where my memory is of Sergey Muravev, whom I loved and had to live without for ten years...and I would have died had I been forced to live those ten years without a friend. He won me over, you know, with his heart. I lost Muravev, but I gained a healer...who restored me with his tears... Now what can I give him if I am here no longer? (*To Diana*) Come here, girl! That's the way, yes, with roses on your lips... Stand here, that's

---

*Mikhail Bestuzhev-Ryumin, one of the leaders of the Decembrist Revolt hanged for his part in the conspiracy. – Ed.

†Pavel Pestel, another leader of the Decembrists who was hanged. – Ed.

right, next to this uhlan and both of you bow to your parents...and I'll make up the third member of the party. Kalmyk, come over here! (*Getting up.*) There, even though I'm wounded, there we are, that's it, I'm standing and now I'll get down on my knees before you, the way you're supposed to...that's it... (*Kneels*) For God's sake, no, don't refuse me! I beg you with my blood, don't refuse me!

RESPEKT: But this is a marriage ceremony you're going through!

MAJOR: Listen to me! You see, I've put together a lot of money. For my own needs, I was able to get by on my salary, my garden, my house. Well, anyway, once upon a time I was rather hard on some merchants during a port quarantine. They wanted their goods out faster, so I shortened the quarantine...for a price. There I was taking my afternoon tea and letting the ship slip out between my legs with its sails and mast. And I grabbed hold of a bag for myself as though it were the anchor itself. So, Count, here you are, these banknotes. (*To the Kalmyk*) Get out of here, go on now! Sh, now! He's giving his daughter in marriage! We're millionaires, eh, ha!

RESPEKT: But Major! In this instance, the money – even though there is quite a bit of it – doesn't mean anything.

MAJOR: Yes, I know, but...

COUNTESS: Oh, my heavens! The Major probably thinks that...

MAJOR: No, I don't think anything...

RESPEKT: But Mr. Fantazy has our word.

MAJOR: Yes, yes, of course, Mr. Fantazy. I'll be in the grave long before he will.

FANTAZY: Wait, for God's sake!

MAJOR: Long before he will...

FANTAZY: Your commands are like those of an angel. (*To Diana*) Your noble hand has not yet been mine. Until now, it's been free. You entranced me like a holy star. I believe that in your heart you'll be able to judge the reason why I must release your hand from mine...forever... (*To Idalia*) Your brother, Countess. Today I leave for Rome and I believe that your heart, the gentlest of hearts, will treat me generously, taking less than I can give...

IDALIA: My heart desires only respect.

FANTAZY: My lady! This dark and bloody death has cleansed me as a man. This person is worth a kiss on the heart. Farewell, Major! I'll send my doctor; don't give up hope!

MAJOR: Now you see, Count, you can't refuse your daughter. Blood is pouring out of me, pouring out of my side like a stream, and I beg your grace and mercy...

RESPEKT: You have them, Major. Take the children to you; give them your blessings. They have ours.

MAJOR: There we are! My Diana and Jan together, forever! I can't do any more! Owww, there must have been a hundred fiery swords in that little pistol shell... Diana... Jan... Diana... You'll have to come to me in the casket... I can't hold on any longer... (*Dies.*)

THE END

Selected Bibliography

Bizan, Marian, and Paweł Hertz. *Juliusz Słowacki Kordian: Głosy do Kordiana.* Warsaw, 1967.

Csato, Edward. *The Polish Theatre.* Warsaw, 1963.

——. *Szkice o dramatach Słowackiego.* Warsaw, 1960.

Descotes, Maurice, *Le Drame romantique et ses grands créatures.* Paris, 1955.

Duker, Abraham G. "Some Cabbalist and Frankist Elements in Adam Mickiewicz's *Dziady*." In *Studies in Polish Civilization*, ed. Damian Wandycz. New York, 1966. p. 213–35.

Gardner, Monica M. *The Anonymous Poet of Poland: Zygmunt Krasiński.* Cambridge, England, 1919.

Grzymała-Siedlecki, Adam. *Z teatrów warszawskich 1926–1939.* Warsaw, 1972.

Inglot, Zdzisław. *"Kordian" Juliusza Słowackiego.* Warsaw, 1993.

Jackiewicz, Alexander. "Model dramatu romantycznego a współczesna polska literatura i film," *Kultura i społeczeństwo*, XV, No. 1 (January–March, 1971), 63–86.

Janion, Maria. *Zygmunt Krasiński: Debiut i dojrzałość.* Warsaw, 1962.

——. *Romantyzm: Studia o ideach i stylu.* Warsaw, 1969.

Kepiński, Zdzisław. *Mickiewicz hermetyczny.* Warsaw, 1980.

Kijowski, Andrzej, *Listopadowy wieczór.* Warsaw, 1972.

Kott, Jan. *Theatre Notebook: 1947–1967.* Trans. Bolesław Taborski. Garden City, New York, 1968.

Krasiński, Zygmunt. *Nie-Boska komedia.* 10th ed., rev. Ed. Maria Grabowska; Intro. by Maria Janion. Wrocław, Warsaw, and Cracow, 1969.

——. *Nie-Boska komedia.* Ed. Stefan Treugutt. Warsaw, 1974.

——. *The Un-Divine Comedy.* Trans. Harriette E. Kennedy and Zofia Umińska. London and Warsaw, 1924.

Krasiński żywy. Ed. Władysław Günther. London, 1959.

Kridl, Manfred, ed. *Adam Mickiewicz: Poet of Poland.* New York, 1951; rpt. 1969.

Krzyżanowski, Julian. *Polish Romantic Literature.* London, 1930.

——. *W świecie romantycznym*, Cracow, 1961.

Lednicki, Waclaw, ed. *Adam Mickiewicz in World Literature.* Berkeley and Los Angeles, 1956.

———. ed. *Zygmunt Krasiński, Romantic Universalist: An International Tribute.* New York, 1964.

Lubieniewska, Ewa. *"Fantazy" Juliusza Słowackiego, czyli komedia na opak wywrócona.* Wrocław, 1985.

Maciejewski, Jarosław. *Trzy szkice romantyczne.* Poznań, 1967.

Makowski, Stanisław. *"Kordian" Juliusza Słowackiego.* Warsaw, 1973.

———. *Nie-boska komedia Zygmunta Krasińskiego.* Warsaw, 1991.

Masłowski, Michał. *Dzieje bohatera: teatralne wizje "Dziadów", "Kordiana", "Nie-boskiej komedii" do II wojny światowej.* Wrocław, 1978.

Mickiewicz, Adam. *Dzieła.* Literatura słowiańska, Kurs trzeci i czwarty. Vol. XI. Trans. Leon Płoszewski. Warsaw, 1955.

———. *Forefathers.* Trans. Count Potocki of Montalk. London, 1968.

———. *Pan Tadeusz.* Trans., with Intro., by Kenneth Mackenzie. London and New York, 1966.

Mickiewicz żywy. Ed. Herminia Naglerowa. London, 1955.

Miłosz, Czesław. *The History of Polish Literature.* London and New York, 1969; 2nd ed., 1983.

Pacewicz, Tadeusz, ed. *Mickiewicz na scenach polskich.* Wrocław, 1959.

Piasecka, Maria. *Mistrzowie snu: Mickiewicz, Słowacki, Krasiński.* Wrocław. 1992.

Prochnicki, Włodzimierz. *Romantyczne światy: czas i przestrzeń w dramatach Słowackiego.* Cracow, 1992.

Revue des Sciences Humaines (Jules Slowacki, 1809–1849). April–June 1961, Fasc. 102.

Sivert, Tadeusz, ed. *Słowacki na scenach polskich.* Wrocław, Warsaw, and Cracow, 1963.

Skuczyński, Janusz. *O przestrzeni teatralnej w dramatach Juliusza Słowackiego.* Warsaw, 1986.

———. *Odmiany form dramatycznych w okresie romantyzmu: Słowacki, Mickiewicz, Krasiński.* Toruń. 1993.

Skwarczyńska, Stefania. *Leona Schillera trzy opracowania teatralne "Nie-boskiej komedii" w dziejach jej inscenizacji w Polsce.* Warsaw, 1959.

———. *W kręgu wielkich romantyków polskich.* Warsaw, 1966.

Sławińska, Irena, *Sceniczny gest poety.* Cracow, 1960.

Słowacki, Juliusz. *Fantazy.* 2nd rev. ed. Ed. Mieczysław Inglot. Wrocław, Warsaw, and Cracow, 1966.

———. *Kordian.* 7th ed. Ed. Eugeniusz Sawrymowicz. Wrocław, 1965.

Sofronova, L. A. *Pol'skaia romanticheskaia drama: Mitskevich, Krasin'skii, Slovatskii.* Moscow, 1992.

Stefanowska, Zofia. *Historia i profecja*: *Studium o Księgach narodu i pielgrzymstwa*. Warsaw, 1962.

Straszewska, Maria. *Życie literackie Wielkiej Emigracji we Francji 1831 1840*. Warsaw, 1970.

Strzelecki, Zenobiusz. *Polska plastyka teatralna*. Vol. I. Warsaw, 1963.

Timoszewicz, Jerzy. *"Dziady" w inscenizacji Leona Schillera*. Warsaw, 1970.

Treugutt, Stefan. *Juliusz Słowacki: Romantic Poet*. Warsaw, 1959.

Weintraub, Wiktor. *Literature as Prophecy: Scholarship and Martinist Poetics in Mickiewicz's Parisian Lectures*. The Hague, 1959.

——. *The Poetry of Adam Mickiewicz*. The Hague, 1954.

——. *Profecja i profesura: Mickiewicz, Michelet i Quinet*. Warsaw, 1975.

Welsh, David. *Adam Mickiewicz*. New York, 1966.

Witkowska, Alina. *Mickiewicz: Słowo i czyn*. Warsaw, 1975.

——. *Wielcy romantycy polscy: Mickiewicz, Słowacki, Krasiński*. Warsaw, 1980.

Witkowski, Michał. *Świat teatralny młodego Mickiewicza*. Warsaw, 1971.

Wyspiański, Stanisław. *Dzieła wybrane*. Vol. XII. Gen. ed. Leon Płoszewski. Cracow, 1961.